Living Languages: An Integrated Approach to Teaching Foreign Languages in Secondary Schools

Living Languages is simply bursting with practical and original ideas aimed at teachers and trainee teachers of foreign languages in secondary schools. Written by a team of experienced linguists, this book will inspire and motivate the foreign language classroom and the teachers who work within it.

Living Languages comprises eight chapters and is structured around the integrated classroom, merging language learning with different aspects of the wider curriculum, such as multimedia, theatre and music, celebrations and festivals, sport, and alternative approaches to teaching languages. A CD is also included with the book, containing additional teaching materials and the associated films and audio recordings which make this a fully-developed and effective teaching resource.

Twenty-eight real-life case studies and projects are presented, all of which have been tried and tested in the classroom, with many having won recent educational awards. Ideas and activities outlined in this unique resource include:

- **Languages and multi-media projects** involving different uses of technology such as film-making, Digital Storytelling and subtitling in different languages;
- **Languages and theatre and music**, including the work of the Théâtre Sans Frontières with its *Marie Curie Science Project*;
- Motivating pupils to **learn languages whilst keeping fit**, including examples from *Score in French*, *The German Orienteering Festival* and *Handball in Spanish*;
- **Continuing Professional Development** to inspire secondary language teachers to continue their individual professional development. The chapter contains concrete examples of others' experiences in this area and includes details of support organisations and practical opportunities.

Each project is explored from the teachers' perspective with practical tips, lesson plans and reflections woven throughout the text, such as what to budget, how to organise the pre-event period, how to evaluate the activity and whom to contact for further advice in each case. Activities and examples throughout are given in three languages – French, German and Spanish.

Catherine Watts is currently Director of the Routes into Languages South consortium and is Principal Lecturer in English Language and German with the Faculty of Arts as well as contributing to the EdD, PGCE and MA in Education at the University of Brighton, UK.

Clare Forder is the Programme Manager for the regional Routes into Languages South consortium at the University of Brighton and has had sustained contact with teachers and pupils in the secondary sector over the past few years.

Living Languages:
An Integrated Approach to Teaching Foreign Languages in Secondary Schools

Edited by Catherine Watts

Catherine Watts and Clare Forder

Routledge
Taylor & Francis Group

LONDON AND NEW YORK

First published 2013
by Routledge
2 Park Square, Milton Park, Abingdon, Oxon OX14 4RN

Simultaneously published in the USA and Canada
by Routledge
711 Third Avenue, New York, NY 10017

Routledge is an imprint of the Taylor & Francis Group, an informa business

British Library Cataloguing in Publication Data
A catalogue record for this book is available from the British Library

Library of Congress Cataloging in Publication Data

Living languages : an integrated approach to teaching foreign languages in secondary schools /
edited by Catherine Watts.
p. cm.
ISBN 978-0-415-67566-6 -- ISBN 978-0-415-67567-3 (pbk.) -- ISBN 978-0-203-80938-9
(ebook) 1. Language and languages--Study and teaching (Secondary) 2. Project method in teaching.
3. Interdisciplinary approach in education. I. Watts, Catherine.
P53.67.L58 2012
418.0071'2--dc23
2012007720

ISBN: 978-0-415-67566-6 (hbk)
ISBN: 978-0-415-67567-3 (pbk)
ISBN: 978-0-203-80938-9 (ebk)

Typeset in Bembo
by Fish Books Ltd., London

MIX
Paper from
responsible sources
FSC
www.fsc.org   FSC® C004839

Printed and bound in Great Britain by the MPG Books Group

Contents

To our families and friends
CW, CF

Contributors

Catherine Watts is a Principal Lecturer at The University of Brighton (School of Humanities) where she has worked for nearly thirty years. Catherine teaches German and English and works with the PGCE teacher trainees in modern languages. In 2002 she was awarded her doctorate by King's College, University of London in the field of foreign languages in education. She led the research team for Brighton and Hove City Council's MFL Primary Pathfinder project in 2002/3 and since 2007 has directed the Routes into Languages regional consortium in the South.

Clare Forder is based at the University of Brighton and works as a project manager for the Routes into Languages regional consortium in the South, part of the national Routes into Languages initiative. Over the last five years she has planned, designed and delivered small- and large-scale activities for students studying languages at secondary school and college. She was part of a seven-country research project into early language learning in Europe and is currently studying for a Professional Doctorate in Education where her research field is languages education in England.

Acknowledgements

The authors and publishers would like to thank the following for helping us to organise each project contained in this book. Our thanks are due to a great many people and we have tried to make this list as comprehensive as possible! We hope we have not left anyone out!

Score in French

Original project design: Ian McCall, Clare Forder, Morgan Schneiderlin, Romain Gasmi,
Artwork: Nicola Goodland (and Alex Chown)
Photography: Andy Vowles
Photograph permission: Chris Letteriello
Translation assistance: Olivier Boulocher

The German orienteering festival

Original project design: Bev Whiteside, Youth Sport Trust, Kat Stevenson.

Spanish handball

Original project design: Bev Whiteside, Youth Sport Trust, Rhys Bearder and Sarah Schechter.
Schedule of Work: Lymm High School
Artwork: Alex Chown
Translation assistance: María Emmerson and Luz Del Carmen Broadbridge

The foreign languages mini-olympics

Original project design: Clare Forder
Translation Assistance: Monika Lind, Luz Del Carmen Broadbridge

Languages, camera, action

Original project design: Jedge Pilbrow, Catherine Watts, Clare Forder
Original project delivery: Jedge Pilbrow, Robyn Steer
Artwork: Claire Ross

Digital storytelling

Project design: Helen Mayer and Matteo Fumagalli
Project organisation: Renata Albuquerque
With thanks to the French and Spanish Departments, LSE Language Centre

Languages and subtitling

Original project design: Andrés García-García, Iria Gonzalez-Becerra, Renata Albuquerque

Language on film

Original project design: Rachel Hawkes, Jane Driver and Leigh McClelland, Sarah Gibson-Yates, Sarah Schechter. With thanks to the Cambridge Arts Picturehouse and the Cambridgeshire Film Consortium.

It's Christmas!

Original project design: Catherine Watts
Advent Calendar: Bettina Meyer, German Embassy, London.
Artwork: Nicola Goodland
Translation assistance: Monika Lind, Anja Merkel
Final photograph: Louis Kirby

Day of the Dead

Original project design: Clare Forder
Artwork: Claire Ross
Translation assistance: Luz Del Carmen Broadbridge, María C Cooke and María Emmerson

Bastille Day

Playscript authors: Eric Urvoy and Dawn Marley
Translation assistance: Dora Carpenter-Laitri; Vanessa Samandi
For the interview: Corrine Bywaters

The European Day of Languages

Project Assistance: The National Centre for Languages (CILT), part of CfBT Education Trust

Eurofest

Original project design: Selby Modern Language Forum; University of Hull; NYBEP.

Languages and the world of work

Original project design: Tanya Riordan, Pat Suttman, Malcolm Lloyd
With thanks to The NatWest Island Games 2011; Gurit UK; Carnival UK

The Language Leader award

Devised by Rachel Hawkes and run by Sarah Schechter

Reaching out to parents

Original project design: Tanya Riordan
Project assistance: Maggi McEwan and Bob Gould

Language live

Original project design: Yvonne Clerehugh and Joc Mack
Translation assistance: Valerie Letondeur and Cristina Molina.

The Marie Curie project

Original project design: Noel Jackson, John Cobb and Sarah Kemp.
Project assistance from: Mark Hanly, Jane Williamson and Simon Henderson (Théâtre Sans Frontières), Margaret Turner and Jacqui Cameron, Hugh Beattie, Rella LaRoe. And funding from The Wellcome Trust. Preparatory resource materials for teachers created by Jane Dawson and Mike Butler with Karen Jeff.
Audio recording: Benjamin Bâcle
Translation assistance: Olivier Boulocher

Spanglovision

Original project design: Rachel Hawkes

Die Mauer

Original project and creation: the University of Hull; the Goethe Institut Manchester; Routes into Languages Yorkshire and The Humber; Links into Languages Yorkshire and The Humber; IdentityCreation.com.

Taking steps towards CLIL (Exploring Antarctica in French and Spanish)

Project created by: Links into Languages
Translation assistance: María Emmerson and Olivier Boulocher
Artwork: Catherine Watts

European geography (Introducing Austria and Switzerland)

Project created by: Elizabeth Wielander
Artwork: Nicola Goodland

Recipes for MFL success!

Project created by: Tamsin Day
Translation assistance: the Burkart family

Foreign Language Spelling Bee

Original project design: Jane Driver, Rachel Hawkes, Sarah Schechter.

The Gold Award for Languages

Project design: Tanya Riordan, Linda Cadier, Di Bowes-Read

The mini-book-making project

Original project design: Jane Breen, Linda Cairns and the Quartier Rouge Schools network

The Foreign Languages Draw

Original project design: Catherine Watts inspired by The Campaign for Drawing.

Continuing Professional Development

This chapter was written by Daryl Bailey and based around professional development workshops she has recently delivered together with Hilary Phillips in East Sussex.

List of abbreviations

CLIL	=	Content and Language Integrated Learning
CPD	=	Continuing Professional Development
EDL	=	European Day of Languages
FL	=	Foreign Language
INSET	=	In-Service Training
IT	=	Information Technology
ITT	=	Initial Teacher Training
MFL	=	Modern Foreign Languages
PE	=	Physical Education
PGCE	=	Post Graduate Certificate in Education
PLTS	=	Personal Learning and Thinking Skills
TiR	=	Teacher in Role
TL	=	Target language

Preface

This book is set against the shifting landscape of foreign-language teaching in secondary schools in England, where the new secondary curriculum for all schools in the maintained sector has now come into effect. This places the emphasis on a much more blended curriculum than was previously the case, reflecting an important shift away from prioritizing coverage of content towards more emphasis on the acquisition of key concepts and skills. However, this book would also fit in well if a reversal to a knowledge-based curriculum were to take place, and we, as a language community, could refocus our attention on Content and Language Integrated Learning (CLIL), where the foreign language is used to teach other areas of the curriculum. All of the projects and activities presented in this book have been designed by language teachers for language teachers, and all have been tried and tested in different learning situations. They seek to motivate and inspire: all are replicable/adaptable and all contain a wealth of resources to extend and enhance the main projects. They aim to help language teachers in secondary schools (both experienced and novice) to combine their language teaching with other parts of the curriculum in new, imaginative and creative ways.

This volume is divided into eight Parts which, in turn, present a wide range of projects combining languages with different aspects of the secondary curriculum, for example, sport, media and drama. Such combinations are in line with recommendations in *The Languages Review*, which mentions "the many possibilities for less ambitious embedding of languages in cooperation with subjects such as Sport, Performing Arts, and Enterprise" (Dearing and King, 2007, 14–15). Each Part in *Living Languages: an integrated approach to teaching foreign languages in secondary schools* comprises four projects; one in Spanish, one in French, one in German, with a final project combining any one or all of these three languages. The projects are of differing lengths. Some are designed to fit into a themed day, for example. Others may straddle six lessons or more, whilst others will fit happily into one lesson. Each project is accompanied by extra language teaching resources on the additional DVD. The DVD material aims to extend the project's possibilities where appropriate, but may just include a list of useful websites indicating where additional resources can be found. Alternatively, the additional materials may include a picture gallery showing the finished results of a particular project, a full translation of the work presented in another language, or a film of the finished project in action.

Over twenty-eight examples of fully-developed projects and activities are brought together here, many of which have won awards and prizes in recent years. One of the prizes mentioned frequently in connection with the work presented in this book is the

European Award for Languages, now called *The European Language Label.* This prestigious award is a Europe-wide initiative supported by the European Commission and co-ordinated in the UK by CILT, the National Centre for Languages, part of the CfBT Education Trust. We are delighted to be able to include in this book so many projects that have won this award which recognises innovation in language teaching and learning.

Many of the projects derive from the work of *Routes into Languages,* a national initiative established in 2007 (www.routesintolanguages.ac.uk). *Routes into Languages* is designed to promote the take-up and continued study of foreign languages in the 14–19 age range by motivating students in secondary schools to participate in a wide variety of events, projects and activities initiated by universities in many regions across the country. Routes into Languages is structured around nine regional consortia comprising 67 universities across the country, and we are very grateful to everyone concerned for allowing us to draw on project materials for inclusion in this book.

Thus, a wealth of exciting, and often award-winning, teaching materials is presented here, which we hope will inspire your teaching, motivate your students and offer further possibilities for your foreign-language classrooms and beyond, to be enjoyed by everyone.

Viel Spass!   **¡que lo pase bien!**   **Amusez-vous bien!**

1

Languages and Sport

routes into
LANGUAGES

Introduction

The idea of combining language learning with various sporting activities is very attractive to many young people, particularly for boys, who may be reluctant to take up or continue with languages. This first Part presents four projects, each based around the theme of sport and each one easy to deliver across one year group. All four projects were developed as part of the national Routes into Languages initiative (see the list of useful websites on the accompanying DVD), and the main aim of each one is to motivate and maximise active target language use. *The German Orienteering Festival* (Project 2) and *Handball in Spanish* (Project 3) both originated from the Youth Sport Trust (see list of useful websites on the accompanying DVD) a charity established in 1994 with a mission to build a brighter future for young people through Physical Education (PE) and Sport.

Project 1 is entitled *Score in French* and is based around a football tournament presented in French. Football is seen here as an ideal way for languages departments to exploit cross-curricular links, raise the profile of languages in the school and motivate those less keen on more traditional classroom methods of teaching and learning. The second project, *The German Orienteering Festival*, takes language learning outside the classroom, but within the school grounds, where students are encouraged to complete a marked-out course, all whilst using the target language! This is followed by *Handball in Spanish*, which can straddle six lessons, is as active as the others and, like the others, encourages full use of the target language, in this case Spanish. The fourth and final project in this Part, *The Foreign Languages Mini-olympics*, just like the others, could be delivered in any foreign language, but is presented here in French, German and Spanish. It contains a wealth of ideas for sports and languages activities which can be used either at the end of a lesson or else as the basis for a more formal Languages and Physical Education day. All of the projects are fun, all will appeal to young people interested in sports and languages and all have great potential for cross-curricular links.

Project 1   Score in French

Project Outline

Requirements: a classroom and a final-stage tournament venue
Event time: six lessons
Language targeted: French
Impact: medium to high. The final tournament can be held between different schools

Introduction

This project was first developed by the University of Southampton in 2009 as part of the work of Routes South. A full report has also been published (McCall, 2011) which explores the project in more detail and considers its impact in greater depth. The published article presents a detailed analysis of questionnaire responses from the 634 students and twenty teachers involved in the project's pilot phase and reflects too on the responses with regard to gender. Further materials to accompany those presented in this Part are available from the Routes South website (see useful internet sites listed on the accompanying DVD) which cover over forty hours of class contact. A less extensive version of the *Score in French* material is presented in this Part, which focuses mainly on the football tournaments that take place in six stages. Students are encouraged to select and introduce their teams to each other; show support for their team; describe parts of the body and talk about injuries. Among the additional DVD materials for this project is an interview in French with two French football-players together with a full transcript in French, a sample certificate you could use at the end of the tournament, a small picture gallery and a list of useful related websites.

Organisation

The heart of the *Score in French* project is designed around six stages, with each stage taking one lesson to complete. The final stage culminates in the football final, whilst the remaining five stages work up to this.

Stage One (tirage au sort)

The first activity involves organising the in–class World Cup Tournament. Students have the opportunity through this activity to practise and reinforce: parts of *être* and *avoir*; numbers up to 32; colours; languages; adjectives of nationality. Each pupil needs to be assigned a national team. The countries represented in this '*coupe du monde*' are detailed in the boxes overleaf. The list can either be cut up, with each student drawing their country's box from a hat, or else each student can draw a number (1–32) which represents their team. A flag for each country can easily be added to each box before you cut them out (see the list of useful internet sites on the accompanying DVD); alternatively, students could research the flag themselves once they have selected their team and draw this in colour alongside the text.

1 **Pays:** *l'Algérie* **Langues:** *l'arabe, le français* **Adjectif:** *algérien/ne*	**2** **Pays:** *l'Australie* **Langue:** *l'anglais* **Adjectif:** *australien/ne*	**3** **Pays:** *le Cameroun* **Langues:** *le français, l'anglais* **Adjectif:** *camerounais/e*
4 **Pays:** *l'Indonésie* **Langues:** *l'indonésien, le français* **Adjectif:** *indonésien/ne*	**5** **Pays:** *le Japon* **Langue:** *le japonais* **Adjectif:** *japonais/e*	**6** **Pays:** *le Maroc* **Langues:** *l'arabe, le français* **Adjectif:** *marocain/e*
7 **Pays:** *le Sénégal* **Langue:** *le français* **Adjectif:** *sénégalais/e*	**8** **Pays:** *la Corée du Sud* **Langues:** *le coréen, le français* **Adjectif:** *sud-coréen/ne*	**9** **Pays:** *la Tunisie* **Langues:** *l'arabe, le français* **Adjectif:** *tunisien/ne*
10 **Pays:** *le Vietnam* **Langues:** *le vietnamien, le français* **Adjectif:** *vietnamien/ne*	**11** **Pays:** *la France* **Langue:** *le français* **Adjectif:** *français/e*	**12** **Pays:** *la Belgique* **Langues:** *le néerlandais, le français, l'allemand* **Adjectif:** *belge*
13 **Pays:** *le Luxembourg* **Langues:** *l'allemand, le français, le luxembourgeois* **Adjectif:** *luxembourgeois/e*	**14** **Pays:** *la Suisse* **Langues:** *l'allemand, le français, l'italien, le romanche* **Adjectif:** *suisse*	**15** **Pays:** *l'Argentine* **Langue:** *l'espagnol* **Adjectif:** *argentin/e*
16 **Pays:** *le Brésil* **Langue:** *le portugais* **Adjectif:** *brésilien/ne*	**17** **Pays:** *le Canada* **Langues:** *l'anglais, le français* **Adjectif:** *canadien/ne*	**18** **Pays:** *le Chili* **Langue:** *l'espagnol* **Adjectif:** *chilien/ne*
19 **Pays:** *la Colombie* **Langue:** *l'espagnol* **Adjectif:** *colombien/ne*	**20** **Pays:** *l'Écosse* **Langue:** *l'anglais* **Adjectif:** *écossais/e*	**21** **Pays:** *la République tchèque* **Langue:** *le tchèque* **Adjectif:** *tchèque*
22 **Pays:** *l'Angleterre* **Langue:** *l'anglais* **Adjectif:** *anglais/e*	**23** **Pays:** *l'Allemagne* **Langue:** *l'allemand* **Adjectif:** *allemand/e*	**24** **Pays:** *la Grèce* **Langue:** *le grec* **Adjectif:** *grec/grecque*
25 **Pays:** *le pays de Galles* **Langues:** *l'anglais, le gallois* **Adjectif:** *gallois/e*	**26** **Pays:** *l'Italie* **Langue:** *l'italien* **Adjectif:** *italien/ne*	**27** **Pays:** *le Pays-Bas* **Langue:** *le néerlandais* **Adjectif:** *néerlandais/e*
28 **Pays:** *le Portugal* **Langue:** *le portugais* **Adjectif:** *portugais/e*	**29** **Pays:** *l'Espagne* **Langue:** *l'espagnol* **Adjectif:** *espagnol/e*	**30** **Pays:** *l'Irlande* **Langue:** *l'anglais* **Adjectif:** *irlandais/e*
31 **Pays:** *les États-Unis* **Langue:** *l'anglais* **Adjectif:** *américain/e*	**32** **Pays:** *la Pologne* **Langue:** *le polonais* **Adjectif:** *polonais/e*	

Students introduce their team in French to the rest of the class. Some of the following structures can be practised:

Je suis manager/capitaine de l'équipe de....

Mes joueurs sont... et parlent....

Notre drapeau est (+ colour)....

Stage Two (tirage au sort and matchs de groupes)

The teams now have to be put into eight qualifying groups (A–H). This can be done by means of a draw, or else teams one to four are '*Groupe A*', teams five to eight '*Groupe B*', etc. Put students into groups of four according to the country they have drawn, to 'play' the matches between all the teams in their group. Matches are played using dice as follows.

Each manager/captain throws for his/her team. Each match is five pairs of throws with a goal awarded to the highest score in each pair (this will allow for various, realistic scores). If time is limited, each match can be decided on a single pair of throws.

At the end, each group reports back the scores of its matches in French and the group table is created. A win for a match gives the team three points and a draw one point. The top two teams from each group go through to the *huitièmes de finale*. If two teams draw on points, the winning team is decided on who won the game they played against each other!

(N.B. There are unlikely to be exactly 32 pupils in a class, so one pupil in each group may need to be given an extra team. Alternatively, keen pupils may play a group's matches in a break and report back the result.)

In order to prepare for the third stage of the tournament, the following activities about being a supporter are useful. They allow students to choose a team and express their support using appropriate vocabulary which will, in turn, engage pupils whose teams were eliminated in the previous round.

Task 1: Matching expressions

This activity helps students learn how to encourage, praise and criticise in French. Ask students to match the expressions in the box to the correct picture.

(N.B. Some of the pictures can be used more than once!)

> ALLEZ LES BLEUS! ON VA GAGNER! AUX ARMES!
>
> ZUT! AFFREUX! ABOMINABLE!
>
> DOMMAGE! IL EST NUL! LAMENTABLE! PURÉE!
>
> CHOUETTE! FORMIDABLE! GÉNIAL! SUPER!
> EXCELLENT! SENSATIONNEL! MAGNIFIQUE!
>
> BRAVO! INCROYABLE!

Suggested answers:

Picture 1 = *Dommage!* Picture 2 = *On va gagner!* Picture 3 = *Zut!*

Picture 4 = *Chouette!* Picture 5 = *Lamentable!* Picture 6 = *Formidable!*

Picture 7 = *Aux armes!* Picture 8 = *Allez les bleus!* Picture 9 = *Génial!*

Task 2: Word search

This word search reinforces key vocabulary presented in Task 1 and adds some extra items too.

Word search – *Trouvez les mots!*   *Trouvez les mots suivants:*

```
S  S  U  N  D  I  S  C  U  T  E  R  B  H  W
T  N  E  L  L  E  C  X  E  C  B  N  G  W  J
J  R  T  S  E  N  S  A  T  I  O  N  N  E  L
M  C  T  U  B  L  D  O  M  M  A  G  E  B  D
I  R  E  I  E  L  B  A  D  I  M  R  O  F  T
X  E  U  E  A  P  I  U  Q  E  I  Z  W  A
Y  N  O  Z  L  B  X  U  E  R  F  F  A  L  L
E  G  H  X  S  B  R  R  O  R  R  D  L  T  Y
R  A  C  U  K  U  A  W  E  P  K  E  K  E  I
D  G  W  U  R  Y  P  T  X  H  Z  R  P  R  C
R  T  Z  N  Y  Q  N  E  N  K  W  H  W  R  S
E  C  X  M  D  A  O  J  R  E  U  P  N  I  P
P  R  V  F  H  Z  P  H  T  R  M  C  B  B  D
G  S  F  C  E  A  B  O  M  I  N  A  B  L  E
S  K  Q  N  J  D  U  R  F  J  L  H  L  E  O
```

ALLEZ	
FORMIDABLE	
SUPER	
CHOUETTE	
EXCELLENT	
SENSATIONNEL	
DOMMAGE	
TERRIBLE	
AFFREUX	
LAMENTABLE	
ABOMINABLE	
GAGNER	
PERDRE	
EQUIPE	
CHANTER	
DISCUTER	

Answers:

```
S  S  U  N  D  I  S  C  U  T  E  R  B  H  W
T  N  E  L  L  E  C  X  E  C  B  N  G  W  J
J  R  T  S  E  N  S  A  T  I  O  N  N  E  L
M  C  T  U  B  L  D  O  M  M  A  G  E  B  D
I  R  E  I  E  L  B  A  D  I  M  R  O  F  T
X  E  U  E  A  P  I  U  Q  E  I  Z  W  A
Y  N  O  Z  L  B  X  U  E  R  F  F  A  L  L
E  G  H  X  S  B  R  R  O  R  R  D  L  T  Y
R  A  C  U  K  U  A  W  E  P  K  E  K  E  I
D  G  W  U  R  Y  P  T  X  H  Z  R  P  R  C
R  T  Z  N  Y  Q  N  E  N  K  W  H  W  R  S
E  C  X  M  D  A  O  J  R  E  U  P  N  I  P
P  R  V  F  H  Z  P  H  T  R  M  C  B  B  D
G  S  F  C  E  A  B  O  M  I  N  A  B  L  E
S  K  Q  N  J  D  U  R  F  J  L  H  L  E  O
```

ALLEZ
FORMIDABLE
SUPER
CHOUETTE
EXCELLENT
SENSATIONNEL
DOMMAGE
TERRIBLE
AFFREUX
LAMENTABLE
ABOMINABLE
GAGNER
PERDRE
EQUIPE
CHANTER
DISCUTER

Task 3: Quiz

This quiz will allow you to practise *aller* and words like *quelquefois* and *souvent*. Pupils can be asked to write some sentences in simple French about what good supporters do, based on the questions in the quiz itself. For example:

un bon supporter regarde toujours son équipe à la télé
un bon supporter a des affiches de son équipe dans sa chambre, etc.

What sort of supporter are you?
Quel type de supporter es-tu?

Tu vas aux matchs à domicile:

a)   plus de dix fois par an

b)   plus de quatre fois par an

c)   moins de quatre fois par an

Tu connais les noms de:

a)   plus de six joueurs de ton équipe

b)   plus de trois joueurs de ton équipe

c)   moins de trois joueurs de ton équipe

Tu connais le score du dernier match:

a)   toujours

b)   quelquefois

c)   jamais

Tu rêves de ton équipe:

a)   souvent

b)   quelquefois

c)   jamais

Tu vas aux matchs à l'extérieur:

a)   plus de quatre fois par an

b)   plus d'une fois par an

c)   jamais

Tu connais le nom de l'équipe adverse du prochain match:

a)   toujours

b)   quelquefois

c)   jamais

Tu portes le maillot de ton équipe:

a)   souvent

b)   quelquefois

c)   jamais

Réponse A = 2 points
Réponse B = 1 point
Réponse C = 0 point

Tu as plus de 12 points:
Tu es un supporter magnifique. Bravo!

Tu as plus de 7 points:
Tu es un bon supporter. Pas mal!

Tu as moins de 7 points:
Tu es nul(le) comme supporter!

Stage Three (Huitièmes de finale)

This phase is played between the top two teams from each group as follows:

Match One: Winner of Group A plays Second of Group B

Match Two: Winner of Group B plays Second of Group A

Match Three: Winner of Group C plays Second of Group D

Match Four: Winner of Group D plays Second of Group C

Match Five: Winner of Group E plays Second of Group F

Match Six: Winner of Group F plays Second of Group E

Match Seven: Winner of Group G plays Second of Group H

Match Eight: Winner of Group H plays Second of Group G

These matches can be played with dice in the same way as the previous phase. If after five throws it is a draw, a further throw will be needed as a decider, as all rounds from now on are knockout ones! You may wish to space these matches out over several classes as a five-minute end-of-class activity.

Stage Four (Quarts de finale)

A)   Winner of Match One plays Winner of Match Two.

B)   Winner of Match Three plays Winner of Match Four.

C)   Winner of Match Five plays Winner of Match Six.

D)   Winner of Match Seven plays Winner of Match Eight.

Stage Five (Demi-finales)

Winner of A plays Winner of B

Winner of C plays Winner of D

Stage Six (Finale)

We would recommend that you play the final at the end of the project. Why not set up a table-football game in the middle of the classroom or the playground and play the final using this? You could film your final too and/or play the final for real on the football pitch with your students representing the two teams, with supporters, etc. You could also involve another school and play the final tournament together all in the target language of course!

Reflections

Score in French is an exciting way of engaging young learners in French. The idea of learning a new language through a familiar topic is appealing, as students feel comfortable and more motivated as a result. This motivation is further harnessed when students are presented with the opportunity of participating in a football tournament at the end of the project, perhaps involving another school. The need to work hard in order to be able to take part ensures even the most reluctant learner makes an effort. For those less keen on the idea of running around a football pitch, the wide array of other cross-curricular activities, such as cheerleading, singing and art projects is also attractive. Finally, the project is inviting, as it can be developed in school and embedded in the curriculum, as well as being used as a model for inter-school collaboration.

Describing bodies and faces

Four activities follow which introduce or revise parts of the face and body. They will also allow you to introduce or revise possessives and expressions relating to injury.

Task 1: Describing the body

As a preliminary question, ask your students if they can work out why some words are in grey bubbles whilst others are in white (the grey ones are feminine and the white ones are masculine).

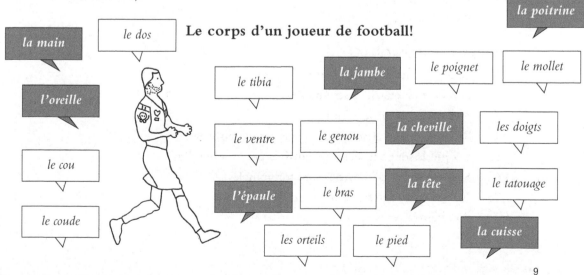

Le corps d'un joueur de football!

9

The first task is to label the body parts by drawing an arrow from the word in French to the appropriate part of the body. Or, if you have an interactive whiteboard, project the picture and ask students to label it. Or, if you can, print the task on A4 sticky-back labels. Let the students cut out the words and label each other!

You can give the body in the picture a name: e.g. Bernard. Then try playing "Simon says...", but here it is obviously "*Bernard dit touche la tête*," etc.

Answers: The body of the football player

le tibia: shinbone	*le tatouage*: tattoo	*les orteils*: toes
le poignet: wrist	*la main*: hand	*le pied*: foot
l'épaule: shoulder	*la cuisse*: thigh	*le dos*: back
le mollet: calf	*la cheville*: ankle	*le bras*: arm
le ventre: stomach	*la tête*: head	*le coude*: elbow
la jambe: leg	*le cou*: neck	*l'oreille* (f): ear
le genou: knee	*la poitrine*: chest	*les doigts*: fingers

Two further activites follow to practise the body vocabulary.

Task 2: Revising possessives

This exercise allows you to revise possessives. Looking at the body of Bernard, encourage students to complete the gaps in the sentences with a word from the list of body parts above.

1. Sa tête est attachée à son…
2. Son… est attaché à ses…
3. Son… et ses… sont larges.
4. Ses… sont attachées à ses bras par ses…
5. Ses… sont attachés a ses… par ses…
6. Sa… et ses… sont très musclés.
7. Il a un… sur le…
8. Son… est plat.

Suggested answers:

1. Sa tête est attachée à son **cou**.
2. Son **cou** est attaché à ses **épaules**.
3. Son **cou** et ses **bras** sont larges.
4. Ses **mains** sont attachées à ses bras par ses **poignets**.
5. Ses **pieds** sont attachés a ses **jambes** par ses **chevilles**.
6. Sa **poitrine** et ses **jambes** sont très musclés.
7. Il a un **tatouage** sur le **bras.**
8. Son **ventre** est plat.

Now consider asking your students to write about how they are put together themselves using *"mon, ma, mes… /notre, nos…,* etc. They should be encouraged to write five sensible sentences each.

Task 3: Mots croisés!

This is a crossword puzzle. As a follow up, ask your students if they can write a clue for a part of the body that isn't represented in the crossword.

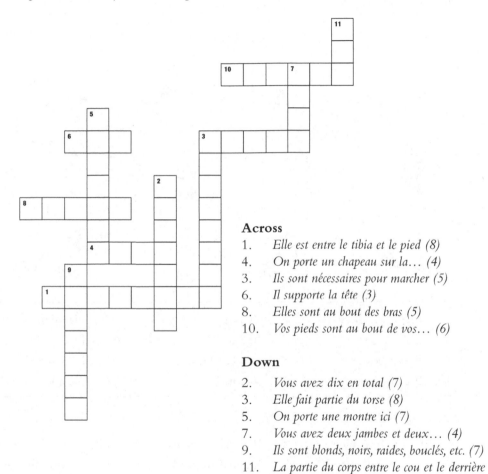

Across

1.   *Elle est entre le tibia et le pied (8)*
4.   *On porte un chapeau sur la… (4)*
3.   *Ils sont nécessaires pour marcher (5)*
6.   *Il supporte la tête (3)*
8.   *Elles sont au bout des bras (5)*
10.   *Vos pieds sont au bout de vos… (6)*

Down

2.   *Vous avez dix en total (7)*
3.   *Elle fait partie du torse (8)*
5.   *On porte une montre ici (7)*
7.   *Vous avez deux jambes et deux… (4)*
9.   *Ils sont blonds, noirs, raides, bouclés, etc. (7)*
11.   *La partie du corps entre le cou et le derrière*

Answers:

Across		*Down*	
1.	*cheville*	2.	*orteils*
4.	*tête*	3.	*poitrine*
3.	*pieds*	5.	*poignet*
6.	*cou*	7.	*bras*
8.	*mains*	9.	*cheveux*
10.	*jambes*	11.	*dos*

Task 4: Talking about injuries

Once your students have mastered the parts of the body, they are ready to move on to thinking about injuries. After doing this gap-fill exercise, ask your students to imagine they are the person in the picture. They need to express their pain and say what is wrong with them!

Hopefully your students will never need these expressions, but they may come in handy one day!

Les blessures

1. 2. 3. 4.

5. 6. 7. 8.

9. 10. 11. 12.

1. Elle a le…blessé.	2. Il a mal au…	3. Elle saigne de la…
4. Il a la…cassée	5. Il a mal au…	6. Il a l'…blessée
7. Il a le…cassé	8. Il a la…blessée	9. Il a mal à la…
10. Il a mal à la…	11. Il a mal aux…	12. Elle a le…blessé

Answers

1. Elle a le **bras** blessé.	2. Il a mal au **genou.**	3. Elle saigne de la **tête.**
4. Il a la **jambe** cassée.	5. Il a mal au **pied**.	6. Il a **l'oreille** blessée.
7. Il a le **bras** cassé.	8. Il a la **tête** blessée.	9. Il a mal a la **cheville**.
10. Il a mal à la **jambe**.	11. Il a mal aux **bras.**	12. Elle a le **genou** blessé.

Score in French: Additional DVD materials

1. An interview with two footballers
2. Full interview transcript in French
3. Example of an end-of-tournament certifictate
4. *Score in French*: small picture gallery
5. Useful websites

Project 2   The German orienteering festival

Project Outline

Requirements: classrooms for early stages; school field or large outdoor space for competition.
Event time: 3 × usual lesson time (although this can be extended if necessary) plus organisation time.
Language targeted: German
Impact: medium-high (can be used with small and large groups)

Introduction

Originally an idea proposed by the Youth Sport Trust and developed by the Routes into Languages consortium in the West Midlands in partnership with a local school, *The German Orienteering Festival* is an innovative way to combine language learning with an outdoor activity. The aim is to devise a marked course with a number of control points between which students must navigate in order to complete it in the fastest time – all whilst working together in the target language. Languages and PE departments can work together to organise and deliver the project. It is suitable not only for language learners of all abilities, but also for those of different ages, with older students providing support by acting as *Language Leaders* (see Part IV, Project 3). Here we outline the preparation and delivery of the activity and include such materials as sample maps, clue examples, core vocabulary, a classroom game, a comprehension task and a sample reporter's interview. The accompanying DVD also includes the following additional materials: clues for higher- and lower-ability groups, a blank grid for maps, a sample marker sheet, a themed quiz and certificate templates.

Organisation

The activity is divided into three stages, each taking a minimum of one lesson to complete. However, this time frame can be extended if it is felt that more sessions are needed to introduce and learn new target language vocabulary or to prepare for the 'Grand Finale'. Before delivering the activity, some organisation and setting up time should also be built in and shared amongst the languages and PE teachers involved.

Setting up

Before implementing the project, languages and PE teachers should work together to devise a course within the school grounds. This should then be mapped onto a simple grid, with buildings and any other features clearly marked. The course should have a series of numbered markers which will be used as navigation points. Here is an example of a completed basic map.

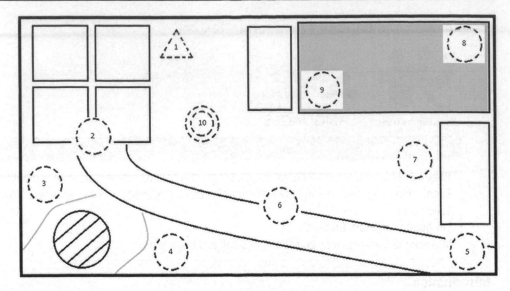

Legend

> **Black:** man-made structures, such as buildings, paths, etc.
>
> **Grey:** vegetation that can be easily navigated, such as playing fields, open spaces, etc.
>
> **Striped:** water such as ponds, lakes, rivers etc.
>
> **Circles with broken lines:** course markers
>
> **Triangle with broken lines:** starting point
>
> **Double circle with broken lines:** finish

Once the course and corresponding map have been designed, clue sheets should be prepared in German to help students navigate the course. Clues should match the numbered markers on the course and can be differentiated according to the target language level of those taking part. The table below offers examples of clues for a general-level class. The questions are given in English and students should be encouraged to answer them in German. Clues for higher- and lower-ability groups can be found in the material for this project on the accompanying DVD.

Sample clues (corresponding to the sample map presented previously)

Markierer	Hinweis	Antwort (auf Deutsch!)
1	What is the name of the room you have just left?	
2	What colour are the doors in this building?	
3	Name an animal that lives in the pond	
4	How many trees can you see from here?	
5	List two lessons that are taught in the building opposite you.	
6	What is the name of the area you can see ahead of you?	
7	Give directions to the canteen from here.	
8	Name two sports you can play here.	
9	Name a type of food and a type of drink you can get here.	
10	How many windows does the building in front of you have?	

To help reiterate the importance of using the target language during this activity, it may also help if participating PE teachers learn some of the basic vocabulary, as in doing so they will act as good role models for the students.

A last step in the setting up and design of the activity is to decide how the markers should physically appear on the course. Ideally they should be large and colourful enough to be easily identified. Cones, hoops or even chairs and tables can be used. Each marker should also be equipped with a pen or pencil and a sheet of paper listing all partici-pating teams so that a member of each team can sign or mark that they have been to that part of the course. Only teams that have identified themselves at each marker can qualify for the 'Grand Finale'. It may also be helpful for the languages and PE teachers to familiarise themselves with the course by walking it through a couple of times to ensure the map and clues are clear and accurate.

It is also useful to consider how older students can act as *Language Leaders* (see also Part IV, Project 3) not only to support the event (for example, staffing markers, giving out maps, helping at refreshment stands and so on) but also to help and encourage younger learners. One Language Leader could be assigned to each team to help with target language clues and navigation.

Stage One: Student briefing

Before students take part in this activity, a briefing session during the language lesson should be held. This session can be used as an opportunity to learn or revisit useful vocabulary for the task, such as colours, numbers, school buildings and so on. It also provides time for students to learn some new motivational language so that they can cheer on their teams. Here is a list of useful core vocabulary.

Core vocabulary

Deutsch	English	*Deutsch*	English
der Orientierungslauf	orienteering	das Gebäude	building
die Landkarte	map	die Umkleidekabine	changing room
der Kompass	compass	der Baum	tree
nord	north	der Weg	path
süd	south	das Fenster	window
ost	east	die Tür	door
west	west	die Sperre	gate
links	left	der Zaun	fence
rechts	right	unterstützen	to support
geradeaus	straight on	der Anhänger	supporter (male)
die Mannschaft	team	die Anhängerin	supporter (female)
der Mannschaftskapitän	team captain	hochrufen	to cheer
der Lauf	course	der Gesang	chant
die Markierung	marker	das Lied	song
die Konkurrenz	competition	der Reporter	reporter (male)
der Gewinner	winner	die Reporterin	reporter (female)
das große Finale	grand finale	der Fotograf	photographer (male)
das Wörterbuch	dictionary	die Fotografin	photographer (female)
schnell	fast	die Erfrischungen	refreshments
schnellste	fastest	Erfrischungen reichen	to serve refreshments
laufen	to run	die Getränke	drinks
die Schule	school	das Plakat	poster
die Sportplätze	playing fields	das Banner	banner
die Kantine	canteen	machen	to make/do
das Klassenzimmer	classroom	winken	to wave

Classroom game

A quick game can also be played in the classroom, so that everyone can familiarise themselves with the main compass points and their target language equivalent. Students are asked to stand facing the teacher – this position is 'north'. 'East' is to the students' right, 'south' behind them and 'west' to their left. The teacher then calls the compass points at random and everyone must quickly turn so that they are facing in the right direction. This can be practised in English first and then in German, using 'nord', 'süd', 'ost' and 'west' as the commands. If someone turns in the wrong direction they are out and must sit down. The game continues until the winner is the last person left standing.

You may also wish to refer the third project in Part Six of this book (*European Geography: Introducing Austria and Switzerland*) for further work in German with maps and compass points which can be easily adapted to fit this task.

Comprehension task

Depending on the number of sessions allocated for this activity, another game can also be played which helps reinforce students' understanding of the target language. This can be done either in pairs or as a whole class. The aim of the game is for students to recreate a basic map with a path marked on it by following simple instructions in the target language such as *Es gibt einen Baum auf der rechten Seite*. If working in pairs, one person will hold a picture of the map (the sample map above could be used) and will slowly describe it without letting the other person see what it looks like. The other person must then draw what they think their partner is describing (or, if a whole class activity, everyone draws what the teacher describes). Once the drawings have been completed, the person whose drawing best matches the original is the winner.

By the end of the briefing session (or sessions) students should possess at least a basic knowledge of the core vocabulary necessary for the activity and an understanding of what will happen in the next stage.

Stage Two: Class competition

Stage Two is also completed during a language lesson. Here students put to practical use the vocabulary learned in the previous session (or sessions) in order to decipher clues and successfully navigate the course. The class should be divided into teams and each one given a map of the course and – depending on its ability in the target language – one of three diffferent versions of clues in that language. The aim is to complete the course in the fastest possible time, communicating only in German. Teams do not have to follow the markers in numerical order but must work together to identify the quickest way round. However, teams must remember to sign against their team name on the sheet at each marker, or risk being disqualified. It may be useful to stagger each team's start times by a couple of minutes, so that groups have time to spread out along the course. A dictionary can be placed in the middle of the course and teams can be allocated three uses of the dictionary each should they need help in answering the clues. A teacher (or Language Leader) should be on hand to monitor fair use of the dictionary and also to encourage students to use their linguistic skills as far as possible before resorting to the dictionary. Those completing the course in the fastest time go through to the 'Grand Finale' to compete against the fastest teams from other classes.

Stage Three: The Grand Finale

Whilst the final stage of the project brings together the winning teams from the class competition, those who will not be competing should remain involved in the activity.

A range of target language tasks can be arranged to help prepare for the 'Grand Finale'. Popular ones include: creating target-language banners and posters, as well as learning team cheers and songs to support the class representatives (see list of useful websites for this project on the accompanying DVD); allocating the roles of event reporter and event photographer to some students; setting up a refreshments table where thirsty competitors must ask for their drink (and perhaps pieces of fruit) in German!

Reporter interviews

Event reporters should be encouraged to interview finalists in German. Students can follow the interview questions below or make up their own questions in either German or English, depending on ability.

1.   *Was hältst du vom Orientierungslauf?*
2.   *Hat dir heute Spaß gemacht?*
3.   *Welche Mannschaft hat gewonnen?*
4.   *Was hat dir am besten gefallen?*
5.   *Würdest du es wieder machen?*

Following the event, winners can be presented with certificates either on the day or in assembly. Prizes can be awarded not only to the winning orienteering team, but also for the best cheers or songs, the best banners, the best event report and/or photograph and the best refreshment stall. Certificate templates can be found in the materials section for this project on the accompanying DVD.

Reflections

Groups who have participated in this activity have reported its positive impact not only on language learning, but also on the sense of support and competition within and between classes. This has consequently improved the atmosphere and camaraderie in the teaching groups, resulting in greater productivity during lessons in general. In some instances using older students as Language Leaders has inspired younger learners to become future Language Leaders themselves. The project has also had a more far-reaching effect at home, with parents mentioning it at parents' evenings. On a wider school level it has provided a basis for the development of further cross-curricular activities.

The German Orienteering Festival: Additional DVD materials

1.   Clues for higher-ability groups
2.   Clues for lower-ability groups
3.   Blank grid for maps
4.   Sample marker sheet
5.   Themed quiz
6.   Certificate templates
7.   Useful websites

Project 3   Handball in Spanish

Youth Sport Trust

routes into
LANGUAGES

Project outline

Requirements: a classroom and a tournament hall
Event time: six lessons
Language targeted: Spanish
Impact: medium (30+ pupils)

Introduction

Handball is in some ways the perfect sport to introduce in the context of a modern foreign language. Whilst relatively unknown in the UK, the sport is immensely popular in Spain, which immediately presents a welcome aspect of intercultural awareness. Originally an idea proposed by the Youth Sport Trust (see list of useful websites on the accompanying DVD), it was developed into the project presented here by Routes East at Anglia Ruskin University by Rhys Bearder and Sarah Schechter. Routes East has been awarded the London 2012 Inspire Mark for all its Language & Sport events, including this one. As your students are unlikely to have played handball before, it is easy for everyone to get involved, regardless of ability. The session naturally focuses on using the new vocabulary and simply having fun without getting too tied up in the rules and technicalities of the game itself! To set the scene in your classroom, the Royal Spanish Handball Federation has some interesting photographs in its photo gallery (see useful internet sites on the accompanying DVD).

Your handball session would ideally be run indoors using five-a-side football goals. Officially, a team consists of six outfield players and one goalkeeper per team. The outfield players pass a ball and throw it into the goal of the other team. The team with the most goals after two periods of 30 minutes wins. You can assign players' positions and introduce vocabulary such as *delantero, defensa* or *centrocampista*. The game is quite fast and includes body contact as the defenders try to stop the ball from reaching the goal. Goals are scored quite frequently (usually both teams score around 20 goals each) which adds to the general excitement.

The rules of handball allow you to conduct the session mostly in the target language. For example, when receiving the ball a player must pass, shoot or dribble within three seconds – you could encourage any spectators to enforce this rule by shouting *uno*, *dos*, *tres* each time. Before shooting, the attacking player can shout *lanza* at the right time as well. If team mates want to receive the ball, they will quickly fall into the habit of calling *pasa* to their classmate.

Generally, you should feel free to make the session your own. Cast away any game rules which will put obstacles in the way of learning and introduce rules of your own which will encourage the use of the target language. The six-lesson version presented below is aimed at Year Sevens and is divided into various stages: warm-up; practice; revising key rules; using new skills; reinforcement of rules; mini-tournament. Each lesson is presented with the necessary key vocabulary and in sequence. All commands and body parts can be taught using gestures/touch, making the project highly practical and fun!

> The sessions I ran for Routes into Languages were a great success and nobody corrected my knowledge of the beautiful game of handball!
>
> *Rhys Bearder, Spanish handball teacher*

The main rules of Spanish handball (summary)

The handball playing field resembles an indoor soccer field. Two teams of seven players (six outfielders and a goalkeeper) attempt to score points by putting the game ball into the opposing team's goal. The following restrictions apply to players handling the ball:

- After receiving the ball, players can only hold it for up to three seconds before passing it on, dribbling with it or shooting;
- After receiving the ball, players can take up to three steps without dribbling. If they then dribble they may take an additional three steps;
- Players who stop dribbling have three seconds either to pass or shoot. They may take three additional steps during this time;
- No players other than the defending goalkeeper are allowed within the goal line. Goalkeepers are allowed outside this line.

Revising body parts in Spanish

head	*la cabeza*	neck	*el cuello*
shoulder	*el hombre*	chest	*el pecho*
arm	*el brazo*	elbow	*el codo*
leg	*la pierna*	knee	*la rodilla*
ankle	*el tobillo*	foot	*el pie*

Lesson One

Objectives

- Warming up – *calentamiento* in Spanish;
- Introduction of key rules (team, travelling, passing, shooting, bouncing, throwing, foul);
- Presentation of key Spanish vocabulary used in the game and drills.

Activities

1. Warming up (10 minutes)
   Drills: *corre, rápido/despacio, para, derecha/izquierda* (commands have to be repeated aloud by students);
2. In groups, practise passing skills (direct and bouncing) (10 minutes)

3. Whole group passes, moves about and shoots (10 minutes)
   Vocabulary: *pasa, bota, tira* (commands have to be repeated by students);

4. Recognise pitch markings including AREA before shooting;

5. Game between two teams using Spanish (15 minutes).
   Key Vocabulary: *corre, rápido, despacio, para, derecha, izquierda, pasa, bota, tira, calentamiento.*

Lesson Two

Objectives

- Warming up – *calentamiento* in Spanish;
- Revision of key rules;
- Practise Spanish vocabulary using known drills and game;
- Students to repeat key actions when involved in drills and game.

Activities

1. Warming up and revision of Lesson One vocabulary with parts of the body
   Drills: *cabeza, mano, pie, rodilla, pecho* (10 minutes);

2. In groups, practise passing and bouncing skills and warming up drill (10 minutes)
   Vocabulary: *pasa, bota;*

3. In groups practise shooting (10 minutes)
   Vocabulary: *tira;*

4. Ask for and discuss key rules including pitch marking

5. Warm down game in Spanish (10 minutes) following the 'line of attack' and 'line of defence' movements (seven-a-side).
   Key Vocabulary: *cabeza, mano, pecho, rodilla, pie, pasa, bota, tira*

Lesson Three

Objectives

- Warming up – *calentamiento* in Spanish;
- Using vocabulary from Lessons One and Two;
- Revision of key rules including attack/defence;
- Introduction of further frequently-used key vocabulary and phrases;
- Involvement of **all** students in using Spanish in drills and the game.

Activities

1. Warming up: revision of vocabulary from Lessons One and Two in a large group and then in a small group (10 minutes);

2. Practise short/long passing, straight and hitting the ground (5 minutes);

3. Practise shooting, straight and hitting the ground (5 minutes);

4. In groups organise *linea de defensa* and *linea de ataque* (10 minutes)
   Movement without the ball;

5. 5-a-side games practising defence and attack movements (15 minutes).
   Key Vocabulary: previous + *portero, defensa, ataque, ¡mia!*

Lesson Four

Objectives

- Warming up – *calentamiento* in Spanish;
- Using new skills, new Spanish vocabulary;
- Reinforcing rules and main skills;
- All students to be involved in using Spanish during drills and game.

Activities/Drills

1. Warming up in large and smaller groups, as in Lesson Three
   Vocabulary: *salta, detrás, delante, para* (10 minutes);
2. In small groups practise passing when running and shooting (10 minutes);
3. In groups practise drill for "passing on line" (attack) and defending with the ball (10 minutes);
4. Warming down game in Spanish (7-a-side) with four teams (15 minutes).
   Key Vocabulary: previous + *salta, detrás, delante, para*

Lesson Five

Objectives

- Warming up – *calentamiento* in Spanish;
- Reinforce rules and main skills;
- All students involved in using Spanish during the drill and the game.

Activities/Drills

1. Warming up using a combination of previous Spanish words (10 minutes);
2. In groups practise skills
   Vocabulary: *pasa, tira, corre* (10 minutes);
3. Revise the lined attack and defence (in groups) with the ball;
4. Full game (7-a-side) with four teams.
   Key Vocabulary: previous

Lesson Six

Objectives

- All students to participate in a mini-tournament after drills and warm-up in Spanish;
- All students to use Spanish whilst playing the game.

Mini Tournament

1. Organise four balanced teams;
2. Conduct a seven-minute game – "everyone plays everyone".

Handball in Spanish: Additional DVD materials

1. List of useful websites.

Project 4   The foreign languages mini-Olympics

Project Outline

Requirements: a sports hall or playing field; volley/net/basketballs; laminated letters; masking tape or chalk; scarves or similar to use as blindfolds; stopwatch; loudhailer (if necessary).
Event time: can range from doing one or two activities to start or end a lesson to doing all activities for a whole lesson
Languages targeted: any (materials here are presented in French, German and Spanish)
Impact: medium-high

Introduction

The other sections of this Part have focused on linking a language with a specific sport. In this section we look at ways of engaging students in language learning through different PE activities that can be used independently of each other to start or end a lesson, or collectively if you are looking for ideas for a cross-curricular Languages and PE Day. The ideas presented here give just a flavour of the things that can be done in such a setting. Staff in your PE department will no doubt have further suggestions, so it is certainly worth involving them if you are planning a whole-day event. Don't forget either that non-languages staff members willing to try a few words in a new language are great role models for younger students. It has also been noted (e.g. Johnson, 2008; Felder and Henriques, 1995) that students adopt different language learning styles. Offering a language lesson in a PE context will appeal to those who are active learners and will also provide others with an opportunity to try out new or different ways of learning.

The following section describes a number of different physical activities that can be combined with French. Additional materials, such as German and Spanish versions of warm-up exercises and game vocabulary, can be found on the DVD accompanying this book.

Organisation

Organising a Foreign Languages Mini-Olympics is relatively straightforward. If you opt for a whole lesson, or even a whole day event, you will need a space large enough for students to participate in team games. This could be in the school gym or sports hall, or even outside on the playing field or tennis courts if the weather allows. Alternatively, most of the activities outlined below can also be played in the classroom (or can be adapted to suit a classroom environment), providing it is possible to move tables and chairs around to create a suitable space.

To save time on the day, it is useful to get students into teams in advance, each team 'representing' a different country. Students can form their own teams or they can be assigned to a team, depending on ability, target language and so on. An ideal number of people per team for the type of games being played is seven or eight, although teams can be smaller or larger if necessary. Encourage students to pick a country where the language they will be playing the games in is spoken. They may wish to find out more about the country they have chosen: e.g. its flag; the colours the national sports team plays in; what sports are typically played there, etc. This could provide a useful motivational activity in the lead-up to the day.

Most of the games presented here do not require any advanced preparation apart from coming up with some themes (which could simply be the topics already covered in lessons). However the spelling relay requires some prior preparation of sets of letters (including the special characters needed depending on the target language used). Again, this is straightforward and you may already have the necessary materials to hand. If not, simply print out and laminate sufficient individual letters for each team to use during the game (and keep them safe to reuse at a later date). It may help to think ahead about which words you might call out (see the following Games section) so that you need only prepare the necessary letters.

You may also wish to prepare a scoreboard which can be placed in the sports hall or on the playing field where everyone can see. Other items you may need to source beforehand include a stopwatch, loudhailer (if working outside or with a large group of students) and different coloured bibs or T-shirts to identify the various teams.

The Games

Before any games are played it is advisable to run a short warm-up session, which will help to minimise the risk of any injuries. This can be done in the target language and is a good way of getting students into the spirit of the day. The warm-up instructions below are in French; German and Spanish versions can be found in the additional materials on the DVD.

Warm-up exercises	L'échauffement
Stand up!	Levez-vous!
Sit down!	Asseyez-vous!
Stretch (with arms in the air)!	Étirez (avec les bras en l'air)
Circle your head	Tournez la tête
Roll your shoulders (backwards /forwards)	Roulez les épaules (en avant / en arrière)
Lean forwards (hands on hips)	Penchez-vous en avant (avec les mains sur les hanches)
Lean backwards (hands on hips)	Penchez-vous en arrière (avec les mains sur les hanches)
Jogging on the spot (for 3 minutes)	Jogging sur place (pendant 3 minutes)

Once everyone has warmed up they can start playing the games below. Depending on available time and space you may wish to organise it so that all teams play the same game at the same time. In this instance you can implement a scoring system with five points awarded to the winning team, three to the second-place team and one to the team in third place. Alternatively, teams could start with different activities and rotate until each team has played each game. In this situation it is harder to award points on the above scoring system, so teams could be given a time limit for completing their game, and points could be awarded depending on who has successfully completed their game in the allotted time.

Vocabulary Volleyball

This game requires teams to keep a volleyball (or netball or other lightweight ball) in the air for a count of ten words relating to a specific theme. The aim is for the ball to be passed around the group with each team member calling out a word as they volley the ball into the air for the next player. If a word is missed or repeated, or the ball is dropped, then the team must start again from the beginning. The word count for this game can be increased depending on target language ability, and it can be further differentiated by asking students to include the correct article with the word. Suggested themes include: colours; body parts; hobbies; sports; holidays/travel; animals/pets; and so on.

Spelling Relay

Identify a start line and ask teams to line up in single file behind it. Place a pile of laminated letters (see above) some distance from the starting line and then give each team a word in English. Teams need to translate the word into the target language and then run relay-style to the pile of letters. Each student must pick up one letter until the target language word is spelled out. Students must take care to choose the appropriate special characters, such as accents. Again, this game can be made slightly harder by asking teams to also pick out letters to make the word's article.

Basketball/Netball Shoot

Ask teams to spread out along the length of a basketball or netball court (if you do not have access to either of these, ask teams to spread out in the available space and use a bin or bucket as the goal) with everyone facing in the same direction. Announce a theme to the group (see under *Vocabulary Volleyball* for suggested themes). The first person in each team passes/throws the ball to the next person in line and shouts out a word in the target language according to the theme. The next person must then catch the ball and pass it on, but they must call out a word that begins with the last letter of the word that the person before called out. This continues until the ball reaches the last person. The last person must then run back (with the ball) to the front of the line. The winning team can then try to extend their lead by shooting the basket- or netball.

Captain's Deck

This activity is based on the familiar game of Captain's Deck. It is useful to play this directly after the basketball shoot game, as teams can remain in their lines. The game is played by a 'captain' (usually a teacher) calling out the various commands which the players must match with appropriate actions. If a player does not understand the command or performs the wrong action, they are out and must sit down. As this game could last for a relatively long time, it is perhaps a good idea to set a time limit, with the winning team being the one with the most players left in once the time is up. A French version of the commands and matching actions follows, with German and Spanish versions in the additional materials for this project on the accompanying DVD.

Commands	Actions	Les ordres
Port	Run to the left	*Bâbord*
Starboard	Run to the right	*Tribord*
Stern	Run to the back	*Arrière*
Bow	Run to the front	*Proue*
Attention, Captain!	Salute and shout 'Aye, aye captain!' (players cannot move until the captain calls out 'at ease' – the captain can use this as a trick move by calling out another order before saying 'at ease'. Those who do the action – even if it is correct – will be out, as the captain did not say 'at ease' first.	*Attention, Capitaine!* (players shout *à vos ordres, Capitaine!*)
All hands on deck	Crouch or lie down	*Tout le monde sur le pont*
Scrub the deck	Get on knees and mime scrubbing	*Briquez le pont*
Man overboard!	Mime looking out over the sea with hand up to forehead.	*Un homme à la mer!*
Shark!	Before the game starts, identify a 'base' where players should run to if 'shark' is called. The last player to the base is out.	*Requin!*
Periscope	Kneel with one arm in the air	*Périscope*

Blindfold Walk

Ask teams to mark out a short path on the floor (if indoors, masking tape could be used; if outside, chalk could be used). Once the path has been marked out, a member of each team should be picked to be the 'walker'. The walker is then positioned at the beginning of the path and the rest of the team can be stationed either along the route or at the end, providing they have a clear view of the path. The walker is then blindfolded and the rest of the team members need to guide them to the end of the path by calling out instructions in the target language. The team who gets their walker to the end of the route in the quickest time is the winner. Teams should be encouraged to spread out where possible so that the blindfolded walkers are not confused by instructions shouted by teams on either side of them. Some suggested French vocabulary for this game is provided below. German and Spanish versions can be found in the additional materials for this project on the accompanying DVD.

Instructions	Les instructions
Forwards	*En avant*
Backwards	*à reculons*
Right	*à droite*
Left	*à gauche*
Step	*au pas*
Turn around	*Retournez-vous*
Straight on	*Tout droit*
Continue	*Continuez*
Stop	*Arrêtez*
Faster	*Plus vite*

Reflections

Games such as those described above are a great way of engaging students in language learning. Not only do they bring languages outside the classroom and into a different environment, they also encourage active learning and are a great motivational tool. These activities are also flexible and easily adaptable, meaning they can be used at any point throughout the school year and are particularly useful for introducing novel ways of revising or learning new vocabulary.

The Foreign Languages Mini-Olympics: Additional DVD materials

1. Warm-up instructions in German
2. Warm-up instructions in Spanish
3. Captain's Deck, commands and matching actions in German
4. Captain's Deck, commands and matching actions in Spanish
5. Blindfold Walk, vocabulary in German
6. Blindfold Walk, vocabulary in Spanish

2

Languages and multi-media

Introduction

The idea of combining language learning and various forms of technology is very attractive to young people, many of whom feel completely at home harnessing new technologies. This Part presents four projects, all developed as part of the national Routes into Languages initiative and each based around the use of different media linked to language teaching. Each project is easy to adapt into other languages and all aim to motivate and maximise active target-language use. The first project, *Languages, camera, action*, involves film-making in the target language and examples are given in German in the book, with translations of key material in French included in the accompanying DVD materials. The second project, *Digital Storytelling*, is presented in Spanish and helps students to create animated presentations, complete with a soundtrack in the target language, using specific computer software. This is followed by another very practical project, *Languages and Subtitling*, which again links language skills with film and media technology, whilst also providing insight into potential careers in this area and the skills required in real-life subtitling. The final project, *Language on Film*, again captures the best of the new secondary curriculum, combining language learning with the applied use of technology and learning new media skills. Students involved with the project have an open-ended task which allows them to explore their own creativity and imagination, whilst the project itself provides a meaningful context for using and developing language skills.

Project 1: Languages, camera, action

Project Outline

Requirements: a television studio (not essential)
Event time: the project presented has been delivered in the following modes: a one-day version; a four-month version; a two-day version; an international version.
Languages targeted: German and French
Impact: medium (30 pupils)

Introduction

This first project in this Part was developed by the University of Brighton in 2005 and reflects the growing popularity of media-related study programmes in schools. It also responds to the suggestion in *Languages Review* (Dearing & King, 3.37) that language learning can be embedded successfully in other areas of the curriculum such as, in this case, script-writing, stage management and team-building. The project presented here has been delivered to well over 1,500 students to date and remains one of the most popular events offered by The University of Brighton to local schools. The project was 'highly commended' in the European Award for Languages 2010 competition organised by the National Centre for Languages (CILT), part of CfBT Education Trust (see useful web addresses in the accompanying DVD materials). *Languages, camera, action* is presented in this section in German. The additional materials on the accompanying DVD contain a translation of the practice storyboard in French, along with key vocabulary items, as well as a short film in English to demonstrate finished outcomes. A template of a photography consent form (crucial for this project) is in Appendix One of this book. The project has four delivery modes: a one-day version; a four-month version; a two-day version; an international version. The last received partial funding in 2011 from the UK–German Connection (see useful web addresses in the accompanying DVD materials) and was also awarded a Springboard Grant in 2012 by the University of Brighton. The main format, which underpins all four modes of delivery, is presented in the next section.

Organisation (One-day version filmed in a tv studio)

It is ambitious to introduce students to a television studio and create a film in the target language in one day, but it can be done to good effect. The key is in the planning and rehearsal beforehand, the importance of which cannot be emphasised too strongly. The schedule below is how the day can run, in terms of who does what, assuming two groups (15 students per group) working in two different languages. If everyone arrives knowing what they are going to do, the film produced can even be pressed on to a DVD before the end of the day for each school to take away with them!

Schedule

0900–0930 – Arrival and welcome

0930–1100 – Introduction to TV studios (Student *Crimewatch* in English)

1100–1130 – Break

1130–1300 – Group A record film/Group B operate studio

1300–1330 – Lunch

1330–1500 – Group B record film/Group A operate studio

1500–1530 – Closing plenary

It is important for the students to familiarise themselves with the way the television studio works before they film their own work. This is partly for reasons of health and safety and partly to ensure the smooth running of the day. If cameras are tilted up towards the bright overhead lights for example, they will break. By using a short film with pre-

prepared storyboard and images, a trial run can be made to troubleshoot at the start of the day. The first storyboard presented here is just a sample in English (resultant film is included in the DVD additional materials) and has the main aim of allowing everyone to see how the different activities fit together. It is simple but nevertheless effective and has the advantage of putting people at ease, as it is easy to understand. A different example of a storyboard can also be found in Project 4 in this Part (*Language on Film*).

Page

Shot	Cam. no.	Video/ Capt.	Vision Instr.	Script	Sound inst.
1	1	Junior Crimewatch presenters	slow zoom in 2 shot	music	fade up
2	2			**Presenter A:** Good evening and welcome to another edition of Junior Crimewatch	present mikes
				Presenter B: Today we shall be looking at two rather nasty school crimes. The first crime involves a hungry phantom with a taste for sandwiches.	
3	3	Caption		**Presenter A:** Hundreds of school children in the Brighton area have fallen victim to the phantom sandwich-eater. Sandwiches are disappearing fast, but some are found nibbled in the children's desks.	

Following the recording of the English version of Student Crimewatch, students record their own films in the target language. Here is the German version of the storyboard above in full (a version in French is contained in the additional materials on the accompanying DVD).

Kinder Krimiserie

Auftritt	Kamera	Untertitel	Bild	Drehbuch	Sonde
1	1	Langsam heranzoomen			Musik einblenden
2	2	2. Auftritt		**Moderator/in A:** Guten Abend und herzlich willkommen bei der Sendung Kinder Krimiserie. **Mod. B:** Heute betrachten wir zwei ziemlich ernste Verbrechen in der Schule. **Mod. A:** Im ersten Verbrechen geht es um einen hungrigen Geist mit einem Geschmack für Brötchen.	Anschalten der Mikrofone des Moderators
3	3			**Mod. B:** Hunderte von Schulkindern in Raum von Brighton sind die Opfer von diesem Brötchen essenden Geist. **Mod. A:** Die Brötchen verschwinden schnell, aber einige werden abgeknabbert in den Schreibtischen der Kinder gefunden.	
4	1			**Mod. B:** Die Lehrer sind verblüfft und bis jetzt gibt es wenige Hinweise darauf, wer die Brötchen der Kinder isst. **Mod. A:** Wenn Sie irgendwelche Informationen über dieses ernste Verbrechen haben, schreiben Sie bitte an diese Adresse:	

Auftritt	Kamera	Untertitel	Bild	Drehbuch	Sonde
5	3	**Kinder Krimiserie BTV Falmer Sussex BN1 9PH**		*Mod. A:* "Kinder Krimiserie", BTV, Falmer, Sussex, BN1 9PH *Mod. B:* Vergessen Sie nicht, Ihre Briefe mit "Brötchen Klage" zu markieren!	
6	1			*Mod. A:* Unser zweites Verbrechen verursacht viel Fu schmerz für Kinder von der Pondside Schule in Brighton.	
7	2		Nahaufnahme	*Mod. B:* Dieser Fu schmerz wird verursacht vom Verschwinden von hunderten Trainingsschuhen in Größe zwei.	
8	3		Schwenken rechts	*Mod. A:* Diese Fu spuren sind überall auf dem Spielfeld gesehen worden. Könnten Sie dem Trainerdieb gehören?	
9	1		Schwenken bis der Blase	*Mod. B:* Kennen Sie jemanden mit der Schuhgröße zwei?	
10	3	**Kinder Krimiserie BTV Falmer Sussex BN1 9PH**	2. Auftritt	*Mod. B:* Wenn ja, bitte an diese Adresse schreiben: "Kinder Krimiserie", BTV, Falmer, Sussex, BN1 9PH *Mod. A:* Vergessen Sie nicht, Ihre Briefe mit "Trainingsschuhe Klage" zu markieren!	

Auftritt	Kamera	Untertitel	Bild	Drehbuch	Sonde
11	2			**Mod. B:** Nun gut, das ist alles für diese Woche. Vergessen Sie nicht, wir sind auf Ihre Hinweise angewiesen. **Mod. A & B:** Guten Abend.	Mikrofon abschalten
12	1			Nicht heranzoomen	Musik ausblenden

Tips

- Students need to be aware that all roles are equally important
- Students rather than staff need to take responsibility for the direction and production of the film. Their active involvement at all stages maximises enjoyment and increases motivation
- Rehearsals should be conducted in the target language
- Students should be advised not to wear heavy jewellery, as microphones can pick up jingles and jangles
- It should be agreed from the outset where the use of the target language is appropriate – i.e., just for the output, or also for the stage/production work as well as the actual film

Reflections

The more autonomy the students have regarding the whole production the better, as they will feel they have really achieved something by the end of the day.

An effective end to the day is to present certificates in an Oscars-style ceremony with those involved selecting the best use of the target language, or the best film made, or the most co-operative team perhaps. This does depend on the aim of the film-making session, and a balance needs to be struck between linguistic output versus film-making skills. An example of a certificate which could easily be adapted is included in the additional DVD materials for Project 2 in Part VII (*The Gold Award for Languages*).

Useful vocabulary list in German

(a version in French is included in the accompanying DVD)

Film Script Vocabulary

der Auftritt	shot; scene
die Kamera	camera
der Untertitel	caption
das Bild	vision
das Drehbuch	script
die Sonde	sound
heranzoomen/wegzoomen	to zoom in/out
einblenden	to fade in
ausblenden	to fade out
der Moderator; die Moderatorin	presenter
die Sendung	edition (of a programme)
das Verbrechen	crime
ernst	serious
anschalten	to switch something on
der Geist	ghost
hungrig	hungry
mit einem Geschmack für	with a taste for
verschwinden	To disappear
abgeknabbert	nibbled
verblüfft	confused
die Hinweise	clues
der Fußschmerz	foot ache
die Nahaufnahme medium	close-up
verursacht	caused
die Trainingsschuhe	trainers
in Größe zwei	in size two
schwenken	to pan (camera)
die Fußspuren	footprints
das Spielfeld	playing field
gehören zu	to belong to
der Dieb	thief
die Blase	(speech; thought) bubble
abschalten	to switch off
angewiesen sein	to rely on

Studio Roles Vocabulary

die Kamerafrau/der Kameramann	camera operator
die Studioleiterin/der Studioleiter	studio manager
die Toningenieurin/der Toningenieur	sound engineer (or sound mixer)
die Bildmischerin/der Bildmischer	vision mixer
die Produzentin/der Produzent	producer
die Regisseurin/der Regisseur	director
die Beleuchtungleiterin/der Beleuchtungleiter	lighting manager

General Film Vocabulary

die Schauspielerin/der Schauspieler	actress/actor
hinter den Kulissen	behind the scenes; backstage
die Kinokasse	box office
hinter der Kamera	behind the camera
das Kino	cinema
der Abspann	credits
die Hauptrolle	leading role
die Nebenrolle	supporting role
die Handlung	plot
die Leinwand	movie screen
der Bildschirm	tv screen
die Bühne	set
bei den Dreharbeiten	on set
das Ende	the end

Movie titles quiz

Can you guess the English titles of these films?

Ace Ventura – Ein tierischer Detektiv ....

Im 80 Tagen um die Welt ....

Harry Potter und die Kammer des Schreckens ....

Der König der Löwen ....

Der Herr der Ringe – Die zwei Türme ....

Krieg der Sterne ....

Zurück in die Zukunft ....

Die Bourne Identität ....

Die Unglaublichen ....

Natürlich blond ....

Adaptations on delivery mode

To create a film in the target language using different delivery modes, the storyboard should be used in each case to plan the film in advance. Hand-held cameras produce effects just as good as the use of a TV studio. During the two-day mode, students have more time for script-writing, although they still need to start the first session with ideas in place regarding what they want to film and how they are going to organise the process. The same applies to the two-month version, but the scripts are devised and written over a longer time span of two hours per week for example. This can be arranged as an after-school club or during lunch breaks. The international version of the *Languages on Film* project is the most ambitious format and obviously has the most linguistic benefits, as students are fully immersed in the target language. This is hugely motivating for individuals, enhances co-operation and reinforces ongoing cultural dialogues. Financial support can frequently be obtained through various bodies, such as the ones listed in the useful internet sites at the end of the accompanying DVD materials.

Languages, camera, action: Additional DVD materials

1. Student Crimewatch storyboard in French
2. Useful vocabulary list in French
3. Movie titles quiz
4. Student Crimewatch example filmed in English
5. Useful websites

Project 2   Digital storytelling

routes into
LANGUAGES

Project Outline

Requirements: a computer room; headsets with microphones.
Event time: varies, but presented as 2.5 hours here
Language targeted: Spanish
Impact: medium (30 pupils)

Introduction

This project is presented in Spanish and was developed by The London School of Economics and Political Science in 2010. It was first used with undergraduates and then adapted to school pupils. *Digital Storytelling* promotes an alternative and exciting way of supporting language learning with the use of multimedia IT resources in schools in different contexts. Its main aims are to support learner autonomy and promote productive skills in the target language. This exciting project has five main learning outcomes: to improve writing skills in the target language; to improve speaking skills (with specific emphasis being placed on pronunciation and intonation); to develop self-expression skills; to create and animate a story; to learn how to use *Movie Maker* software. Students work in groups and create their digital story collaboratively. They narrate stories in the target language based on selected images; an animated presentation is then developed on accessible computer software. An example of a completed story in both Spanish and English is included in the accompanying DVD materials, along with extra support materials in the two languages and full instructions relating to the use of the software *Movie Maker*. English and Spanish versions of the worksheet for pupils, to help them plan their stories, are also included in the additional DVD materials for this project.

The project presented here lasts approximately 2.5 hours and is suitable for all year groups. Students choose a story they want to tell from topics such as: a summer experience in a different country; the summary of a life story; and, for higher levels, themes such as the search for personal and national identity. They go through a planning stage, thinking about the images they would like to use to illustrate their story and then write a script closely linked to the images. The script is corrected by a teacher/classroom assistant and suggestions are made to help improve language and grammar, as well as finding the best way to express feelings and ideas.

The next stage involves working with personal computers. Students search for images and upload them to the software to create a sequence. Using the same software, students record the commentary for their story, thereby practising oral skills and working on their pronunciation, intonation and cadence in the process. The final stage involves animating their story through transitions, effects, titles and a soundtrack.

Organisation

The idea behind the project is simple but effective. The workshop was originally designed to launch a project of several weeks' duration. However, it can be delivered effectively as an activity in its own right, with students completing a digital story by the end of the time allocated (2.5 hours in the version presented here). Alternatively, if teachers wish to prepare students beforehand by having planning sessions before the workshop, then it can be adapted and delivered in a shorter time. The software *Movie Maker* is a basic programme already included in Windows XP Professional.

Demonstration phase

1. Show an example of a Digital Story. One is included in both English and Spanish in the accompanying DVD;

2. Demonstrate how to use *Movie Maker*. Full instructions are included in both Spanish and English in the materials on the accompanying DVD, together with a short demonstration film aimed at teachers. You should include the following points in the demonstration to your students:
   - how to find copyright-free images on the internet (see links on the accompanying DVD);
   - how to upload the selected images;
   - how to import the images to the storyboard;

- how to record a commentary;
- how to add a soundtrack;
- how to add transitions;
- how to finish by exporting the project to make a file which is readable on any computer.

Hands-on phase

Students work in groups of two or three.

1. Each group plans their digital story. This can be done in English or, ideally, in the target language (there is a model planning worksheet in both English and Spanish in the materials on the accompanying DVD).

2. Once the groups have completed their outline, they write their scripts. Teachers monitor the groups helping with language queries and encouraging pupils to use the target language effectively.

3. Groups follow the steps on the handout (see "*Movie Maker* Instructions" in the accompanying DVD materials to create their Digital Story using the software.

4. An important stage is recording the commentary. Students should have the chance to make several recordings in order to perfect their pronunciation and intonation. Teachers monitor the groups, helping with linguistic accuracy.

5. Students export their stories and send them to their teacher or save them in a shared space.

Story première

Final versions of the stories are presented to the whole class using the projector. The presentations can be followed by discussion and reflection on the part of all participants.

Reflections

Groupwork: although this can be an individual project, students especially enjoy doing this activity as a group. Students tend to help each other with language skills and/or technical aspects and the whole creative process becomes more dynamic.

Supervision: for larger groups having an extra teacher who speaks the target language is advisable to help monitoring.

IT Support: technical issues can arise, such as microphones not working or computers crashing, so testing before the workshop and good IT support are advisable in order to minimise disruptions.

Adapting the Workshop: this workshop can be tailored quite easily to different language levels and age groups. For lower levels the target language is normally used for writing the script and recording the commentary only. For higher levels the whole workshop can be done in the target language.

Useful phrases for digital storytelling

Theme: My Holiday	*Tema: Las Vacaciones*
My story is about…	*Mi relato trata de…*
I'm going to talk about…	*Voy a hablar sobre…*
This is…/These are…	*Esto es…/Estos/as son…*
There is/there are…	*Hay…*
In the foreground/background	*En primer plano/en el fondo aparece*
Here you can see…	*Aquí se puede ver/apreciar…*
Last year/two years ago I went to…	*El año pasado/Hace dos años fui a…*
Typical food in this country is…	*La comida típica de ese país es…*
I ate…	*Comí…*
I travelled by train/plane/boat	*Viajé en tren/avión/barco*
I was there for one/two week(s)	*Estuve/Pasé allí una/dos semanas*
I visited…	*Visité…*
The thing I like the most was…	*Lo que más me gustó fue…*
I stayed in a	*Me quedé en un*
hotel/campsite/apartment	*hotel/camping/apartamento*
The people were	*La gente era*
friendly/unfriendly/polite/	*simpática/antipática/educada*
I went with my family/my friends	*Fui con mi familia/mis amigos*
The weather was nice/hot/cold/rainy	*Llovió/Hizo buen tiempo/calor/frío*
The funniest thing that happened was…	*Lo más divertido que me pasó fue que…*

Digital Storytelling: Additional DVD materials

1. An example of a Digital Story in Spanish.
2. An example of a Digital Story in English.
3. Model planning worksheet for students to use in Spanish
4. Model planning worksheet for students to use in English
5. Using *Movie maker* (Spanish version)
6. Using *Movie maker* (English version)
7. Useful websites

Project 3   Languages and Subtitling

routes into
LANGUAGES

Project Outline

Requirements: access to computers with free-to-download software *Aegisub* installed; short film clips
Event time: two 50-minute sessions
Languages: any
Impact: medium-high

Introduction

Learners of another language often need to see how their skills can be applied in a practical context. This project offers a simple but appealing way of demonstrating this. It also shows how languages can be combined with other subjects, in this case film and media technology, whilst providing insight into potential careers in this area and the skills required in real-life subtitling.

Introducing a subtitling project to students may seem ambitious, but software which is easily accessible and often free to download makes this relatively straightforward. It is exciting and engaging and offers a stimulating way of developing students' oral and written skills. Once students are familiar with the concept of subtitling and a subtitling programme, activities to tackle listening comprehension, writing, vocabulary or grammar can be planned. Students can also create and subtitle their own videos about culture, language or grammar. A wide range of programmes are available for this type of activity. Certain websites such as Classik TV, Bombay TV and Futebol TV have videos with easy-to-follow instructions which could be used with younger students as a basic introduction to subtitling. The web addresses can be found in the list of useful websites on the accomapanying DVD.

This section describes a project created by staff at Imperial College, London, as part of Capital L, the Routes into Languages initiative in London. It outlines what subtitling is, explores a free-to-download subtitling software package and offers lesson plans for two 50-minute subtitling workshops. It is aimed at older students (years 11–13) and part of its challenge and appeal is the opportunity of working with a realistic subtitling programme and with the same constraints that a real-life situation might involve.

Lesson plan

Year Group	Years 11 and 12
Overview	This workshop introduces students to professional subtitling using a basic software package, which allows them to gain a better understanding of the issues that arise when translating and

creating subtitles. Students are given the opportunity to create subtitles for a short film clip they have studied, or they may create their own films for fellow students to prepare subtitles.

Duration
Two approximately 50-minute sessions:
Session one: familiarisation with software and the role of the subtitler;
Session two: practical subtitling project.

Objectives
Introduce students to translation and subtitling techniques;
Demonstrate the use of software to prepare subtitles;
Improve language skills related to film;
Understanding the role of a subtitler.

Learning outcomes
Demonstrate independent translation skills;
Use a professional subtitling programme;
Identify online resources to clarify language questions;
Practise target language on film.

Resources
Workshop outline (see below);
Introduction to translation and subtitling (see below);
Access to computers with *Aegisub* (www.aegisub.com) installed;
Instructions for using *Aegisub* (see below).

Workshop outlines

Session 1

Introduction to subtitling (10 minutes)

It is useful to give students a definition of subtitling as a way of introducing the session. A good definition could be:

> *Subtitles are a textual representation of the dialogue in a video programme and the main medium for language transfer in audiovisual programming. Subtitling can be intralingual (in the same language as spoken in the programme) or interlingual (in another language) but in neither case is the textual representation a verbatim transcription or translation of the spoken words.*

(www.subtitlers.org.uk)

Once student have been given the definition, lead into a short discussion about subtitles in real life. Possible questions could be:

- Have any of the students seen subtitles before?
- If they have, where have they seen them?
- Are they useful?
- Has anyone ever spotted an error in a subtitle?
- Have the students noticed the differences between standard subtitles and subtitles for those who are deaf or hard of hearing?
- Following this, show a short clip from a DVD, YouTube or iplayer with subtitles and link it back to the points made during the discussion.

Professional subtitling (10 minutes)

Next, briefly describe and discuss the role of a professional subtitler; what skills might a subtitler need? What is the difference between intralingual and interlingual subtitles and what might a subtitler need to consider in each situation? Refer back to the definition above if necessary. The following points may be useful:

Professional subtitling

- A professional subtitler presents written text to accompany the audiovisual message on screen.
- There should be coherence between the audiovisual message and the text.
- There are space limits: subtitles should take up to two lines and no more than 39 characters per line.
- There are time limits: subtitles should not last less than one second or more than six seconds. There should also be a minimum gap of two frames so viewers notice the change of subtitles.
- Subtitlers need to consider reading speed. We can read much more in six seconds than we can in two seconds.

Required skills
A subtitler should:

- Have excellent reading and writing skills;
- Be competent in a foreign language or languages if doing interlingual subtitling;
- Be proficient in typing and using a computer;
- Be succinct – i.e. able to communicate in only one or two lines per frame;
- Be able to work quickly and efficiently.

Difference between intralingual and interlingual subtitling
What are the main differences between the two types of subtitling?

> Intralingual subtitles are in the same language as the audiovisual programme and interlingual subtitles are in a different language (refer to definition above).

What problems might interlingual subtitling present?

> For exmple, the subtitler might not know what a word or phrase in the foreign language means; there might not be a direct or easy translation for the foreign language word or phrase; there might be cultural elements that are hard to explain or communicate.

Introduction to the Aegisub programme (10 minutes)

NOTE: it is extremely useful to have already prepared a range of video clips for use during the workshops. Not only does this save time, it will also allow students to focus on learning how to use the subtitling programme properly which will ensure that everyone has the best experience possible.

Aegisub can read DVDs, but it is much better to work from other video file formats with the extensions *.avi* or.*mpg*, as these involve much smaller file sizes. DVD formats can be easily converted into either of these by simple programmes such as *Any Video Converter* (www.any-video-converter.com/). Similarly, clips from websites such as YouTube can be converted using "tube-catcher" software, downloadable from http://atube-catcher.dsnetwb.com/video/.

Importantly, students should be made aware that if they download a video, subtitle it and then upload or "re-publish" it on other websites, they may be infringing copyright laws.

Once the students have been provided with background information about subtitling and have engaged in the above discussions, they can be introduced to the subtitling software programme *Aegisub*, which ideally will have been installed on computers in advance of the session. However, before working directly with the software, it is helpful to consider the following questions:

- Will students begin working immediately in the target language, or will you familiarise them with the software by doing a "trial run" in English?
- Will the students watch the film clip first as a target-language listening exercise?
- Would it be better for students to watch the clip and create their own transcripts before using the software?

These points can help differentiate the workshops according to the students' level of ability.

If working with a film in the target language it can be very useful to provide students with, or ask them to create, a transcript of the clip to be subtitled. An advanced class could also translate an English transcript and practise intralingual subtitling in the target language.

Ask students to open the *Aegisub* application and then open a specific video file, so that everyone sees the same thing. They will notice that if they click on ***play***, there will be no sound. This is because they still need to open the audio track. To do this, go to the ***Audio*** tab and click on ***open audio from video***. After following these steps, the students' work surfaces should appear with the video window in the top left corner and the audio window adjacent to it. The numbers below the audio window indicate seconds, whilst the red bracket in the audio window indicates the beginning of a subtitle and the orange bracket the end. Sound is shown visually by the green vibration line. This turns white when it is within the brackets and the brackets can be easily adjusted to the sound by using the mouse. Pink vertical lines indicate shot changes in the video window. However, pink lines can also appear when there is a change of light within the same shot, or when on-screen text comes in and out.

Using the Aegisub programme (20 minutes)

For the remainder of the workshop students should be encouraged to find a clip they like and transcribe the script. Working with a song previously used in class so that students are familiar with it works well here, but students can follow their own ideas. If they prefer, instead of transcribing the words they hear, they can annotate the clip with comments, such as the biography of the singer or actor, cultural elements or an explanation of what is happening in the video.

The list below introduces each of the main commands for the programme (including their shortcut keys). You can compare these with the screengrab image and start subtitling!

And these instructions:

Go to previous line, discarding any unsaved changes (previous syllable when in KARAOKE MODE)

Go to next line, discarding any unsaved changes (next syllable when in karaoke mode)

Play selected area of the audio waveform

Play currently selected line

Pause playback

Play 500ms before selection start

Play 500ms after selection end

Play first 500ms of selection

Play last 500ms of selection

Play from selection start to end of file (or until pause is pressed)

Add lead-in (how much is determined by the audio lead in setting)

Add lead-out (exactly like the above, but the setting is called audio lead out, logically enough)

Commit (save) changes

Scroll view to selection/go to selection

Toggle auto-commit (all timing changes will be committed immediately, without the user pressing commit, if this is enabled)

Toggle auto next line on commit (if this is enabled, Aegisub will automatically select the next line when the current line is committed; enabling both this and auto-commit at the same time is strongly discouraged)

Toggle auto-scrolling (will center waveform on the currently selected line automatically when enabled)

Toggle spectrum analyzer mode (see below)

Toggle Medusa-style timing shortcuts

Audio display zoom (horizontal)

Audio display zoom (vertical)

Audio volume

Toggle linking of vertical audio zoom slider with volume slider

Toggle karaoke mode

Join selected syllables (karaoke mode only)

Split selected syllables (karaoke mode only)
(from http://docs.aegisub.org.manual/Audio)

1. *Play* – note that when you click here you will play both the video and the audio files
2. *Play selected subtitle*
3. *Pause*
4. *Toggle* – autoscroll of video
5. *Drag subtitles* – this is the only tool students may need from the menu on the left-hand side of the video window. It might become useful for cases with on-screen text where the subtitle may need moving if the text is occupying the subtitle area.
6. *Previous subtitle (Left/Z)*
7. *Next subtitle (Right/X)*
8. *Play selection (Space/S)* – note that when you click on it, you are playing the audio. It is very helpful to have the visual aspects in mind, so that you can anticipate information for the viewer.
9. *Play current subtitle (R)* – to select a subtitle you click on it in the subtitles table, which is found in the lower half of the screen.
10. *Stop (H)*
11. *Play 500 milliseconds before selection (Q)* – this will guarantee the subtitle is not going in too late.
12. *Play 500 ms after selection (W)*
13. *Play first 500ms of selection (E)*
14. *Play last 500ms of selection (D)*
15. *Play from selection start to end of file (T)*
16. *Add lead in (C)* – this command adds 200ms to the beginning of the subtitle
17. *Add lead out (V)*
18. *Commit changes (F8/G)* – you can also commit (i.e. save) changes by clicking on "commit" or pressing Enter. Remember to commit every change before you proceed to the following action or it will get lost.
19. *Go to selection*
20. *Automatically commit all changes*
21. *Go to next line – on commit automatically*
22. *Scroll audio display* – to selected line automatically
23. The nine keys on the last row beneath the audio window allow you to change the style, font and font colour
24. **Commit**
25. **Text box**
26. **Subtitle box**

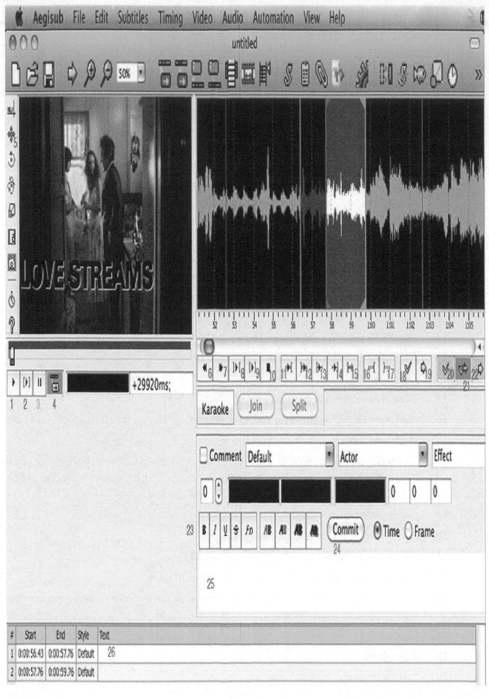

Encourage students to familiarise themselves with the layout of the work surface and the above commands. They should now be ready to start creating their own subtitles. Remind everyone to save their files frequently! Files can be saved by clicking on the *File* tab and then *Save subtitles as*. Saved files will have a *.ass* extension.

Subtitled videos can be opened with a multimedia player called VLC (available free online from http://www.videolan.org/vlc/), which can open any video format and/or subtitle file. This programme may look complicated at first glance but, once you get started, it does not take long to get used to its format.

Session 2

Introduction and recap of previous session (5 minutes)

Begin the session with a short recap of the points covered in the previous workshop. Give the students a couple of minutes to consider what sort of translation and/or subtitling problems they may encounter. Next ask them to go over the main instructions for using the software and any issues they will need to take into account when working independently with the programme.

Independent subtitling (35 minutes)

Students should watch the video to be subtitled while reading the transcription (prepared in the previous session). If dictionaries are available, these can be used. If not, students can always use online resources such as Word Reference (www.wordreference.com). Online machine translations such as Google Translate should be avoided, as they are not always accurate.

To produce their subtitles each student or group of students should set the timings of the subtitles in *Aegisub*, indicating where they think each sentence should appear. They can input the text whilst setting the timings, or they can add it to each relevant box after the timings have been set. Students should be reminded that they need to commit changes (i.e. save their work) every time they input a new line.

Feedback (10 minutes)

Each student or group should be asked to show their translation/subtitled video to the rest of the class. Encourage the class to discuss the following:

- Any difficulties experienced;
- Any cultural elements that were challenging to translate;
- A comparison of both languages and their structures;
- Choices for their timings, words or utterances they had to leave out.

Conclude the workshop by reiterating how languages can be used in professional contexts such as subtitling and that students now have a real taste of what it might be like to forge a career in this profession.

Reflections

This short project effectively engages students in a real-life context where they can combine their language skills with professional software to create a short subtitled video. Not only does this help to improve target language listening skills as well as competence in the use of media and technology, but it also provides a taste of what a career with languages could look like.

Comments from teacher:

> "The workshop was a great way of showing A level students other ways in which they can use languages. The students really enjoyed using their knowledge of Spanish for something practical"

Comments from students:

> **Question:** What did you like about it?
>
> - The whole concept of subtitling and how the complexity of it can be resolved is interesting
> - Challenging, made me think
> - Good to practise grammar and vocab
> - Improved listening and reading skills
> - Taught me more about languages and technology and my future in languages

Languages and subtitling: Additional DVD materials

1.　Useful websites

Project 4:　Language on Film

Project Outline

Requirements: Flip cameras or similar; Microsoft *Moviemaker*
Event time: ongoing throughout the academic year
Languages targeted: any
Impact: high. Some schools have now integrated it into the Year 9 curriculum

Introduction

The *Language on Film* project grew, almost by chance, out of discussions between Routes into Languages East and Rachel Hawkes, Jane Driver and Leigh McClelland of Comberton Village College, Cambridge. The discussions were actually about our Language from Film project, creating a cache of pre- and post-film materials for Key Stage Three. These are available from the Routes East website (see list of useful websites on the accompanying DVD). A film-making competition was mentioned and immediately agreed on. The teachers felt very strongly that it should include film-making training and so the project was born with training from Anglia Ruskin University Film & Media Studies lecturer, Sarah Gibson-Yates. This resulting *Language on Film* project presented here was awarded a prestigious European Language Label in 2011.

Teachers from around the Region were invited, in an attempt to ensure that every county was represented. Teachers were expected to disseminate all training to colleagues in cluster schools as well as in their own schools. The first session was to deliver an overview of film-making techniques to the teachers and this was followed by three more sessions with teachers and pupils attending together (pre-production, production and post-production), where a competition for pupils to produce a five-minute film in any language with English subtitles was also launched. The pupils were then expected to help disseminate their new skills to their peers back at school.

The competition was very structured and based around the training sessions, so that the pupils and teachers felt supported with their newly-acquired skills. It was decided that only basic equipment would be allowed, so that all schools would be in a position to participate. A training DVD (created by Leigh McClelland from footage filmed during the first year of the project as part of the training course at Anglia Ruskin University) was sent to every school in the Eastern Region. Copies are available from the Routes East website and a freely-downloadable version is available on the Routes into Languages website (see list of useful internet sites on the accompanying DVD for both addresses). The following material is taken from the Teacher's Pack compiled by Jane Driver.

Project Overview

Aim

The aim of the film competition is for students in Key Stage Three to write, direct and produce a short film of any genre (with a maximum length of five minutes) in a foreign language (with English subtitles).

Process

- Making a short film is a complicated and lengthy process, so schools should launch the competition at the beginning of the autumn term. Students should be encouraged to work independently on the project during their lunch/break/after school. They should meet regularly with the School Co-ordinator to ensure that they are on schedule to meet each deadline.
- The competition has five stages to guide the participating groups through the film-making process.
- There is a deadline for completion of each stage of the competition, which is worth a percentage of the overall score for the film. Participating groups must submit evidence of completion of each stage through their School Co-ordinator (submission forms to be sent in at each stage are included on the accompanying DVD materials).
- Submissions are assessed centrally by a judging panel (in this case Routes East, Anglia Ruskin University, judged each stage as well as the final films together with Language and Film Studies Student Ambassadors) and allocated scores at each stage. Judges could also be your Language Leaders (see Project 3 in Part IV).

- Films may be produced in any language apart from English and all films must have English subtitles.
- Participating groups are only permitted to use digital video cameras/Flip cameras and Microsoft *Movie-Maker* – no professional film-making software is permitted.
- Films should be a maximum of five minutes in duration and should not be animated films.
- A Première Evening with a formal awards ceremony takes place at the end of the project, with the best entries premièred.

Stage 1 – Development

Teams should:

a) allocate pre-production roles which are:
   1. The Producer
   2. The Director (has the overall vision for the film)
   3. The Art Director (has a more visual role – thinks about lighting, camera angles, set, etc.)
   4. The Cameraperson

b) decide on an idea and genre for a film – i.e. an action film, fly-on-the-wall documentary, comedy sketches, etc.

c) pitch their idea to their supervisor, who will provide feedback about the feasibility of the idea. The pitch should be a short presentation to sell their idea. This should be videoed and submitted to the central judging panel.

d) write a film proposal. This is a written version of the pitch and should consist of a two-line idea proposal.

e) produce an outline of the film. This is a short paragraph detailing what happens in the film.

Deadline: end of November
Percentage of overall score: 5 per cent

Stage 2 – Preproduction: Scripting

Teams should:

a) produce a script for the film in the Target Language (TL).

b) submit the script using the film industry script format (example presented later)
   Deadline: Mid-December
   Percentage of overall mark: 30 per cent

Example: industry script format

"STYLING WITH MICROSOFT WORD XP"
by
Cynthia Randall
(Title with author(s) – centrally justified)

1234 Your Street
City, State ZIP Code
Telephone Number
(address and contact details centrally justified)

FADE IN:

IN A PICKLE IS CATHY

Cathy is sitting at her computer. She is frustrated and mumbling to herself.
(camera instructions are in capitals and left justified. Instructions for the set are not in capitals but are also left-justified)

JOHN
How's it going, Cath? You don't sound so
good.

CATHY
No, I'm not. I've been messing with styles
and formatting in Word, and I can't figure
out how to show just the ones I want.

JOHN
Yeah, they changed the styles and
formatting feature in XP – you are using
Word XP, right?

CATHY
Yes.

JOHN
It's a bit weird at first but is an
improvement over the last version. Here,
let me show you.

(the script is centrally justified and not capitalized – apart from the character's name)

John takes hold of the mouse and pokes around in Word for a few minutes to
see what styles Cathy has been working with.

JOHN

So you're building a screenwriting
template, eh?

CATHY

Trying to.

JOHN

It's these 11 styles you want, right? –
character, dialog,

Cathy, interjecting, points to each style in the task pane…

CATHY

Scene heading, the end, title, trans in,
trans out, your address, your name, and
action.

JOHN

A girl who can finish my sentences -
powerful stuff, Cath. And speaking of
action: You've been a bit low on the gas
lately, if you know what I mean…
    (John has been trying to date
    Cathy since the second grade;
    they're now in first year university
    and Cathy still has no interest.)

(extra background information is centrally justified in small letters in brackets)

CATHY

John, stop it! I need to get this done!

JOHN

Okay, okay, now where was I? So when
you've got all the styles you want, the
way to show just them and not all the
others – which, by the way, belong to
Normal.dot – is to first enter each style in
the document, and then here at the
bottom of the task pane in the Show box,
choose Formatting in use. See, now
when you go to choose a style from the
Formatting toolbar or from the task pane,
just your 11 styles appear.

CATHY

And these styles will always be here?
I mean, when I close the template and
open it again, everything will be the
same?

JOHN

Word saves the last state you were
working in – this is called "sticky". Just
your 11 styles will be in the styles list on
the Formatting toolbar and shown in the
task pane. But when you reopen Word,
the task pane won't be open. You'll need
to click the Formatting and styles button
on the Formatting toolbar to open it back
up again.

CATHY

Okay. And it looks like I can still add,
modify, and delete styles in Formatting in
use view, yes?

JOHN

Yep.

CATHY

Thanks, John! You've been a big help.

JOHN

Yeah, you probably owe me one come to
think of it.

CATHY

Owe you one! Owe you one what?

JOHN

Relax Cathy. I've had enough action for
one day. See you in Biology.

Smiling, John closes the door behind him.

FADE OUT:

THE END

Stage 3 – Preproduction: Storyboarding and shot list

Teams should:

■ **produce a storyboard** of each shot in their film. The storyboard is a series of sketches. Each sketch depicts a shot in the film and helps the directors and the camera to set up and frame the shot adequately. An example of a simple storyboard and a storyboard template are presented below. There is also an example of a more complex storyboard in the project *Languages, camera, action* earlier in this Part (Project 1). The storyboard can be in the form of stick figures, as no extra points are allocated for the quality of the artwork!

Example of a simple storyboard

Storyboard template

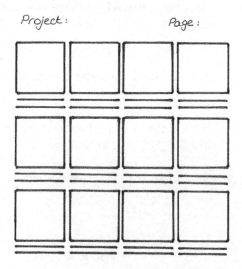

- **produce a shot list**. Each of the shots on the storyboard should be given a number. During the shoot, it may not be feasible to shoot each shot in the order depicted in the storyboard. It may be better to shoot all shots in each location together. The shot list is a list of numbers showing the order that all the shots will be filmed.

Example of a shot list

The film première – shots one to six

Shot 1:   **Long Shot** establishing the view of a limousine transporting the film star heading to the venue.

Shot 2:   **Medium Shot** of the mayor stepping forwards to meet the approaching limo.

Shot 3:   **Big Close Up Shot** of the limo door opening. Nothing else in shot. Create suspense.

Shot 4:   **Medium Long Shot** of the crowd cheering in anticipation.

Shot 5:   **Close Up Shot** of the drums playing. Adds to suspense.

Shot 6:   **Extreme close-up shot** of the film star emerging from the limo and greeting the crowd!

Shot list template (six shots)

Shot	Description of the Shot
Shot 1	
Shot 2	
Shot 3	
Shot 4	
Shot 5	
Shot 6	

Deadline: End of January
Percentage of overall mark: 15 per cent

Stage 4 – Production

Teams should:

- **film the movie.** Students should film the shots using their shot list and storyboard to help them.

- **save the shots they are going to use in Microsoft *Moviemaker*.** They should now put the shots in the correct order, so that they are ready for editing and they should delete any out-takes. See also the additional DVD materials for Project 2 in this Part (*Digital Storytelling*) for further details on using Microsoft *Moviemaker*.

Suggested deadline: Mid-March

PLEASE NOTE: THIS DATE IS FOR GUIDANCE ONLY – THERE IS NOTHING TO SUBMIT

Stage 5 – Post-production

Teams should:

- **edit the movie.** Teams should use Microsoft *Moviemaker* to edit the shots, ensuring that the film runs in sequence and that the transitions between shots are smooth.
- **add subtitles.** Teams should use Microsoft *Moviemaker* to add English subtitles to their films. This enables parents, judges and other viewers to understand the film.
- **add music.** If required, teams can add music to their films to add ambience. Please note that this music must be open-source and not subject to copyright rules.

Deadline: Mid-May
Percentage of overall score: 50 per cent

Having completed your film, you should now submit it to your central judging panel. All the submission forms you need are contained on the accompanying DVD for this project. Good luck with the judging!

Responses to the *Language on Film* project presented here have been overwhelmingly positive, with schools reporting a high level of positive impact on GCSE language choices and some subsequently integrating the project and competition into their Year Nine Schemes of Work. Some schools used class-time to work on the projects, whilst others set up film clubs in break-times and after school, or expected pupils to work on the films in their own time and away from school (no risk assessments to fill in). One school holds its own awards ceremony, with the previous year's winners on the judging panel.

Here is an excerpt from a report by Kate Muscroft of Birchwood School on what went really well during their *Language on Film* project:

- Tolerance of other staff to having groups of language students filming on site after school – I think this really raised the profile of languages within the school and many staff are curious to see the finished films.
- Collaboration – there were some students who could not always get themselves organised, but we had the most amazing collaboration between students who otherwise tend to quietly get on with things on their own. I was also impressed with the way some students got non-language students involved.
- Two of my slightly negative Year Nine French students have told me on countless occasions that this is the best thing they have done at school and they are now much more positive towards their language learning.

"I found this project incredibly helpful. It has really helped me to develop my languages and go out and use them confidently and has put them into context. When we were learning the scripts, I found this very helpful for my French and German, as we had to learn our lines off by heart, so they were now stuck in our heads. I have really enjoyed this project and would love to do this again. *J'adore le projet de film, weil es sehr lustig ist!*"

(*Year Nine girl*)

"…the film project inspired me to make more films and try to enjoy French. I'm quite pleased with my results recently in practice exams and have now learnt to make an effort in class…"

(*Year Nine boy*)

"This is the best thing we have ever done in school!"

(*Year 9 student*)

"…we gave the boys no curriculum time to do the film and so they dedicated many lunchtimes, after schools and even a Saturday to work on their film. The result of this was that the boys nearly all opted to take German at GCSE…One of the boys still quotes his lines from the film in the warm-up activities in the German lesson. We have shown the film to colleagues throughout Hertfordshire and also locally during INSET on at least two occasions, and this has inspired other MFL colleagues to try and use film in the classroom more creatively. We even showed the film in assemblies to all students, to showcase what the boys had done and to encourage further uptake of languages at GCSE, and we have used it in our Year 6 Open Evening. Each time we have had amazing feedback from parents and students about how professional, exciting, innovative and creative the project is, and how impressive the language skills are."

(*Teacher*)

Shopping list
Flip cameras
Mini Oscars for the winning team overall
Certificates for each member of the winning team of each stage of the competition. (a sample certificate is included in the accompanying DVD materials)
Commended and Highly Commended certificates for all pupils who would not otherwise receive a certificate

Language on Film: Additional DVD materials

1.   Sample marksheet
2.   Sample certificate
3.   Submission forms
4.   Useful websites

3

Languages, celebrations and festivals

routes into
LANGUAGES

Introduction

This chapter explores four projects which are based around different celebrations in various countries. Each project combines language study with performance skills in some way and each can be delivered at different levels very easily in a variety of languages. All four were designed and delivered under the auspices of the national Routes into Languages initiative (Routes South).

The first project explored is in German and is called *It's Christmas!*. It combines one hour of student-led entertainment with a visit to a range of market stalls where a host of different items/activities are 'on sale'. A range of Christmas-themed activities are also presented, with extra materials included in the accompanying DVD materials.

The second project is based around the *Day of the Dead* celebrations which take place in Mexico and other Latin American countries on November 2nd each year. The project comprises classroom-based language activities, as well as a selection of exciting and varied cultural events in Spanish. Extension materials around the same theme are included in the additional materials section on the DVD.

The third project explores *Bastille Day*, celebrated in French-speaking countries each year on July 14th. The celebration is presented in the form of a playscript in which the key events between May and October 1789 are documented. A short interview with a French person is included about how Bastille Day is traditionally celebrated each year, whilst the additional materials on the accompanying DVD offer background support to the event itself and include ideas for making a variety of props to support the play.

The fourth project in this chapter is *The European Day of Languages*, which is celebrated each year on (or as close as possible to) September 26th. The project presents an overview of this celebration followed by twelve practical ideas to deliver in your school to help celebrate the day.

Project 1   It's Christmas!

Project Outline

Requirements: large hall with space for (a) the entertainment and (b) the market stalls
Event time: two hours
Languages targeted: any languages from countries which have the tradition of Christmas markets: e.g. Germany, Belgium, Denmark, Holland, France, Sweden, Switzerland, Norway, Hungary, Estonia, Poland, Italy, Spain, Finland, etc. The project here is presented in German.
Impact: high (100+ pupils)

Introduction

The main attraction of this project is its flexibility and replicability, as the model can be easily adopted/adapted and aimed at those whose target-language speaking skills in particular need enhancing, with more or less vocabulary being provided as required. Prizes for the most effort made throughout the event can be awarded, as can prizes for the best use of the target language, for example (see sample certificate in Part I, project 1, *Score in French*). The project was designed and developed in 2010 by the University of Brighton. The event can be filmed (see Appendix One for a sample consent form), and this can motivate younger peer groups as well as providing a good record for the participants themselves. Outside companies belonging to the target-language group can be approached to provide promotional items for one of the stalls or for prizes – many are very generous when it comes to giving away 'freebies' to such events (see additional materials on the accompanying DVD for a sample letter in German). The project can accommodate up to 150 pupils realistically, otherwise too many stalls are needed to avoid long queues. Why not invite similar year groups in other schools to join in with your celebrations? All you need is a hall large enough to hold everyone.

The additional materials that accompany this section include: the translation of a Christmas story in English and a reading suggestion from *Harry Potter und der Stein der Weisen*; a language game; a Christmas carol; a sample letter to outside organisations in German; a photograph gallery. Useful internet sites for further material are also included at the end of the section.

Organisation

This Christmas event takes place over approximately two hours (one hour for the entertainment and one hour to visit the market stalls). Set-up time is also required to: prepare the 'money'; contact in advance any outside organisations you think might offer promotional items (see sample letter in the additional DVD materials); set up the market stalls; rehearse the acts.

Part One: The entertainment

The first hour comprises a show to which all participants contribute with a song, a sketch, a story etc in the target language. A Christmas story in German is included in the Additional Activities at the end of this section (Activity 4), whilst a German Christmas carol and a suggested reading are contained in the accompanying DVD materials as examples of appropriate activities. A time limit should be set for each act of approximately eight minutes (five minutes at most would be suitable for beginners, while more advanced pupils could cope with around ten minutes). It is important to incorporate a range of acts, otherwise the audience could get restless! Rehearsal time can be built into class time or organised over lunch periods/after-school clubs.

Part Two: the market

After the performances the pupils are invited to visit a row of market stalls. Between eight and ten stalls are needed, depending on the number of pupils involved; about one stall per twelve pupils is appropriate. Pupils 'buy' items from the stallholders in the target language. The pupils do not use real money. Instead, items found in the locality are used. For example, each pupil gets ten shells in a bag (which need to be collected/sorted in advance and then replaced after the event) to 'spend' on items/activities at each stall which cost one shell each. Teachers/native speakers should be the stallholders, to maximise target-language use and speakers of the target language in the wider school community, such as parents, visitors, etc., could also be recruited as stallholders. Ordinary tables can serve as stalls (these would need to be decorated in advance), or else real market stalls could be hired from local markets, depending on the budget available. The stalls may be set up along the back of the performance hall or in a different (but nearby) space. Posters can be hung around the stalls displaying key vocabulary in the target language if needed, depending on the level of the pupils. Prices of items 'on sale' should not be displayed, as the pupils should be encouraged to ask for items and do the activities in the target language.

Below are some examples of what can be provided cheaply at a German Christmas Market on ten stalls, to accommodate around 120 pupils. Pupils should visit a stall once only and do *all* the activities on offer, otherwise the more popular stalls will get swamped! Each item/activity below costs one shell or equivalent.

Stall 1: Der Lebkuchentisch (the gingerbread stall)

Buy bags of German gingerbread biscuits from English supermarkets and white/coloured writing icing tubes. Pupils decorate their biscuits before eating them! Alternatively, students could make piped biscuits at home, using the recipe in the Additional Activities section (Activity 1), and decorate them at the market stall.

Stall 2: Der Glühweintisch (the mulled wine stall)

An urn of hot, non-alcoholic mulled wine or spiced, hot apple juice can be sold by the glass (pupils can bring their own cups to the event).

Stall 3: Der Wühltisch (the 'freebie' table)

All items on this table are donated by German companies, which need to be approached in advance of the event. Examples of possible items are: jelly sweets; pens; post-it notes; pencils; biscuits; mousemats.

Stall 4: Der Luckydiptisch (the lucky dip stall)

Donations of small items such as rubbers, playing cards, wooden Christmas tree decorations, pencils, etc., can be bought at this stall. Each item needs to be wrapped in advance and put in a big bag or dustbin full of shredded waste paper. Pupils can help wrap the items before the event.

Stall 5: Der Strohdekorationstisch (the straw decoration stall)

These can either be purchased (budget permitting) or made in advance by pupils using the target language and hung around the stall on sale. Instructions in the target language for making straw decorations can be given to pupils when they buy one (see the useful internet sites on the accompanying DVD for the instructions).

Stall 6: Der Quiztisch (the quiz table)

Clues are given out relating to the target-language country (a large map with pins to stick in the appropriate place(s) or small post-it notes can be used to good effect) and the person closest to the correct place or with the most correct answers wins a prize. A quiz based around German Christmas traditions is included in the Additional Activities section below (Activity 2).

Stall 7: Der Ballontisch (the balloon stall)

Pupils can ask for balloons to be twisted into the shape of animals, such as poodles, giraffes, etc. It is a good idea to inflate the balloons in advance of the event to avoid long queues forming.

Stall 8: Der Wunschsterntisch (the wishing star table)

Each pupil writes in the target language on a coloured cardboard star his or her wish for Christmas. This could be for example 'peace on earth' or even 'a pair of slippers'! Cardboard stars need to be cut out in advance, using the template in the Additional Activities section below (Activity 3). Completed stars are then hung up on display around the stall to inspire others.

Stall 9: Der Umtauschtisch (the swap table)

If any pupil has received an item which s/he would prefer to exchange (for example from the Lucky Dip stall), s/he can offer to swap it (using the target language of course!).

Stall 10: Die Tombola (the raffle table)

Each pupil buys a raffle ticket. Numbers are called out in the target language at the end of the event and the lucky winner chooses a donated prize from the table.

Budget tips

A small charge of 50p per pupil could be levied, which (assuming 120 pupils) would raise £60 to cover the costs of the small items needed for the market stalls.

Shopping List

- Bags of gingerbread biscuits and writing icing (Stall 1). Try Lidl or Waitrose stores for authentic German varieties.
- Non-alcoholic Glühwein (Stall 2). This can be made with blackcurrant squash, cordial or apple juice, mixed with spices and heated.
- Small items for the lucky dip stall (Stall 4). If too few are collected from friends/family/colleagues, 99p shops are a good source of these items.
- Packs of straws for star-making (see various internet sites). If a larger budget is available, packs of ready-made straw stars can be bought quite cheaply (Stall 5).
- A large map of the target-language country is required (Stall 6), along with small post-it notes or pins.
- Balloons and a hand pump (Stall 7) are needed to make the balloon animals. These can be bought cheaply and are often supplied with instructions!
- Coloured cardboard for the wishing stars (Stall 8). Hanging ribbon too.
- Book of raffle tickets (Stall 10)

Reflections

If the pupils have not rehearsed their entertainments sufficiently for the first hour of the event, the audience can become restless!

Additional activities

Six topic-related activities follow which can easily be adapted to suit various levels. The activities can be used in any order.

Activity 1: Recipe for Spritzgebäck (piped biscuits)

These German Christmas biscuits are made by pressing dough through an icing bag to create interesting, swirly forms and decorative details. They are delicate, have a buttery taste and can be decorated by being half-dipped in chocolate or sprinkled with 'hundreds and thousands'. *Spritzgebäck* or piped biscuits are often made in German homes around Christmas time.

Ingredients:	Zutaten:
200g butter	*200g Butter*
200g sugar	*200g Zucker*
3 eggs	*3 Eier*
500g plain flour	*500g Mehl*
1 small packet of vanilla sugar	*Ein kleines Päckchen Vanillezucker*

Method:

Beat the butter until fluffy. Gradually add the sugar mixed with the vanilla sugar and the three eggs. Mix thoroughly. Sift the flour and add to the mixture. Using an icing bag, pipe various shapes on a baking tray covered with baking paper.
Bake at 175°C for around 10–12 minutes. **ENJOY!**

Zubereitung:

Die Butter schaumig schlagen. Nach und nach den mit Vanillezucker vermischten Zucker und die drei Eier hinzufügen. Alles gut verrühren. Dann das gesiebte Mehl einrühren. Ein Backblech mit Backpapier bedecken und mit einer Sahnespritze verschiedene Formen auf das Blech spritzen. Ungefähr 10–12 Minuten bei 170°C backen. **GUTEN APPETIT!**

Activity 2: A Christmas quiz

1. *Was ißt man traditionell in Norddeutschland zu Weihnachten?*

    a) *Eine Pute*   b) *einen Karpfen*   c) *eine Gans*

2. *Wie heißt 'cranberry' auf deutsch?*

    a) *Die Stachelbeere*   b) *die Holunderbeere*   c) *die Preiselbeere*

3. *Wann kommt in Deutschland der Nikolaus?*

    a) *Am 6. Dezember*   b) *am 24. Dezember*   c) *am 31. Dezember*

4. *In welchem Jahr wurde der erste mit Schokolade gefüllte Adventskalender verkauft?*

    a) *1839*   b) *1958*   c) *1977*

5. *Was hält der Nikolaus traditionell in der Hand?*

    a) *einen Sack voller Geschenke*
    b) *einen Sack voller Geschenke und eine Rute*
    c) *eine Rute und einen Weihnachtsstrumpf.*

6. *Welche deutsche Stadt ist für ihren Lebkuchen bekannt?*

    a) *Lübeck*   b) *Frankfurt*   c) *Nürnberg*

7. *Welche deutsche Stadt ist für ihren Stollen bekannt?*

    a) *Hamburg*   b) *Nürnberg*   c) *Dresden*

8. *Welche deutsche Stadt ist für ihr Marzipan bekannt?*

    a) *Frankfurt*   b) *Lübeck*   c) *Hannover*

9. *Welche der folgenden Zutaten gehört auf keinen Fall in Glühwein?*

    a) *Zucker*   b) *Zimt*   c) *Anis*

10. *Wo gibt es in der vorweihnachtszeit den ältesten Christkindlesmarkt?*

    a) *In München*   b) *In Stuttgart*   c) *In Nürnberg*

Antworten zu dem Weihnachtsquiz:

1 – b   2 – c   3 – a   4 – b   5 – b
6 – c   7 – c   8 – b   9 – c   10 – c

Activity 3: Wunschsterne (wishing stars)

This is one of the market stall activities (stall 8) and can also be done in class to good effect. Completed stars can be strung up to decorate the classroom. Use the template below to help you make stars out of cardboard (gold/silver on one side and plain on the reverse for the writing). Glitter or sequins can be stuck onto the shiny side or even around the writing.

Activity 4: A Christmas story

Die drei Wichtelmännchen (the three trolls)

This Christmas story was written by Cathy Watts and illustrated by Nicola Goodland; an English version is included in the accompanying DVD materials. The following German translation was written by Cathy Watts and Monika Lind.

Die drei Wichtelmännchen

Die drei kleinen Wichtelmännchen kamen in jener eiskalten Dezembernacht aus dem Wald und gingen den Berghang hinunter bis auf das Dorf zu, das unten im Tal kauerte. Obwohl sie nur so kleine Füße hatten, krachte das Eis unter ihren holzbesohlten Lederschuhen, das sich in den Rillen des Pfades gebildet hatte. Der Winter ist lang und hart gewesen in diesem Jahr und es gab immer noch keine Anzeichen des Tauens. Millionen Sterne funkelten über ihnen in jenem eisigen und schwarzen Nachthimmel und der Neumond schien ihnen mit seinem silbernen Lichtstrahl den Weg zu leuchten.

Stillschweigen herrschte in dieser zauberhaften Nacht, der Nacht in der jedes der Wichtelmännchen seine eigene Aufgabe zu erfüllen hatte. Als erstes kam Heinzl den Weg entlang mit einem niemals endenden Lebkuchen und an Ende eines langen Stocks hing eine Laterne. Seine Geschenke konnten den hungrigsten Menschen satt machen und das ärmlichste Häuschen erleuchten. Als nächstes kam Berndl, der eine kleinere Laterne und eine Zauberaxt trug, die jeden Baum in jede Anzahl gewünschter Holzscheite zerhacken konnte. Und dann kam Fritzl, der in einer Hand zwei Geschenke und in der anderen einen winzigen Weihnachtsbaum trug, der sogar einen goldenen Stern auf seiner Spitze hatte. Er wollte Weihnachten in das Haus einer Familie bringen, die so gar nichts besaß.

Es schien als ob die Dorflichter unten im Tal Heinzl, Berndl und Fritzl herbeiwinkten als sie durch die eiskalte Nacht knirschten und den dunklen Kiefernwald hinter sich ließen. Jedes der Wichtelmännchen hatte das freundlichste Gesicht das man sich je vorstellen konnte und alle trugen sie Mützen auf dem Kopf. Ihre Kleidung war in verschiedenen Brauntönen und Berndl und Fritzl trugen stolz die prächtigsten silbergrauen Bärte, die zu ihren langen Haarsträhnen passten. Berndls Bart umrahmte sein Gesicht mit wunderschönen, silbergrauen Locken, auf die er mächtig stolz war. Heinzl trug einen braunen Schal statt eines Bartes, denn er war der jüngste. Auf seinem Kopf saß eine hellbraune, gestrickte Bommelmütze, die stolz und hoch auf seinem dunkelbraunen Haar thronte. Die zwei anderen Wichtelmännchen trugen auch Mützen. Fritzls war so wie Heinzls nur mit einem Pelzrand, doch er trug sie über die Schulter gefaltet und hatte einen Stechpalmenzweig an der Vorderseite festgemacht. Berndl trug eine Kappe aus braunem Filz, von der er glaubte, in der er sich recht keck fand.

Als die drei Freunde auf dem gefrorenen Pfad zum Dorf unten im Tal marschierten, sahen sie auf einer Seite des Pfades zwischen den Bäumen ein bescheidenes Häuschen versteckt. Als sie durch ein niedriges Fenster spähten, sahen die Wichtelmännchen einen sehr schwachen Lichtschimmer von einem sehr schwachen Feuer und einen Jungen in zerschlissenen Lumpen, der an einem kahlen Holztisch saß und still vor sich hin weinte. Die drei freundlichen Wichtelmännchen näherten sich dem Jungen, der der Sohn eines Holzfällers war, und erkundigten sich nach seinem Kummer.

"All unsere Holzscheite sind gefroren," sagte er traurig "und wir können noch nicht mal unser eigenes Häuschen heizen, geschweige denn Holzscheite an die Dorfleute verkaufen. Unsere Werkzeuge können die Holzscheite einfach nicht klein hacken und das ganze Dorf verlässt sich auf uns." Und er weinte völlig verzweifelt als er an seine Eltern dachte, die draußen in dieser eiskalten Dezembernacht die Hühner fütterten und an das Dorfvolk, das sich noch nicht mal genug wärmen konnte um Weihnachten zu feiern.

"Komm mit mir nach draußen zu eurem Holzhaufen," sagte Berndl mit freundlicher Stimme und der Junge wischte sich die Tränen von seinen blassen, kalten Wangen und folgte ihm schüchtern. Als sie draußen waren, hob Berndl seine Axt an, die im Mondlicht silbern glitzerte und hackte alle Holzscheite in zwanzig Hieben. "Toll!" hauchte der Sohn des Holzfällers bewundernd und sammelte einen Arm voll Holzscheite und ging ins Häuschen zurück, um das Feuer zu schüren. Im Häuschen hatte Heinzl seinen verzauberten Lebkuchen auf den Tisch neben drei Teller gelegt und Fritzl hatte zwei Weihnachtsgeschenke an den Kamin neben das prasselnde Feuer gelegt. Berndl stellte seine kleinere Laterne auf den Kaminsims über dem Feuer und als der Holzfäller und seine Frau schließlich vom Hühnerfüttern von draußen reinkamen, fanden sie Wärme von dem lodernden Holzfeuer und Licht von Berndls Laterne, Essen auf dem Tisch und sogar zwei Weihnachtsgeschenke zu öffnen. Heinzl, Berndl und Fritzl ließen dem Holzfäller die Zauberaxt zurück und schlichen sich leise davon und machten

sich wieder auf ihren Weg den gefrorenen Pfad entlang zum Dorf unten im Tal. Nun hatten sie nur noch den Weihnachtsbaum und die Laterne am Ende von Heinzls langem Stock.

Als sie sich dem Dorfrand näherten, sahen sie keine Menschenseele. Die Straßenlampen flackerten über ihnen und die holzbesohlten Lederschuhe der Wichtelmännchen machten winzige, kratzende Geräusche auf dem Eis. Sie konnten ihren Atem vor sich sehen wie drei kleine Drachenrauchwolken. Aber es gab keinerlei Lebenszeichen: an allen Häusern waren die Fensterläden geschlossen und es war als ob sich alle eingeschlossen hatten. Fritzl, Heinzl und Berndl liefen schweigend weiter bis sie zum Hauptplatz kamen. Dort hielten sie an und stellten den Weihnachtsbaum auf, der im Mondlicht funkelte und glitzerte. Daneben stellten sie die große Laterne am Ende von Heinzls Stock. Und um den ganzem Baum herum von der Laterne beleuchtet erschienen plötzlich Haufen und Haufen von Holzscheiten wie hingezaubert, in verschiedenen Formen und Größen und alle trocken und zum Verbrennen bereit.

Als Fritzl, Heinzl und Berndl sich umdrehten um auf dem eisigen Pfad wieder zum Kiefernwald zurückzugehen, hörten sie wie sich die Haustür eines Häuschens öffnete und einen Jubelschrei beim Anblick der Holzscheite. Dann kamen mehr und mehr Stimmen hinzu und die Lichter im Dorf leuchteten heller als das Dorfvolk seine Feuer schürte und die Wärme genoss. Und dann hörten die drei Wichtelmännchen Gesang und als sie sich auf dem Pfad umblickten, sahen sie vielleicht hundert Menschen um den Weihnachtsbaum und die Laterne auf dem Hauptplatz herum. Sie hielten sich alle bei den Händen und sangen zusammen. Die Wichtelmännchen lächelten vor sich hin, nun da ihre Aufgaben erfüllt waren und kletterten weiter den gefroren Pfad hoch bis sie die Dunkelheit des Kiefernwaldes aufnahm und sie nicht mehr zu sehen waren.

Activity 5: Advent calendar

This advent calendar comes from the German Embassy, London (see list of useful websites in the accompanying DVD materials) where it is presented in 3D. The closed example here can be adapted to suit your class, with a new question posed each day. One way to exploit this calendar is to ask your class to work out what the word is in German from the jumbled letters, one of which will appear each day behind the door. You can disclose the letters in any order, but the correct word (24 letters) in this example is **die Weihnachtssüßigkeiten**

DESIGN: SAY HELLO! Graphic Design, -www.bettinamayer.com-

Activity 6: Christmas Bingo

Here is an example of a bingo sheet with clues. Clues can be read aloud by a student or teacher and the corresponding picture is ticked each time. The winner is the first person to tick all the pictures correctly and shout out BINGO! The pictures could be displayed on the whiteboard with or without the vocabulary (it is obviously easier if the words are visible).

Clues/Hinweise

Ich habe 24 Türen (der Adventskalender)

Ich schmecke lecker! (der Lebkuchen)

Ich habe 4 Kerzen (der Adventskranz)

Ich habe Geweihe auf meinem Kopf (das Rentier)

Man hängt mich auf den Weihnachtsbaum (die Christbaumkugel)

Ich bin aus Schnee gebaut (der Schneemann)

Ich habe Flügel (der Engel)

Man hört mich überall (die Glocke)

Unter mir liegen oft Geschenke (der Weihnachtsbaum)

Man öffnet mich am 24sten Dezember in Deutschland (das Geschenk)

Ich bin das Weihnachtsmahl (die Weihnachtsgans)

Ich bringe die Geschenke (der Weihnachtsmann)

Normalerweise bin ich aus Wachs gemacht (die Kerze)

Man kann mich oft am Himmel sehen (der Weihnachtsstern)

Hier kannst du auch Tiere finden (die Krippe)

der Adventskalender

die Christbaumkugel

das Geschenk

der Lebkuchen

der Schneemann

die Weihnachtsgans

der Adventskranz   der Engel   die Glocke

das Rentier   der Weihnachtsbaum   der Weihnachtsmann

die Kerze   der Weihnachtsstern   die Krippe

It's Christmas!: Additional DVD materials

1. A Christmas story in English
2, A Christmas reading
3. German towns puzzle
4. A Christmas carol
5. A letter to German companies
6. A photograph gallery
7. Useful internet sites

Project 2   Day of the Dead

routes into
LANGUAGES

Project Outline

Requirements: classroom or hall (depending on number of students taking part)
Event time: two hours
Language targeted: Spanish
Impact: medium-high (can be used with small and large groups)

Introduction

This project combines learning about the traditional Day of the Dead festivals in countries such as Mexico and Spain with taking part in some of the customary cultural activities associated with the event. It can be structured as a basic model to help promote Spanish to new learners or can be made more complex, depending on the targeted learners. It is also suitable for both small and large groups and was first developed in 2008 by the University of Brighton as a Routes South project.

The additional materials that accompany this section include: a Day of the Dead presentation in English; two picture galleries of decorating sugar and paper skulls; a Day of the Dead quiz; a recipe for *pan de muerto* (bread of the dead); a list of useful websites.

Organisation

This event is flexible in its timings and can be reduced or extended depending on the time available (1–2 hours). Preparation time beforehand is required to set up video clips, print out worksheets and prepare materials (depending on which cultural activities are chosen). The event can be divided into two parts, with the first half covering target language tasks and the second half devoted to cultural activities.

Part One: Language activities

It is useful to begin the session with a short presentation about the Day of the Dead festival. This can include showing short video clips of typical celebrations and parades (*desfile*) in Mexico and other Latin American countries (see list of useful internet sites in the materials for this project on the accompanying DVD). The following presentation in Spanish is also available in English in the additional materials section on the DVD. After the presentation, students can take part in various activities designed to help reinforce new vocabulary. Three such activities are presented after the Spanish presentation, (picture/word matching, themed anagrams and a word search). Here is some useful vocabulary to support the project as a whole:

El Día de los Muertos, vocabulario – Day of the Dead, vocabulary

el altar de la ofrenda:	altar (of the offering)
el ataúd:	coffin
la calaca:	skeleton (see also *el esqueleto*)
la calavera:	skull
la calavera de azúcar:	sugar skull
el candelero:	candlestick
las Calaveras:	poems and songs written during *El Día de los Muertos*
las caretas:	masks (see also *la máscara*)
las Catrinas:	female skeletons
el cementerio:	cemetery
la cruz:	cross
el cempasúchil (cempazúchil):	marigold
el desfile:	parade
la flor de muertos:	flower of the dead
los dulces:	sweets
el Día Todos los Santos:	All Saints' Day
la máscara:	mask
el esqueleto:	skeleton
las ofrendas:	offerings
el pan de los muertos:	bread of the dead
la tumba:	grave
el papel picado:	cut-out paper decorations
la vela:	candle

Spanish presentation

> *El Día de los Muertos es una festividad tradicional de origen prehispánico que se celebra en México y en otros países Latinoamericanos el 2 de noviembre todos los años. Coincide con las celebraciones de Día de los Fieles Difuntos y Todos los Santos (1 y 2 noviembre) y se remonta a la civilización azteca.*
>
> *En México la costumbre es reunirse con familiares y con amigos para recordar y celebrar a sus seres queridos difuntos. Estas fiestas no son tristes sino una celebración alegre y colorida en la que la muerte asume una expresión vivaz y amistosa; se recuerda y se honra a los muertos comiendo y bebiendo sus alimentos favoritos. Las familias limpian y decoran las tumbas y van al cementerio en procesiones para dejar flores y otras ofrendas. A veces pasan la noche allí.*
>
> *Mucha gente elabora detallados altares en el cementerio, o en su casa o su oficina. Decoran el altar con ofrendas como retratos de los seres queridos, velas y flores – especialmente cempasúchil – y las comidas y bebidas preferidas de los difuntos. Ofrendas típicas pueden incluir calabaza cristalizada, pan de muerto, calaveras de dulce y otros dulces. También se pueden dejar vasos de*

agua y almohadas por si el alma del difunto tiene sed o quiere descansar. Las familias se sientan alrededor de la tumba para rezar y recordar al difunto y contar historias de su vida. En algunas regiones la gente se prende conchas a la ropa para que, al bailar, hagan ruido para despertar al difunto.

Las calaveras son muy populares en estas fiestas – pueden ser de azúcar o chocolate para consumir o de madera o cartón como decoración. Las calaveras pueden tener el nombre del difunto escrito en la frente y las comen los parientes y amigos para demostrar que no temen la muerte. También populares como símbolos en estas festividades son los esqueletos y los ataúdes que pueden ser de papel o cartón o de chocolate. El esqueleto hace referencia al personaje de la Catrina 'la dama de la muerte' representada como una mujer rica.

Otra tradición de esta festividad son 'las calaveritas' que, aparte de ser dulces para comer o de papel o cartón como decoración o disfraz, también pueden ser rimas y versos humorísticos que hablan sobre el difunto o sobre la muerte misma; la música, cantos y bailes son también características de estas festividades.

Activity 1: Picture/word matching

Match the words to the pictures:

1. Catrina
2. Calaca
3. Ataúd
4. Cempasúchil
5. Cruz
6. Calavera de azúcar

A

B

C

D

E

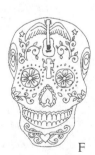
F

Answers: 1 = B, 2 = C, 3 = A, 4 = D, 5 = E, 6 = F

Activity 2: Themed anagrams

Unscramble the letters to make Spanish words relating to *El Día de los Muertos*:

ANAGRAMA	ESPAÑOL	INGLÉS
smrtoeu	....	....
darnerof	....	....
alacsac	....	....
sacmraá	....	....
vrsacaela	....	....
zúarca	....	....
adí	....	....
xiémoc	....	....
poñeasl	....	....
orlf	....	....
sanictra	....	....
zucr	....	....
daaút	....	....

Spanish answers
muertos, ofrenda, calacas, máscara, calaveras, azúcar, día, México, español, flor, Catrinas, cruz, ataúd

English answers
dead, offering, skeletons, mask, skulls, sugar, day, Mexico, Spanish, flower, female skeletons (Catrinas), cross, coffin

Activity Three: Word search

Look for the following Spanish words which are hidden in the word square:

*Ataúd / Azúcar / Calaca / Calavera / Candelero / Catrina / Cruz / Desfile / Día / Dulces
Español / Fiesta / Flor / Máscara / México / Muertos / Ofrenda / Tequila / Vela*

```
S  O  Z  Y  N  E  G  X  W  O  N  R  S  P  J  T
E  F  L  B  U  G  Z  P  T  H  O  W  A  N  E  R
S  D  E  S  F  I  L  E  V  L  G  L  R  V  J  Q
E  C  I  D  Ú  A  T  A  F  E  Y  W  E  R  P  L
C  Y  A  C  A  T  R  I  N  A  T  Y  V  C  V  M
L  E  M  N  A  P  I  U  C  R  E  C  A  R  F  U
U  I  É  R  D  L  G  A  Z  A  Q  E  L  U  L  E
D  T  X  E  I  E  A  C  M  C  U  L  A  Z  H  R
S  C  I  T  L  R  L  C  V  Ú  I  O  C  O  E  T
X  E  C  O  Y  I  C  E  A  Z  L  Ñ  F  Y  M  O
J  X  O  N  Q  Q  A  Q  R  A  A  A  P  H  A  S
A  D  N  E  R  F  O  I  J  O  X  P  L  T  L  V
W  D  T  R  E  E  K  Q  C  W  E  S  S  W  I  E
N  S  A  M  Á  S  C  A  R  A  P  E  A  C  C  L
M  N  F  E  C  S  Y  O  Z  D  Í  A  R  G  D  A
T  C  X  B  V  L  Q  Y  D  F  W  Q  K  J  P  B
```

Answers:

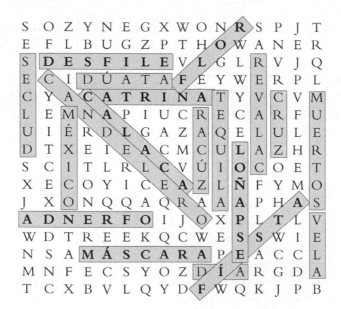

Part Two: Cultural activities

A wide range of cultural activities can be employed to help make the event as realistic as possible. Depending on the time allocated for the event, students can take part in any number of the following tasks:

Calaveras de azúcar (sugar skull decorating)

This is a fun activity for learners of all ages. It involves decorating pre-made sugar skulls, which can then be placed on an *ofrenda* (altar). Skulls can be decorated with a variety of materials, such as sweets, icing, glitter and sequins.[1] Prizes can be awarded for the best-looking skulls. It is advisable that the skulls are made well in advance of the event, so that they have time to dry and harden before decoration. Internet sites selling skull moulds can be found in the list of useful websites in the accompanying DVD materials, as can a selection of photographs of the best-decorated sugar skulls (in our opinion!).

- 450g granulated sugar
- 2 full teaspoons meringue powder
- Water to add

Directions (skulls can also be made out of jelly, plaster of Paris or chocolate):

1. Put the sugar and meringue powder into a large bowl and mix together.
2. Gradually add drops of water until the mixture becomes moist and similar to the texture of wet beach sand.
3. Once the mixture resembles sand it is ready to mould – press it firmly into the skull mould, ensuring all indentations are properly filled.
4. Smooth the back of the mould and ensure it is filled right to the top.
5. Place a square of cardboard on top of the mould then turn it over (as if removing a cake from a tin).
6. Gently remove the mould and set the sugar skull aside to dry and harden.

Note: depending on the type of mould you use, you can either make the skulls in two halves and sandwich them together using icing (so that you have a full skull) or, to save time, you can make just the 'face' half of the skull, leaving the reverse side flat to lay on plates or pieces of card for ease of decorating.

Máscara de calaveras (skull mask making)

If making sugar skulls as described above is not possible, students can make and decorate their own skull mask. Here is a template which can be copied onto cardboard and then decorated. In the accompanying DVD materials there is a picture gallery of skull masks made by Year Seven students.

---

1 Please note that whilst the skulls are made with sugar and can be decorated with sweets, they are not intended to be eaten.

Ofrenda (altar)

Students can work together to construct an altar upon which items such as sugar skulls and masks can be placed. Altars are usually brightly decorated with crosses, candles and flowers – typically the marigold (*flor de muerto or cempasúchil*) – although religious artefacts can be omitted if necessary. The *ofrenda* can be a decorated table, or it can be specifically constructed using items such as cardboard boxes.

Calacas (skeletons)

Skeletons are typical symbols commonly seen throughout the festival. Students can make and decorate individual skeletons, and these can be hung up on the *ofrenda* or throughout the room as decorations. Skeletons can be made as follows.

1. Using the template shown here, draw a skeleton onto thick paper or cardboard.

2. Paint the skeleton in bright colours and leave to dry.

3. Cut around the outline of the shapes. The feet and hands can be kept as one section each (i.e., do not cut out each finger or toe).

4. Make a small hole on each spot, using a needle (or hole puncher if the skeleton is large enough).

5. Tie the bones together using white thread and knot securely.

6. Finally draw a face on the skeleton and hang it up with a loop of thread in the top hole on the head.

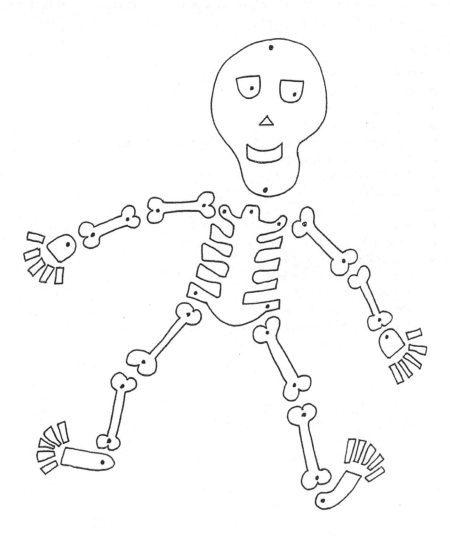

Traditional food and drink tasting

A very popular part of this event involves tasting food and drink traditionally consumed during the Day of the Dead festival. This can be kept quite simple, by choosing only one or two items from the list below, or can be extended to include all of them.

- Cucumber and lime: sticks of cucumber drizzled with fresh lime juice
- Salsa or guacamole with tortilla chips
- Chilli-flavoured chocolate (available at most supermarkets)
- Hot chocolate with mild or strong chilli powder added to taste

A recipe for 'bread of the dead' is also included in the materials for this section on the accompanying DVD.

Tips

- A charge of 50p–£1 can be applied to help cover the costs of materials or ingredients.
- Students can be asked to collect cardboard boxes in advance of the event to help construct the *ofrenda*.

Shopping list

Sugar skull ingredients:

- Granulated sugar
- Meringue powder
- Sugar skull moulds
- Decorating items, such as small sweets, icing, cake decorations, glitter, sequins, glue, etc.
- Paper plates to put skulls on
- Paper bowls for decorating items
- Cucumber
- Limes
- Salsa
- Guacamole
- Tortilla chips
- Chilli-flavoured chocolate
- Hot chocolate powder
- Mild and/or hot chilli powder
- Flowers for the *ofrenda* (marigolds if possible)
- Prizes for best sugar skull or mask

Calaveras poem task

Another traditional activity during this festival is writing short poems. Students can be asked to create their own versions on the model of the traditional one below:

Calavera	**Skull**
Ahi viene el agua	Here comes the water
Por la ladera,	Down the slop,
Y se me moja	And my skull
Mi calavera.	Is getting wet.
La muerte calaca,	Death, a skeleton,
Ni gorda, ni flaca.	Neither fat, nor skinny.
La muerte casera,	A homemade skeleton,
Pegada con cera.	Stuck together with wax.

Reflections

The sugar skulls are certainly a very entertaining and successful part of the event but can be time-consuming to prepare. Be sure to leave enough time to practise making a skull as well as enough time for them to dry once they have been made (at least eight hours or more). The addition of wallpaper paste certainly helps stick the skull together but care must be taken to ensure no one eats the finished product!

Day of the Dead: Additional materials

1. *El Día de los Muertos* presentation in English
2. Picture gallery
3. *El Día de los Muertos* quiz
4. *Una receta para pan de muertos*
5. Useful websites

Project 3   Bastille Day

routes into
LANGUAGES

Project Outline

Requirements: large hall preferably with a raised stage.
Event time: one hour
Language targeted: French
Impact: medium (30+ pupils) plus audience

Introduction

This project explores the annual celebrations in France on July 14th, known in France as *La Fête de la Fédération*, by presenting a short play surrounding the events leading up to the storming of the Bastille and the subsequent revolution that ensued in 1789. It is an exciting project, first developed by the University of Surrey for an Able Linguists Day in 2009. Its aim is to introduce a major event in French history and provide the opportunity to re-enact short sequences using specific vocabulary. Awareness of the historical background to key cultural events is essential to understanding France and the French and the project aims to provide some of this cultural information in a fun and accessible way.

The additional materials accompanying this section provide: key background information as well as a relevant song; an English translation of the playscript; instructions for making props; an English translation of the poem *La nuit d'avant* and a list of useful internet sites.

Organisation

The playscript presented below is complete in itself. Roles need to be allocated, props created, rehearsals organised (these can be built into class time or organised over lunch periods/after-school clubs) and a venue/date/time for the performance identified. The event can be filmed (see Appendix One for sample consent form), which can motivate younger peer groups as well as providing a good record for the participants themselves. Why not invite similar year groups in other schools to join your celebrations? All you need is a hall big enough to hold everyone.

Play: La Révolution Française

Dressing up in some kind of costume helps people to feel the part. The costumes do not have to be particularly elaborate and could be made at home if enough notice is given. Here are some ideas.

- Mop caps are fun for the peasants to wear in the crowd scenes. These are simple to make out of white cotton and elastic (see details in additional materials on the DVD).
- Peasant women can wear long shifts tied at the waist.
- Peasant men can wear dark-coloured leggings and tunics again tied at the waist.
- Noblemen and the king would wear wigs. These can be made of cotton-wool!
- A large map of Paris could be on display showing the locations of the Bastille and the Palace of Versailles.
- A cockade made out of blue, white and red tissue paper (see details in additional DVD materials).
- A bamboo cane and a paper-maché head to parade around the town (see details in additional DVD materials).
- 2 tennis rackets for the real-tennis scene at the start of the play.
- 5 × A3-size posters with a 'human right' declared on each one (see playscript).

Cast

- 2 people playing real tennis
- **Jean Sylvain Bailly:** President of the Third Estate
- **The Marquis de Dreux-Brézé:** Grand Master of Ceremonies
- **Comte de Mirabeau:** politician, orator and member of the National Assembly
- **King Louis XVI:** King of France (*reg.* 1774–1793)
- **Monsieur de Launay:** governor of the Bastille prison
- Messenger from the Swiss Guard
- **Queen Marie-Antoinette**
- Wife of a charcoal burner
- **The Duke of Rochefoucauld-Liancourt:** French social reformer who became president of the National Constituent Assembly
- **The Marquis de la Fayette:** a general with the National Guard
- 5 people, each to read out a declaration of the rights of man and the citizen
- Enough people to represent: the deputies at the National Assembly; the deputies of the Third estate; the group of patriots and the crowd scenes; the officers of the royal guard; the market women of Paris; the royal retinue

Timeframe of the playscript

(**N.B.** a short background to the French Revolution is included in the additional materials for this project on the DVD)

The year is 1789

5 May: Meeting of the deputies at Versailles. No reforms announced.

17 June: Representatives of the Third Estate (le Tiers) adopt the title National Assembly, a body whose purpose was the creation of a French constitution. They meet together on an indoor tennis court and refuse to disperse until constitutional reform has been achieved.

23 June: The deputies of the Third Estate are formally asked to disperse. They refuse.

9 July: The National Assembly declares itself a Constituent Assembly.

13 July: The patriots try to defend themselves against the King's troops. They need arms and gunpowder.

14 July: The crowd goes to the military hospital, Les Invalides, where they secure guns and canons. But they still need gunpowder. They go back to the Bastille to ask the prison governor, Monsieur de Launay, who refuses and orders shots to be fired on the crowd. After some time, the Bastille is taken and Monsieur de Launay is executed. The Bastille was the medieval fortress and prison in the centre of Paris and represented royal authority; its fall was the flashpoint of the French Revolution as the King no longer held supreme authority.

15 July: King Louis XVI withdraws his troops from Paris.

26 August: the National Assembly adopts the Declaration of the Rights of Man and the Citizen.

1 October: the officers of the royal guard trample on the tricolour cockade in front of a royal audience.

5 October: a crowd of Parisian market women send a deputation to the King in his palace to ask him for bread, which has become hugely expensive and almost unavailable. The King agrees. He is now under the control of the Parisian crowd and the independent authority of the French monarch is at an end.

Playscript

(**N.B.** an English translation is included in the additional DVD materials)
Authors: Eric Urvoy and Dawn Marley (University of Surrey)

Le début de la Révolution

Le 5 mai, les 1139 députés sont réunis à Versailles. Aucune réforme n'est annoncée. Les 578 députés du tiers-état décident de se proclamer *Assemblée nationale* le 17 juin. Ils sont priés d'évacuer, mais se réunissent dans la salle du jeu de paume. Là ils font serment de ne plus se séparer jusqu'à ce qu'une constitution soit établie.

2 personnes jouent à la paume. Les députés arrivent.

Un député: Messieurs (ou Mesdames) veuillez sortir. L'Assemblée nationale doit se réunir ici-même.

Les joueurs sortent. Bailly monte sur une table.

Bailly: Nous, membres de cette assemblée, prêtons à l'instant serment de ne jamais nous séparer tant que la Constitution du Royaume ne sera pas établie et affermie sur des fondements solides.

Applaudissements.

Le 23 juin, le Marquis de Dreux-Brézé, grand maître des cérémonies, somme le Tiers de se disperser. Ils refusent.

Dreux-Brézé: Le Roi a levé le séance, il vous ordonne de partir.

Bailly: La Nation assemblée ne peut recevoir d'ordres!

Mirabeau: Allez dire à votre maître que nous sommes ici par la volonté du peuple et que nous n'en sortirons que par la force des baïonnettes!

Dreux-Brézé sort furieux. Il va voir le Roi.

Dreux-Brézé: Sire, le Tiers refuse de lever la séance.

Louis XVI: Ils veulent rester? Eh bien! Fichtre! Qu'ils restent!

Le 9 juillet l'Assemblée nationale se déclare constituante. Cela signifie qu'elle se donne le pouvoir de créer une constitution et de prendre des décisions en dehors du Roi. Louis XVI n'est plus le seul à détenir le pouvoir.

La prise de la Bastille

Le 13 juillet, les patriotes creusent des tranchées et édifient des barricades pour se défendre contre les troupes du Roi, mais il faut des armes. Très tôt, le 14, la foule se porte aux Invalides. Elle s'empare de plusieurs canons et de 32 000 fusils. Ne manque que la poudre.

Tous: A la Bastille! A la Bastille!

Les représentants sont reçus par le Gouverneur de la prison, Monsieur de Launay.

Un patriote: Au nom du peuple, Monsieur, veuillez nous laisser entrer. Nous avons besoin de poudre pour défendre la Patrie.

M. de Launay: non, je ne peux vous la donner.

Un patriote: Alors nous prendrons la Bastille!

M. de Launay fait tirer sur la foule. Il y a presque 100 morts, quand la garnison suisse envoie un messager.

Messager: Nous ferons sauter la poudre si vous n'acceptez pas notre capitulation.

La femme d'un charbonnier cherche le cadavre de son fils. Quand elle le trouve, elle dit:

Femme: Il a donné sa vie pour la Patrie. Il est bienheureux.

Au bout de quelques heures la Bastille est prise. M. de Launay est condamné à mort. Sa tête fera le tour de la ville toute la nuit. Au palais, le Duc de la Rochefoucauld-Liancourt s'entretient avec le Roi.

Le Duc:	Sire, la Bastille a été prise…
Le Roi:	Prise?
Le Duc:	Oui, Sire, par le peuple. Le Gouverneur a été assassiné. On porte sa tête sur une pique dans toute la ville.

Silence.

| **Le Roi:** | Mais alors c'est une révolte ? |
| **Le Duc:** | Non, Sire, c'est une révolution! |

Le 15, Louis XVI décide du retrait de ses troupes de Paris. Le 16, il arrive à la Place de l'Hôtel de Ville.

| **La foule:** | Vive le Roi! Vive la Nation! |

Le Marquis de La Fayette, général de la Garde nationale, lui remet la cocarde tricolore.

| **La Fayette:** | Sire, ceci est le symbole de notre Patrie. Au rouge et au bleu, couleurs de Paris, on a ajouté le blanc, couleur de la monarchie. |

Les Droits de l'Homme

Le 26 août, l'Assemblée adopte la Déclaration des droits de l'Homme et du Citoyen. Celle-là même dont s'est inspiré l'ONU dans sa déclaration universelle des droits de l'Homme le 10 décembre 1948 à Paris.

Les acteurs énoncent chacun leur tour les grands principes du texte:

1: Les hommes naissent et demeurent libres et égaux en droits.

2: Nul ne peut être puni qu'en vertu d'une loi.

3: Nul ne doit être inquiété pour ses opinions, même religieuses.

4: Tout citoyen peut parler, écrire, imprimer librement.

5: La propriété étant un droit inviolable et sacré, nul ne peut en être privé.

Les journées d'octobre

Le 1ᵉʳ octobre, au cours d'un banquet à l'Opéra de Versailles, des officiers de la Garde royale piétinent la cocarde tricolore devant le Roi et la Reine. A cette nouvelle le peuple gronde.

Un officier arrache sa cocarde, la jette par terre, et la piétine. Le Roi et la Reine rient.

Le 5 octobre, les femmes de la Halle de Paris partent à Versailles demander du pain au Roi.

| **Une femme:** | Allons chercher le boulanger, la boulangère et le petit mitron! |
| **Femmes:** | Du pain et le Roi! Du pain et le Roi!! |

Arrivées au palais le lendemain, elles demandent le Roi au balcon.

| **Femmes:** | Le Roi au balcon! Le Roi au balcon! |

Il paraît.

Femmes:	Vive le Roi!
Une femme:	A Paris! A Paris!
Une autre:	La Reine au balcon!

Elle vient accompagnée de ses enfants.

Femmes: Vive la Reine!

Le soir même, le cortège royal se met en route pour Paris, avec des chariots transportant les réserves de blé et de farine. Le Roi et l'Assemblée se trouvent désormais sous le contrôle populaire parisien. Le Roi restera chef de l'état jusqu'au 21 septembre 1792. Il sera guillotiné le 21 janvier 1793.

Vocabulary-matching

Draw a line to join the French word on the left with its correct English translation on the right. All the words are in the playscript.

L'Assemblée nationale	to hold power
une cocarde	a charcoal-burner
un mort	to blow up the gunpowder
un charbonnier	the National Assembly
faire sauter la poudre	a corpse
la foule	a cockade/rosette
un fusil	the crowd
jouer à la paume	the guard
le Tiers	a pike(staff)
détenir pouvoir	a death/fatality
un cadavre	a gun
la garnison	to play real tennis
une pique	deputies of the Third Estate

Task

You could ask students to look back over the French playscript and highlight the words in the box above. This will help them to familiarise themselves with the words.

Reflections

If an audience (perhaps from another school) is invited, small programmes can be made and sold at 50p each to cover any costs. In them, some of the background information in the additional materials section could be reproduced to set the scene, or it could be given to the visiting schools in advance to ensure that everyone knows what is happening. A map of Paris could be put into the programmes too, showing the locations of the Bastille and the Palace of Versailles. Perhaps the five 'human rights' presented in the play could also be added. If *La Marseillaise* (included in the additional materials) is also in the programme, the audience could sing it along with the cast at the end of the performance!

An interview

In the passage which follows, Corrine describes how she and her family spend July 14th, Bastille Day, each year in France:

La prise de la Bastille! La France entière est "bleu-blanc-rouge".

On commence par regarder le défilé sur les Champs-Élysées. Toute notre merveilleuse armée marche au pas et la nation toute entière est devant sa télévision. A midi, repas en famille ou pique-nique avec des amis. Dans les villes et les villages, hommes, femmes et enfants se retrouvent. Toute la journée, garçons et filles font péter des pétards. Les enfants défilent dans les rues avec leur lampion. Dans chaque ville et village, la communauté se regroupe pour assister au feu d'artifice (il est illégal en France de faire un feu d'artifice chez soi). Ensuite, les jeunes se retrouvent autour de l'orchestre sur la place publique pour le grand bal populaire où l'accordéon est roi. En ce jour, toute la France vit au rythme des pétards, des feux d'artifices, des flonflons et du musette.

Key vocabulary

la prise (de la Bastille)	the capture (of the Bastille)
le défilé	procession
le repas	meal
se retrouver	to meet
le pétard	banger/firecracker
le lampion	Chinese lantern
le feu d'artifice	firework
le bal	dance
les flonflons	a type of dance
la musette	accordion

Exploring other historical events

If essential background information is provided, exploring historical events can be both inspiring and motivating to secondary-school students. Some suggestions follow which focus on French/English cultural understanding and shared history.

Battle of Hastings (14/10/1066)	**Battle of Trafalgar** (21/10/1805)
Battle of Agincourt (25/10/1415)	**Battle of Waterloo** (18/6/1815)

One way to exploit historical re-enactments in the classroom is to write short playscripts around the key action points, such as the one presented above. Alternatively, students could be asked to imagine a character from one of the scenes and write creatively about the person, in the form perhaps of a short story or a poem. This will usually involve further research on their part. An example of possible work is follows.

The minstrel Taillefer

The Battle of Hastings, which took place on Saturday October 14th 1066, started with a song according to many accounts. This song was recited by the minstrel/jongleur Taillefer who juggled with his sword in front of the Norman troops as he sang. The song he sang was of heroic deeds in a never-to-be-forgotten battle against impossible odds. Some scholars believe this song was the *Chanson de Roland* or at least a version of it. The purpose of the recital was to awaken the fighting spirit of the Norman troops and motivate them through the warlike examples in the song. Following the entertainment, Taillefer was challenged by an English soldier whom he subsequently killed. Taillefer then charged the lines of the English troops and never emerged. The Battle of Hastings then ensued.

The name Taillefer can be translated as "hewer of iron". His origins are unknown and he is, perhaps surprisingly, not depicted on the Bayeux Tapestry. To find out more about minstrels and their roles in society, the book on medieval lives (Jones & Ereira, 2005: 36–61) is particularly informative.

The short poem that follows was inspired by the life of Taillefer. It is set on the night before the Battle of Hastings (Friday October 13th 1066), after the Norman troops have eaten their evening meal and are settling down before facing King Harold's army in the morning. There is an English translation of the poem in the additional DVD materials.

The night before

Poem written by Cathy Watts and illustrated by Alex Chown.

French translation by Dora Laitri-Carpenter, University of Brighton

La nuit d'avant

L'automne anglais et sa morsure
Remplissent l'air autour de nous.
Et je contemple les étoiles anglaises
De ma couche sur le sol.

Mon cheval a bu et a mangé.
Mes compagnons se reposent maintenant.
Et pourtant quelque chose perturbe mon sommeil
Et m'empêchera de faire de mon mieux.

Oui, c'est moi le ministrel Taillefer
Le jongleur de Guillaume.
Je chante les hauts faits des héros d'autrefois.
Je travaille pour la joie et pour l'argent.

Ma tâche au matin est celle-ci
J'encourage les troupes pour la guerre.
Mais cette nuit, seul sous les étoiles
Je songe à ceux qui vont tomber.

Le vendredi 13 est de mauvais augure.
Je me demande si cette nuit sera la dernière pour moi.
Mais de telles pensées nuisent à mon ardeur
Je les remise dans le passé.

Taillefer, as we know, was the first to die in front of the troops on Saturday October 14th 1066.

Quiz regarding Old French

One of the consequences of The Battle of Hastings in 1066 was that French replaced English as the language of administration and culture in England. This state of linguistic affairs lasted for well over two hundred years. It is often surprising to discover how many words we use today can be traced back to Old French, having been introduced to the English language by William the Conqueror and his successors. It has been estimated (Crystal, 2003: 46) that as many as ten thousand French words colonised English in the three centuries following the Norman Conquest.

Look at the word fields below. In each field **one** word did not enter the English language through French. But which one? Circle the odd one out in each field.

Food	salmon	cake	pork
Fashion	bracelet	skirt	buckle
Law	crime	prison	lock
Religion	altar	abbey	temptation
Entertainment	dance	book	music
Animals	falcon	spaniel	mouse
Medicine	ill	ointment	surgeon
The home	blanket	pillow	towel
Material	leather	lace	satin
Military	soldier	siege	raid

Answers

Food:	cake	(12–14C, from Scandinavian).
Fashion:	skirt	(post-1200, from Old Norse)
Law:	lock	(pre-1200, from Old English/Germanic)
Religion:	altar	(pre-1200, from Old English from Latin)
Entertainment:	book	(pre-1200, from Old English)
Animals:	mouse	(pre-1200, from Old English)
Medicine:	ill	(12–14C, from Old Norse)
The home:	pillow	(pre-1200, from Old English)
Material:	leather	(pre-1200, from Old English/Germanic)
Military:	raid	(post-1200, from Scottish/Old English)

Bastille Day: Additional DVD materials

Below are examples of different materials around the theme of Bastille Day and other historical events which can be used to supplement the main project.

1. Background to the French Revolution.
2. Song (La Marseillaise).
3. English translation of the playscript.
4. Making props for the play a) a mop cap, b) a cockade and c) a paper-mâché head.
5. English translation of the poem '*La nuit d'avant*'.
6. Useful websites.

Project 4   The European Day of Languages

Project Outline

This project presents an overview of The European Day of Languages followed by twelve ideas to deliver in your school to celebrate the day. There are no discrete requirements this time, as each project uses a different format.

Introduction

The European Day of Languages is celebrated each year on September 26th. If this date falls on a weekend, then the Monday closest to the 26th is chosen for the celebrations. The European Day of Languages is a Europe-wide celebration of language and culture and involves 47 countries. The Council of Europe, together with the European Union, initiated the concept over ten years ago and the celebration is co-ordinated in the UK by CILT, the National Centre for Languages, part of CfBT Education Trust (see useful web addresses in the accompanying DVD materials). The first European Day of Languages was held in 2011, which was the European Year of Languages. All languages are involved in the celebration, not just European ones and the day has its own dedicated website (see list of useful websites in the material for this project on the accompanying DVD). The idea is simple but effective and each year all participants have great fun celebrating the language(s) of their choice. The European Day of Languages has three main objectives as stated by the Council of Europe (see useful web addresses in the accompanying DVD materials) which are to raise awareness of:

■ Europe's rich linguistic diversity, which must be preserved and enhanced;
■ the need to diversify the range of languages people learn (to include less widely used languages), which results in plurilingualism;
■ the need for people to develop some degree of proficiency in two languages or more, to be able to play their full part in democratic citizenship in Europe.

Twelve ideas!

Here are twelve ideas for ways to celebrate European Day of Languages. They are easy enough to host in your school and will make it a day to remember all round!

Idea 1: A class quiz.

This is an interesting idea which can be used in class very easily. Follow-on work can involve students working in separate target-language groups researching further details or perhaps adding to the quiz in various languages.

Do you know the answers to these questions? Perhaps your neighbour does?

1.   What is the 'national dish' of Spain?
     a)   *chorizo*   b)   *paella*   c)   *jamón*

2.   How do you say 'thank you' in Spanish
     a)   *hola*   b)   *adios*   c)   *gracias*

3.   In which city is the famous '*El Prado*' museum?
     a)   Barcelona   b)   Sevilla   c)   Madrid

4.   How do you say 'Good morning' in Russian?
     a)   *Dobre utra!*   b)   *Dobryi den'!*   c)   *Dobryi vecher!*

5.   What is the name of the Danish queen?
     a)   Maria   b)   Margrethe   c)   Elizabeth

6.   Where does parmesan cheese come from?
     a)   Italy   b)   Spain   c)   France

7.   What type of stew is bouillabaisse?
     a)   Fish   b)   Lamb   c)   Beef

8.   What docs the word 'spaghetti' literally mean?
     a)   Little laces   b)   Little strings   c)   Little worms

9.   On which river is Paris situated?
     a)   Marne   b)   Seine   c)   Rhine

10.   When is Bastille Day celebrated in France?
     a)   14th July   b)   15th July   c)   16th July

11.   When was the Eiffel Tower built?
     a)   1889   b)   1897   c)   1937

12.   'Number 5' is a perfume by:
     a)   Christian Dior   b)   Coco Chanel   c)   Yves Saint Laurent

13.   When do Germans traditionally open their Christmas presents?
     a)   24th December   b)   25th December   c)   26th December

14.   What is the capital of Germany?
     a)   Bonn   b)   Munich   c)   Berlin

Answers:

1 – b	2 – c	3 – c	4 – a	5 – b	6 – a
7 – a	8 – b	9 – b	10 – a	11 – a	12 – b
13 – a	14 – c				

Here are some other quizzes you could also use. The relevant web sites are included in the material for this project on the accompanying DVD.

The Council of Europe Quiz. A quiz designed to test your knowledge about the languages of our continent. Their web site contains many interesting languages games and materials.

The Think-German Quiz. This is designed to test your knowledge of Germany.

The CILT EDL Business Quiz. Finds out whether your business can talk World Class!

The CILT EDL Quiz. Download this quiz and test your friends, colleagues and classmates!

Idea 2: Organize an international film event

Hold it either during the day or as an after-school club. A Harry Potter film in a foreign language (or a segment from it) is always good fun, as students probably know the English version and can better guess the gist in the target language.

Idea 3: Create a student newspaper with articles and pictures in foreign languages.

Idea 4: Host a multi-lingual student karaoke.

Idea 5: Design a set of greetings cards using words and pictures in the target language(s). These can be printed professionally and sold at the school around major festivals e.g. Christmas, Diwali, Chinese New Year, etc.

Idea 6: Set up a football tournament which can be carried out in the target language(s). One is presented in Part I, Project 1 (*Score in French*), or you could look at the Arsenal Double Club materials (see useful internet sites on the accompanying DVD).

Idea 7: Perform a song, a poem or a short play to the rest of the school or selected classes in a multi-lingual assembly. One idea for an International Talent Evening can be found on Rachel Hawkes's website at Comberton Village College in Cambridgeshire (see useful websites on the accompanying DVD materials).

Idea 8: Set up a foreign language draw

Decorate your classroom or a corridor with a frieze divided into the letters of the alphabet in the target language (or the Roman-alphabet equivalent, where another writing system is used). Invite students (and staff) to find a noun representing each letter, draw a picture of it and decorate it, add it to the frieze with the noun in the target language written alongside – and genders too, where appropriate. A prize could be awarded for the best picture/most imaginative word, etc. (see also Part VII, Project 4 for details: *The Foreign Languages Draw*).

Idea 9: A language café can be set up where food/drinks are on offer but can only be bought in the target language. Students can make food items themselves, such as biscuits, following recipes in the target language (see, for example, Part VI, Project 4: *Recipes for MFL success!*), or else these items can be bought from supermarkets which stock international items. Students can dress up and work in the café and be involved in creating menus, banners, price cards, etc. A language café does not have to be particularly elaborate; the key thing is to encourage target language use. It can take place as a breakfast, lunch or after-school event on the European Day of Languages.

Idea 10: Offer a 20-minute language taster session at lunchtime. Just learning basic numbers, colours and a few phrases in another language is hugely motivating.

Idea 11: Invite local guest speakers into your school for a mini-conference where positive stories about languages and language-learning are shared. A good presentation for a plenary session entitled 'Why Study Languages' is available from the Routes into Languages website (see useful websites in the material for this project on the accompanying DVD). Guest speakers can include representatives from local businesses (see Part IV, Project 2: *Languages and the World of Work*) as well as Language Leaders (see Part IV, Project 3: *The Language Leader award*) and speakers from your nearest university or sixth-form college perhaps.

Idea 12: The European Day of Languages logo

This was designed by CILT, the National Centre for Languages, part of the CfBT Education Trust. It is shown below, together with ten simple ideas for using it in class. Four different two-colour versions of the logo can be found on the accompanying DVD in downloadable format.

Ten things to do with this logo!

- Download the logo from the accompanying DVD or the CILT website.
- Make a bunting
- Print it on your event invitations
- Add it to your website
- Use it to make flags
- Put it on your European Day of Languages posters
- Colour it in
- Send it in an e-card to someone who does not have English as their first language
- Use it to decorate your classroom
- Make it into a hat

We wish you a very Happy European Day of Languages!

The European Day of Languages: Additional DVD materials

1. Electronic version of the CILT logo
2. The CILT EDL characters
3. Useful web sites

4

Inspiring language learning

Introduction

This chapter presents four projects aimed at inspiring and motivating learners of foreign languages. All four projects were developed under the auspices of the national Routes into Languages initiative. The first project in this chapter, entitled *Eurofest,* outlines a trade fair set up and delivered in the target language (in this case French, German and Spanish, with a sample workshop included in Chinese and Japanese). The idea is certainly stimulating and enables students to design, and persuade visitors to buy, items the students have made themselves and to promote their chosen locality in the target language.

The second project is called *Languages and the World of Work* which concentrates on foreign languages used in the workplace. Outside companies are invited to take part in exploring a variety of activities in the target language with the participating students. This project is followed by *The Language Leader Award*, a year-long programme designed to help students learn to lead, through the medium of language teaching.

Finally it is the turn of parents and carers, whose attitudes towards language learning can be hugely influential on young people. In *Reaching Out to Parents*, a presentation is delivered to help persuade those at home of the value in their child or children learning to speak other languages and the importance potential employers place on this. Ideas for involving parents more closely in learning foreign languages themselves are included, as well as handy tips for helping with homework in the home environment.

Project 1   Eurofest

Project Outline

Requirements: large hall for plenary sessions, fair events and workshops
Event time: whole or half day. Time is also needed for product preparation beforehand (6 hours/lessons).
Languages targeted: French, German and Spanish
Impact: high (100+ pupils, plus visitors who take an active role)

> "Eurofest was brilliant – it gave me a taste of being multilingual and being an entrepreneur. I loved it!"
>
> (*Year 9 Student from Brayton College*)

Introduction

Eurofest is an exciting simulated international trade fair developed by the Selby Modern Languages Forum, Routes into Languages (Yorkshire and Humber), NYBEP and the University of Hull in 2008 to encourage the active use of foreign languages and to increase the number of Year Nine students selecting languages as part of their options. In essence, teams of students from local schools come to a central venue to sell products which they have designed themselves and run both trade and tourist information stands – and have a lot of fun at the same time! By incorporating languages, business, enterprise and business partners, the aim is also to raise the profile of the subject area. This serves to help young people identify careers and progression opportunities in these industries and raise their interest and aspirations in pursuing careers in the sector. The *Eurofest* project won a *European Award for Languages* in 2009 and the *Euro London Appointments Business Prize* in the same year.

What is delivered?

Eurofest is an activity which can be delivered either collaboratively across a district or internally across a year group. The model presented here assumes wider collaboration, but this can easily be adapted to suit a more modest event.

Each school sends twenty Year Eight students to the final event, which is made up of four trade stands and one tourist information stand per school. Schools are free to choose the focus of their stand in any way they want. Some develop products and ideas linked to the school's specialism or a particular subject they have been covering in lessons, whilst others give students a free rein. The tourist information stand can be for any destination – most schools base this around the local area, although fictitious places are also acceptable!

A host venue needs to be negotiated. This could be one of the schools in the area, a local FE college or a nearby university. The advantage of involving post-16 institutions is that school students meet older students (ideally studying languages or international students) who can help out as *Language Leaders* (see Project 3 in this Part) and as visitors to the trade fair. This further promotes languages, as Language Leaders are often seen as positive role models.

Who attends?

In addition to the participating students, a number of key stakeholders from the local community can be invited to give the event a sense of gravitas and enhanced credibility. The local mayor has opened the *Selby Eurofest* each year for example and the Chair of the Local Authority along with business people from a variety of local organisations are also invited, including staff and students from the institution where the event is based. Sponsorship from local businesses is also possible.

Unless acting as a judge, only a very basic level of language skill is necessary for visitors to engage with students on the stands, as much of the information is available on the prompt sheets provided later in this section. Therefore as many contacts as possible are invited. Students studying languages in Higher Education are also invited to act as judges, as their foreign-language skills are often high.

Timeframe

Enough notice is needed for all involved to be able to write the *Eurofest* date into their calendars. Invitations to dignitaries and businesses, including requests for sponsorship, need to go out around three months before the event. In this time period all the logistics surrounding transport and the hiring of display boards, a large hall, etc., are put in place. Schools decide individually how and when to start to organise the in-school preparation for *Eurofest*. The 'frequently asked questions' section below offers handy hints and tips on doing this.

Organisation

The 2008 *Eurofest* was organised as a half-day activity which consisted of the trade fair and a few speakers who came to talk to the students about the value of languages in the business world. Following the success of the day, and with the involvement of the local university, *Eurofest* was extended to become a full-day activity. The format of the morning session stayed much the same, but a carousel of workshops in the afternoon, based around language tasters, was added. To achieve this, chairs were moved from the main presentation area and put around the pods, with one workshop being based in each pod. Students were then split into two groups and, whilst one group was taken on a tour of the college campus by Language Leaders, the other half rotated around the workshops at fifteen-minute intervals. The workshop sessions were kept low-tech and interactive in nature. Languages on offer included Russian, Chinese, Japanese and Italian. Sample workshops in Japanese and Chinese are included in the accompanying DVD materials for this project.

Sample Eurofest layout

The project presented here offers the tools needed to develop and run a *Eurofest* project along with some helpful hints and tips to ensure the smooth running of the event itself. It is hoped that, whether you run your *Eurofest* as an internal or collaborative event, you will experience the same success that *Eurofest* has enjoyed during its development, in terms of embedding it not only into the curriculum but also into local consciousness in both education and the business community.

> A wonderful way to put languages into practice.
> (*Student quote*)

> An entertaining educational experience.
> (*Student quote*)

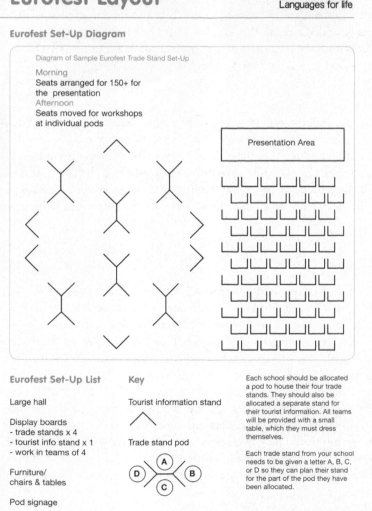

Eurofest Layout

EUROFEST
Languages for life

Eurofest Set-Up Diagram

Diagram of Sample Eurofest Trade Stand Set-Up

Morning
Seats arranged for 150+ for the presentation
Afternoon
Seats moved for workshops at individual pods

Presentation Area

Eurofest Set-Up List

Large hall

Display boards
- trade stands x 4
- tourist info stand x 1
- work in teams of 4

Furniture/
chairs & tables

Pod signage

Key

Tourist information stand

Trade stand pod

Each school should be allocated a pod to house their four trade stands. They should also be allocated a separate stand for their tourist information. All teams will be provided with a small table, which they must dress themselves.

Each trade stand from your school needs to be given a letter A, B, C, or D so they can plan their stand for the part of the pod they have been allocated.

Frequently asked questions

What will Eurofest mean to me as a teacher?

Eurofest will tick a lot of boxes, such as Every Child Matters, Personal Learning and Thinking Skills (PLTS), Enterprise and also, potentially, Employer Engagement, if you involve local businesses/HE/FE in your final event.

What will Eurofest offer my students?

Eurofest will mean a chance for your students to use languages in a practical, non-classroom based environment. It will hopefully increase their motivation and also help them realise that there is a use for what they are learning in a variety of different environments.

How much will involvement cost the school?

This can vary greatly. If you run *Eurofest* as an internal event you may only need the cost of materials to make the products the students design. As a collaborative event run on a large scale between six schools (120 pupils), and with all costs covered including transport and refreshments, you could need £1,000 plus.

Money is needed to:

■ provide materials for the products the students design;
■ provide prizes for the various categories for the students;
■ offer flowers or equivalent to the judges;
■ hire display boards;
■ hire the large hall;
■ provide transport;
■ provide refreshments.

You may not need to spend money on all of these items, as your school may have selected items on hand, for example, the display boards.

How do you get the money to run Eurofest?

The Selby Modern Languages Forum has in the past asked each participating school to contribute up to £500. They have also received sponsorship from local businesses.

Where do you host Eurofest?

Any large hall will suffice. This could be in a sports hall in your local school/college/university for example.

What's a realistic timescale from initial interest to the final trade fair?

The Selby Modern Languages Forum starts to organise the event three to four months before the final event. This is for the collaborative version, with time allowed to find visiting dignitaries and local businesses with enough notice. A smaller-scale, internal event will need less preparation time.

How many hours of preparation does it take the students to choose a product and make the materials?

One hour/one lesson should be allowed for students to choose a product and another five hours/five lessons for the production of materials and practice of the foreign language.

How should the promotional materials be produced?

Students enjoy producing materials on the computer and printing them off in colour, but hand-made items, such as badges, are also good. Other ideas include calendars, cards, food items, key rings, bookmarks. As students have been involved in enterprise activities since Year Seven, they are used to thinking outside the box. They come up with some ingenious and innovative ideas.

How do you introduce students to this enterprise idea?

It is a good idea to whet the students' appetites well in advance and at the beginning of the summer term for example. Setting the scene is very important. You need to explain the enterprise side of the activity and describe what the fair itself will require of the students at the beginning of the first lesson/introductory session.

How are the working groups chosen?

Students should be chosen so that they are not working in friendship groups. Mix the students of differing abilities and skills, so that they learn to work with peers that they haven't worked with before and make new friends.

Which language groups/sets should be involved in the Eurofest event?

The original idea was to involve Year Eight students in the middle sets, in order to stimulate their interest and enthusiasm for modern languages, but top and lower sets who are enthusiastic can take part. It is surprising how much shy or disinterested students are motivated by the methods used to prepare and carry out this event.

How do the students know what to do and when?

It is sensible to give each group a tick-list of the things they need to do in the preparation phase. They should then divide the tasks between them and use the tick-sheet when they have been completed. That way everyone knows what s/he is up to. Once students get started they are quite responsible and take the work seriously.

How do students practise the foreign language items?

Using the role play cards provided later in this section, students can use some time at the end of the materials production stage to practise within their group. Students should also make themselves a small cue card to use on the day of the event to give them confidence when speaking to the buyers at the fair.

How are the groups chosen to represent the school at the event?

Students are enthused when you hold an internal competition to select the representative groups(s). At the end of five weeks, in the last lesson, it makes sense to hold an internal competition in each class or in classes doing the same language. Each group could be asked to do a two-minute presentation about their product in English, each member of the group taking a turn to promote their idea. Each student in the class has one vote, and after the presentations the class votes for the best team. The group(s) with the highest number of votes goes/go on the represent the school at the fair.

What about the tourist information stand? Who prepares that?

The teacher should choose a group of students who would be good at promoting a French/German/Spanish town (you could use an exchange town, a school link or a twin town if you have one). These students would use the internet to provide suitable information for the visitors to the fair: hotels, conference centres, restaurants, maps, entertainment venues, sports facilities and other suitable information.

I'm quite worried about letting my students loose on a project like this, as I'm not used to this way of working in the classroom. How will I cope?

Here's a tip from a member of the Selby Modern Languages Forum.

> From experience I can say that I felt the same initially, but I was pleasantly surprised. The students tackle the project with enthusiasm every year and take responsibility for their own activities – it is a new way of learning. Your job is to hover in the background and maybe make a few suggestions in passing or listen in to the practising of the foreign language to correct mis-pronunciations. Otherwise just relax and let them get on with it!

The following sections of this project present the tools you may like to use to help you to organise your *Eurofest*. Additional materials for this project are also on the accompanying DVD. They include: model invitations/letters/consent forms; judging sheets; a certificate template and sample worksheets in Japanese and Chinese, as well as alphabets in French, German and Spanish.

Teacher checklist

- Consent form
- School-specific risk assessment
- Names of students attending
- Transport (if needed)
- Reviewing vocabulary for specified topics
- Props for trade stands
- Ensure students know orientation of stands, pods, names, etc.

Organiser checklist

- Transport
- Orientation/set-up
- Order/organisation of display
- Venue confirmation
- Certificates and awards
- Refreshments for organisations and guests
- Recruit workshop leaders

- Workshop organisation
- Invite local dignitaries
- Role plays to judges
- Invite guests
- Venue-specific risk assessments
- Publicity
- Sponsorship
- Business partners/colleges and universities
- Judging criteria
- Judges invited and confirmed

Student checklist

- Consent form filled in and returned
- Packed lunch
- Reviewing vocabulary for specified topics
- Marketing and props for trade stands
- Order forms
- Name badge

> The *Eurofest* project is an excellent example of linking languages to the world of work in an effective and meaningful way through a simulation-based approach. When you enter the trade fair simulation, you can feel the buzz of all these young people ready to use their language skills to promote their products to a wider audience of real business people and local community. A very powerful example of engagement across the curriculum and within the community.
>
> (*Teacher quote*)

dministration handout

1. Supervision

Teachers are reminded that they must remain with their own groups of students during the event and over the breaks. Business Partners are not allowed to supervise students.

2. Health and Safety

On hearing the fire alarm, evacuate the building by the nearest exit and assemble on the car park. Please move as far away from the building as possible.

3. Students' List

A list of names of all students including information on gender must be provided to (name) in advance of the event.

4. Coats and Bags

An area will be provided for storage. They may be collected during breaks if required and at the end of the event.

5. Lunch

Lunch will be at 12.00. Students must bring a packed lunch; they will be provided with a drink during the afternoon break.

Lunches are to be eaten in the sports hall or outside if the weather permits.

6. Departure

You need to be outside the college gates to board the buses back to school at (time).

7. *Publicity*

Local media may attend the event to take photographs, film or interview students. Other partners may also wish to take photographs to be used in promotional materials, such as brochures, websites and newsletters. Please inform us in advance if there are any parents who have not given permission for their child/children to be photographed, filmed or interviewed for such purposes. (An example consent form which could be used here is included in Appendix One in this book).

Student information sheet

Aims

- To run a project for young people who may have an interest in taking Modern Languages at the end of Year Nine.
- To help raise the profile of the subject area.
- Help young people identify careers and progression opportunities related to languages.
- Raise the interest and aspirations of young people in pursuing careers incorporating languages.

Timetable of events

Time	Activity
0930	Students arrive and set up stalls
1000	Exhibition opens
1130	Exhibition closes (tidy up time)
1200	Lunch
1230	Talk (Why Study Languages?) and quiz
1310	Workshops and campus tours begin
1410	Break
1430	Award ceremony
1500	Close

Supervision

Once in the Sports Hall you must not leave it unless you have permission from a member of staff from your school.

Behaviour

You will be expected to behave in a mature and sensible manner at all times whilst on the College premises. If a student behaves in an unacceptable manner in the College, they will be asked to leave. They may be escorted back to school and the relevant member of the school staff will be informed. Disciplinary action may be taken by the College/ School after discussion.

Health and Safety

On hearing the fire alarm, evacuate the building by the nearest exit and assemble on the car park. Please move as far away from the building as possible.

Coats/bags

An area will be provided for storage. You may collect your coats and bags during the breaks if required and at the end of the event.

Breaks

You will be provided with a drink during the break. You may only eat during the breaks, either in the Sports Hall or outside with the permission of your school staff.

Departure

You must be ready to leave College at 1500 sharp! Your school staff will give you instructions about where they want you to meet.

Congratulations on being chosen to represent your school!
Good luck and enjoy the day!

Role play cards

These should be distributed to the pairs – one of whom will be the student and one the customer. The players need to highlight their respective parts on the cards and then rehearse before acting them out at the trade fair.

Au Salon Eurofest – At the Exhibition

Produits

S = Student's role
C = Customer's role

S   Bonjour, monsieur/ madame. Est-ce que je peux vous aider?
(Can I help you?)

C   Pouvez-vous me montrer vos produits?
(Can you show me your products?)

S   Voici... (Here...)
(Student presents the products)

C   Avez-vous d'autres... couleurs/tailles..?
(Do you have other... colours/sizes..?)

S   Oui, nous avons... (Yes, we have...)

C   C'est combien? (How much is it?)

S   C'est... l'unité/pour 10/le kilo...
(It's... each/for 10/per kilo...)

C   Je voudrais... (I would like...)
(Say how many or how much)

S   Quel est le nom de votre société?
(What is the name of your firm?) (Student writes out order)

C   Customer gives name of a French company.
(Can be imaginary).

S   Comment ça s'écrit?
(How do you spell that?)

C   Customer spells the French name.

S   Quel est votre adresse et votre numéro de téléphone?
(Address & Telephone number?)

C   Gives an address and telephone number.

S   Merci beaucoup, monsieur/ madame. Au revoir.

C   Au revoir.

Auf dem Eurofest – At the Exhibition

Produkte

S = Student's role
C = Customer's role

S	Guten Tag. Kann ich Ihnen helfen? (Can I help you?)
C	Ja. Können Sie mir bitte Ihre Produkte zeigen? (Can you show me your products?)
S	Hier sind unsere… (Here are our…) (Student presents the products)
C	Haben Sie andere Farben/Größen..? (Have you other colours/sizes..?)
S	Ja, wir haben… (Yes, we have…)
C	Was kostet das? (What does it cost?)
S	Das kostet… das Stück/für 10/pro Kilo… (That costs… each/for 10/per kg…)
C	Ich möchte… (I would like…) (Say how many or how much)
S	Wie heißt die Firma? (What is the name of your firm?) (Student writes out order)
C	Customer gives name of a German company. (Can be imaginary).
S	Wie schreibt man das? (How do you spell that?)
C	Customer spells the German name.
S	Wie ist die Adresse bitte? Und die Telefonnummer? (Address and Telephone number)
C	Gives an address and telephone number.
S	Vielen Dank. Auf Wiedersehen.
C	Auf Wiedersehen.

En el Salón Eurofest – At the Exhibition

Productos

S = Student's role
C = Customer's role

S	Buenos días, Señor/Señora. ¿Le puedo ayudar? (Can I help you?)
C	**¿Puede enseñarme sus productos?** (Can you show me your products?)
S	Aquí tiene... (**Here are...**) (Student presents the products)
C	**¿Tiene usted... otros collores/otras tallas...?** (Do you have other... colours/sizes..?)
S	Sí, tenemos... (Yes, we have...)
C	**¿Cuánto es?** (How much is it?)
S	Son... la unidad/10/por kilo... (It's... each/for 10/per kilo...)
C	**Quisiera...** (I would like...) (Say how many or how much)
S	¿Cómo se llama su empresa? (What is the name of your firm?) (Student writes out order)
C	**Customer gives name of a Spanish company.** (Can be imaginary).
S	¿Cómo se escribe eso? (How do you spell that?)
C	**Customer spells the Spanish name.**
S	¿Cuál es su dirección y número de teléfono? (Address & Telephone number?)
C	**Gives an address and telephone number.**
S	Muchas gracias Señor/Señora. ¡Adiós!
C	¡Adiós!

A l'Office de Tourisme
Carte du Visiteur – Visitor's Card

You are to visit all the tourist stands and speaking in French find out information about the town represented. Below is a check list of questions to ask.

Bonjour

1. Qu'est-ce qu'il y a à faire et à voir dans la ville?
   (What is there to see and do in the town?)

   Student should say at least three things.

2. Vous avez un plan de la ville ou une brochure?
   (Do you have a map of the town or a brochure?)

   Student should show/give a map and/or a leaflet.

3. Est-ce qu'il y a un bon hôtel dans la ville?
   (Is there a good hotel in the town?)

4. Où est l'hôtel?
   (Where is the hotel?)

   Student should show hotel on the map and give directions in French.

5. Est-ce qu'il y a un bon restaurant?
   (Is there a good restaurant?)

6. Où est le restaurant?
   (Where is the restaurant?)

   Student should show restaurant on the map and give directions in French.

7. Est-ce qu'il y a des magasins en ville?
   (Are there any shops in the town?)

   Student should say what kind of shops there are and mention the market.

Au revoir.

An der Touristeninformation
Besucherkarte – Visitor's Card

You are to visit all the tourist stands and speaking in
German find out information about the town represented.
Below is a check list of questions to ask.

Guten Tag.

1. Was gibt es in der Stadt? (What is there to see in the town?)

   Student should say at least two things.

2. Was kann man hier machen? (What is there to do here?)

   Student should say at least two things.

3. Haben Sie einen Stadtplan oder eine Broschüre?
   (Do you have a map of the town or a brochure?)

   Student should show/give a map and/or a leaflet.

4. Gibt es ein gutes Hotel in der Stadt?
   (Is there a good hotel in the town?)

5. Wo ist das Hotel? (Where is the hotel?)

   Student should show hotel on the map and give directions in German.

6. Gibt es ein gutes Restaurant? (Is there a good restaurant?)

7. Wo ist das Restaurant? (Where is the restaurant?)

   Student should show restaurant on the map and give directions
   in German.

8. Was für Geschäfte gibt es in der Stadt?
   (What kind of shops are there in the town?)

   Student should say what kind of shops there are and mention
   the market.

Auf Wiedersehen.

En la Oficina de Turismo
Tarjeta del visitante – Visitor's Card

You are to visit all the tourist stands and speaking in Spanish find out information about the town represented. Below is a check list of questions to ask.

¡Buenos días!

1. ¿Qué hay para ver y hacer en la ciudad?
   (What is there to see and do in the town?)

   Student should say at least three things.

2. ¿Tiene un mapa de la ciudad o un folleto?
   (Do you have a map of the town or a brochure?)

   Student should show/give a map and/or a leaflet.

3. ¿Hay un buen hotel en la ciudad?
   (Is there a good hotel in the town?)

4. ¿Dónde está el hotel?
   (Where is the hotel?)

   Student should show hotel on the map and give directions in Spanish.

5. ¿Hay un buen restaurante?
   (Is there a good restaurant?)

6. ¿Dónde está el restaurante?
   (Where is the restaurant?)

   Student should show restaurant on the map and give directions in Spanish.

7. ¿Qué tiendas hay?
   (What kind of shops are there in the town?)

   Student should say what kind of shops there are and mention the market.

¡Adiós!

Order Form/Formulaire de commande/
Bestellungsformular/Hoja de pedido

Company/Société/Firma/Empresa

....

Address/Adresse/Dirección

....

....

....

Telephone No./Téléphone/Telefonnummer/Número de teléfono

....

Quantity Quantité Menge Cantidad	Description Produit Artikel Descripción	Unit Price Prix unitaire Einzelpreis Precio por unidad	Total

Judging Explanation Sheet

This sheet aims to clearly set out the process and logistics of the judging process:

Twelve to fifteen linguists from local schools, colleges, universities and businesses (where possible) are engaged to facilitate the judging process. This enables two judges to visit each stand.

Each judge receives a judging sheet outlining the scoring criteria on which teams are to be marked. The sheet also clearly identifies which teams they are to judge. Each pair of judges then visits 4 teams and scores each team independently.

Once the judges have visited and scored all their allocated teams, they add up their own scores and return to the organisers. The scores (for each team) are then transferred onto the judging collation sheets.

Once the collation sheets are completed you can then identify which teams from each pod scored the highest totals, and therefore which team scored the highest overall mark.

Awards are presented for the following:

Best use of the French language
Best use of the German language
Best use of the Spanish language
(Depending on which languages you have included in your event).
Best trade stand
Best tourist information stand

Finally by adding together the scores from all teams from each school (pod totals including their tourist information stand) we also come up with an overall winning school, which is our grand prize.

Notes to consider:

As the tourist information stands are often bilingual, judges allocated to these stands need to be comfortable with all the languages used by the team they are judging.

The awards for the best use of each language need to take into account all stands including the tourist information ones.

Judges who are allocated tourist information stands should only include a team's highest language score when adding up their totals. This brings the scores in line with the trade stand teams to allow for fair comparison.

Additional Awards:

In addition to the main awards above, within the pack there is also the option to give star performer and also best effort certificates to allow flexibility in terms of ensuring that all schools/students can be acknowledged as required.

Eurofest is a super example of a hands-on activity that encourages young people to use languages in a work-based context and to give genuine meaning to the link between languages and business. The enthusiasm of the students involved is clearly apparent, together with the huge efforts they make to bring the event to life and a clear sense of fun from taking part.

(*Teacher quote*)

Eurofest: Additional DVD materials

1. Invitation to Eurofest
2. Letter to parents re. consent
3. Medical consent form
4. Letter of participation
5. Judging sheets for French, German and Spanish and the Tourist information
6. Trade stand score-collation sheet
7. Award winners
8. Sample workshops in Japanese and Chinese
9. Certificate template
10. French, German and Spanish alphabets

Project 2   Languages and the world of work

Project Outline

Requirements: one room large enough for the group taking part plus breakout rooms
Event time: one day
Languages targeted: any (depending on the languages spoken by any mentors you use)
Impact: high

Introduction

As the title of this project suggests, this activity concentrates on languages in the work-place. It aims to provide students with tangible links between language lessons and the language skills that are increasingly sought by employers. It also seeks to highlight the large number of careers that require language skills, of which many students can be unaware. Also promoted during these activities are employers' needs for language skills across a wide range, from basic competence to advanced ability – thus dispelling the myth that you need to be fluent in another language for it to be useful. Other common misconceptions among students can also be explored and hopefully reconsidered, such as the belief that British employers do not need staff with language skills (Watts, 2004) and the conviction that other subjects are far more important in terms of career options (Graham, 2004).

World of Work events are appealing, as they can be easily adapted to suit the needs of all year groups. They can also be delivered in various guises. The version described here is a project delivered by the University of Portsmouth, as part of the Routes into Languages initiative in the South, in which Year 11 students embark on a languages challenge involving a fictitious cruise-ship company. However, the Routes South team has also developed versions suitable for Years Eight and Nine in which students are invited to university campuses to hear short talks by business representatives about how they use languages in their job roles, which are then typically followed by taster sessions in new languages. The activity can be further adapted for older students by including mock interview sessions, tips for writing cover letters and CVs, as well as more in–depth discussions about careers with languages and the various options for studying languages at university.

This section includes advice on approaching businesses and inviting them into school or to an event such as the one presented later, along with a basic brief for employers detailing the aims and objectives of a *World of Work* event and what will be expected of them should they attend. It also outlines a work-related event for Year 11 able linguists. Materials on the accompanying DVD include a sample certificate for participants in the Languages Challenge event, an event-evaluation form for teachers and those in supporting roles, an event-evaluation form for students and a list of useful websites.

Contacting local businesses

Local businesses and companies can often provide a wealth of support for work-related events and activities. Larger companies usually welcome opportunities that help them fulfil their statements of corporate social responsibility, whilst smaller firms may be looking for new ways in which to promote their business. A good place to start looking for contacts is to find out whether friends, family members or parents of students are employees of any of the companies you are interested in contacting. This is a worthwhile step, as they may often be able to provide you with the name and details of the right person to get in touch with, thus saving you having to call (or email) 'cold'. But if this route is unavailable to you, another avenue is your local Chamber of Commerce (see list of useful websites on the accompanying DVD). Their websites usually allow you to search a list of members and company contact details are often included. If there is one in your area, your local Education Business Partnership office may also be able to help.

Once you have decided whom to approach, it is worth writing up a short brief about the event which can either be e-mailed or used as a prompt sheet during a telephone conversation. To maximise your chances of a positive response, ensure you can provide details such as the date and time of the event and how long the person might be expected to stay. This may seem obvious, but such details are surprisingly often neglected. Also ensure that you contact people in good time, or you may find that diaries are full, and you have no one to support your event. Once your invitation has been accepted, make a note of when to send out a timely reminder, so that your event is not forgotten. Finally, once the event is over, consider sending a short note of thanks, perhaps noting how valuable the experience was for the participating students. It is also always worth asking if the business representatives would be happy to be contacted regarding similar events in the future.

Your future in languages: A work-related languages challenge for year 11

Overview

The *World of Work* event we focus on here is called *Your Future in Languages*, an event designed specifically for Year 11 able linguists studying for GCSE examinations in French, German, Italian and Spanish. It originates from a joint enterprise between Young Chamber and Ryde High School, a language college on the Isle of Wight, and is supported by the University of Portsmouth. Students are invited to an off-site location (in this instance, the county cricket club), as this helps to create a more 'work-like' atmosphere than a school environment. It also means that accompanying staff are less likely to be disturbed and students can work without being distracted by things like the school bell and people not participating in the event. Tea and coffee are provided on arrival, which also helps to maintain a professional, rather than school, feel to the day.

How the day works

Suggested schedule

Time	Activity
09.00–09.15	Arrival and registration (refreshments served and students treated as if they are attending a business conference)
09.15–09.20	Welcome
09.20–09.40	First business presentation
09.40–10.00	Second business presentation
10.00–10.15	Break
10.15–10.35	Third business speaker
10.35–10.50	Introduction of Language Challenge
10.50–13.00	Students work on the four tasks that make up the challenge
13.00–13.45	Lunch
13.45–14.30	Presentations to tour operators
14.30–15.00	Announcement of winners
15.00	End

Following registration and welcome, students hear short presentations from local business representatives. For the most recent *Your Future in Languages* event, speakers were invited from:

- The NatWest Island Games 2011, an international event where competitors from 25 islands across the world come together to compete in various sporting events;
- Gurit UK, a manufacturer of advanced composite materials based on the Isle of Wight;
- Carnival UK, a cruise company.

Topics covered during the presentations included: how language skills can be helpful when welcoming visitors to the island; how languages are used at various levels in a multi-national organisation; various careers available within certain industries for students with language abilities.

After the presentations students begin work on the main part of the day. This is a language challenge set around a fictitious scenario based at a cruise line. The scenario is as follows: Carnival UK wishes to increase the number of international cruise passengers carried and to improve international relations and communication between foreign passengers, thereby enhancing the passenger experience. Students assume the roles of Carnival UK employees and are asked to put together a proposal for a cruise holiday for international families that can be offered to tour operators in France, Spain, Italy and Germany. Students work in small groups to complete four tasks devised by Carnival UK:

1. develop an itinerary for on-board activities that is fun and interesting for teenagers, including an intercultural event;
2. produce a radio advert to promote the cruise holiday and activities;

3.   make a marketing poster;

4.   present their pitch to a tour operator.

Students should work in the target language to complete each of the tasks. All promotional materials and the radio jingle must also be in the target language. To help complete the first three tasks, students must visit the tour operators (presented later) to find out what information should be included in the itinerary they develop. Students must then pitch their ideas in the form of a presentation, which is also in the target language. Student groups will be assigned a mentor (presented later) to help them with the language aspect of the challenge. Judges (presented later) will observe each group throughout the day and will award marks for tasks 1–3 above according to a set of criteria. They will also watch each of the presentations with the tour operators and will confer with the operators to award marks. A sample scoring sheet is presented later. The team(s) with the highest marks will win the Language Challenge. In the case of the event described here, the cruise company kindly provided prizes of a day on board one of their ships. Other companies approached for events of a similar nature may also be interested in providing prizes, so it is worth asking if they can.

Supporting roles

To ensure the smooth running of the day, a number of supporting roles also need to be filled. These include mentors, tour operators and judges. In this instance, the University of Portsmouth asks its cohort of PGCE trainees to fill these positions during the event. If inviting groups of PGCE trainees to similar events at your school is not feasible, then other groups can be considered. The teachers accompanying the groups of students could be approached to take on these roles, as could older students in Years 12 or 13, languages undergraduates from local universities, or even parents.

It is helpful to acquaint mentors, tour operators and judges with the aims of the day beforehand, perhaps in a short briefing session in a lunch break or after school, depending on the schedules of those volunteering. This will ensure that everyone understands their role and how to carry it out. It also gives people an opportunity to ask questions or make suggestions. The main aims of the day are:

■   to promote enterprise and language learning in young people through a real-life business context, during which they can apply and develop their language and enterprise skills;

■   to give students the opportunity to apply their skills and knowledge in a business environment outside the classroom, working to tight deadlines on individual tasks and as a team;

■   to raise awareness of the use of languages and intercultural activity in the workplace and to develop an appreciation of the cruise industry.

The sections below explain each of the supporting roles in more detail.

Mentors

Mentors are usually native or near-native speakers of the target language(s) being used during the challenge. One mentor is assigned to each team of Year 11 students and remains on hand to advise and help them in using the target language. Mentors can also guide students in the production of their presentations, jingles and promotional artwork, making sure each task is completed on time and that as much target language as possible is used. Mentors stay with their group for the whole day and can assist students when they meet with the tour operators. They can also watch their group's presentation of their pitch at the end of the challenge.

Tour operators

Tour operators will hold information about what should be included in the activity itinerary and it is up to the students to meet with them to find out the details. All exchanges of information must be conducted in the target language. The information that tour operators should advise students to include is as follows.

1. Five days' worth of activity.
2. Dates of each activity.
3. Times of each activity.
4. The age group to which each activity relates.
5. At least one intercultural activity per day.

Each group's meeting with the tour operators will be scored by both the judges and the tour operators themselves. Points awarded here will contribute to the teams' overall scores.

Judges

Those acting as judges will also need to be reasonably fluent in the target language(s) used during the challenge. They are assigned teams according to the language(s) they speak and will observe them throughout the day. Each task must be judged and scored. The meeting with the tour operator will also be judged by the tour operators themselves. Here is a sample scoring sheet:

Team Name................................. **Judge Name**...................................

Task 1 – Itinerary (maximum 15 marks)

Judging criteria	Max	
Innovation and diversity in the activities suggested	5	
Ability to use the foreign language in an effective and accurate way	5	
Intercultural activities for each day	5	

Task 2 – Meet with Tour Operator (maximum 15 marks)

Judging criteria	Max	
Ability to use the foreign language in an effective and accurate way	5	
Asking questions for more information in MFL	5	
Suitability of questions	5	

Task 3 – Marketing poster (maximum 20 marks)

Judging criteria	Max	
Creativity	5	
Relevance of activity to promote intercultural activity	5	
Ability to use MFL in an effective and accurate way	5	
Appeal of the display to the target audience and overall design	5	

Current Total	Max	
	50	

Task 4 – Radio Advert (maximum 20 marks)

Judging criteria	Max	
Creativity of radio advert	5	
Ability to use the foreign language in an effective and accurate way	5	
Confidence and ability to interact in a natural way with the judges	5	
Relevance of answers given to the questions asked	5	

Criteria for good team-work: max 10 marks

■ Everyone knows what to do and the team's goals are clear. ■ Full and active participation by all team members. ■ The team members enjoy working together.	■ Everyone takes responsibility. ■ Team members listen to each other. ■ Different opinions are respected. ■ Everyone feels appreciated and is supported by other team members.

Criteria for effective use of MFL: max 10 marks

■ Liaise with team members in MFL wherever possible when discussing ideas. ■ Request support from Mentors using MFL.	■ Use MFL as often as possible in marketing poster, radio advert, and itinerary and tour operator.

Final Total	Max	
	90	

As already mentioned, in this example those in the winning team were awarded the prize of a day on board one of Carnival UK's cruise ships. However, if the companies supporting your event cannot offer prizes of a similar nature, winners could be presented with vouchers for a meal in a restaurant typical of the country or countries where the language they worked in is spoken. Alternatively a Language Challenge cup or trophy could be purchased. It might also be of interest (and add to the competitive nature of the day) to offer prizes for the best radio jingle, best marketing poster, best use of the target language and so on. Certificates could also be awarded to everyone who took part. A sample certificate for this event can be found on the accompanying DVD.

As with any event, feedback and evaluation are key elements that help sustain activity and iron out any issues that may arise. A selection of comments from students who took part in this event in 2010 can be found below. A sample evaluation form for students and a sample evaluation form for teachers, mentors, tour operators and judges can also be found in the DVD of accompanying materials.

My mentor has inspired me to continue with my languages and think about my career choices.	The challenge combined languages with arts and creativity too.	It was great – a real challenge, and we worked well as a team.

Teachers also commented that:

> It was a very positive experience and the learning objectives were met in a real context.

> It was a lot of fun and students showed interest in the target language.

Reflections

An event of this type is ideal for emphasising the important link between languages and the workplace. Giving students the opportunity to hear from those who use languages in their careers can broaden their understanding of why language skills are valuable as well as inform them of the many different ways in which they can be applied. Providing an active challenge in a real–life work setting lends a certain gravitas and maturity to the situation, to which students respond well and positively. In turn, this helps them to put language learning in context and think about how they might be able to use their own language skills in the future. More immediately, the event often leads to a renewed focus on the subject in the classroom.

Languages and the World of Work: Additional DVD materials

1. A sample certificate for those who take part in the Languages Challenge event
2. An event evaluation form for teachers and those in supporting roles
3. An event evaluation form for students
4. Useful websites

Project 3   The Language Leader Award

routes into
LANGUAGES

COMBERTON
VILLAGECOLLEGE

Project Outline

Requirements: copies of the Language Leader Award application form and log book (in the additional DVD materials).

Event time: one academic year to complete the award

Languages targeted: any

Impact: medium-high (can be used with small and large groups), plus impact on primary school groups. Many Year Nine students who apply to be Language Leaders first learnt about the Award when they received a visit as primary pupils!

Introduction

This project, known as the Language Leader Award, was originally developed by Rachel Hawkes of Comberton Village College in Cambridge. It is a year-long programme designed to help students learn to lead, using language teaching as the medium. Throughout the year students are encouraged to develop their leadership skills and confidence whilst enhancing their language knowledge. It can be completed as a stand-alone award or it can be used as a platform for completing the Gold Award for Languages (see Part VII, Project 2). This section explains how the award works and provides answers to frequently asked questions. The additional materials on the accompanying DVD contain the Language Leader Award application form, log book details and a list of useful websites.

Rationale

The Language Leader Award develops students' leadership skills as well as their linguistic skills. Learners of all abilities gain a tremendous amount of satisfaction and confidence from sharing what they know with others. It is also known that we retain the knowledge that we teach actively to others far more effectively than the knowledge that we take on board in a more passive way.

The points below summarise the principal gains of the Language Leader Award programme. It:

- rewards students' language learning;
- gives them a purpose and context for their language skills;
- develops their generic communication and leadership skills;
- gives them a better understanding of themselves as learners;
- gives a better understanding of the role of the teacher;
- enhances their self-esteem and confidence;
- improves their evaluative and analytical skills;
- increases their own attainment in a foreign language.

How does it work?

The scheme runs over three terms and culminates with students delivering a total of one-hour's independent language teaching at a local primary school. The most typical model involves three separate visits with a 20-minute teaching session in each. It is run in school and begins with interested pupils submitting an application form to their languages teacher before they can be considered for participation.

If the student's application is successful (i.e. they can demonstrate genuine interest in and commitment to the programme) they are given a log book to complete over the course of the year. It is in here that training, activities and reflections are recorded. A sample application form and log book can be found on the accompanying DVD materials.

The course comprises a series of sessions over the academic year (ideally September to May). During these sessions learners develop their teaching skills and prepare lessons to deliver to younger language learners. In preparing to teach, students take part in micro-teaching as well as peer and teacher feedback. Teachers who deliver this award devise their own schedules but include all of the elements described in the Award Programme Overview (see below).

At the end of the course the students submit their log books and their teacher assesses these as well as the students' performance during the year. Once the assessments have been completed and log books signed off, students can then be awarded their Language Leader certificate and lapel pin. Many teachers have asked the Head Teacher to sign off the students' log books, as this not only ensures that they are aware of different projects being implemented, but also helps to raise the profile of languages in the school.

Key requirements of the programme

- 25–30 course hours delivered by a languages teacher
- a languages teacher who can be explicit about aspects of pedagogy (for example, an ITT mentor)
- Continuous assessment and feedback by the teacher
- Minimum of one hour (usually 3 × 20 minutes) language activity planned and taught to whole class of younger learners and evaluated by the language leader (teacher to assess)

The Language Leader Award Programme overview

Week	Activity
Autumn term	
1.	Students must: 1. Put themselves at the front of the room, address the class and introduce themselves. 2. Concentrate on eye contact, body language, movement, gestures, smiling. 3. Give peer feedback and improvements for the second time around.

Week	Activity
Autumn term (continued)	
2.	1. Repeat Week 1's activity, having been given the week to observe their teachers closely in their lessons. 2. Brainstorm the qualities of an excellent teacher.
3.	1. Discuss how to gain the attention of learners (in the target language). 2. Practise this and take peer feedback. 3. Begin to brainstorm a list of classroom language needed (to be continued during the week by all leaders).
4.	1. Share the lists of target language produced by all leaders. 2. Practise using this language and responding to it in small groups. 3. Give peer feedback and suggest improvements.
5.	Vocal workshop to focus on projection, volume and tone of voice, as well as how to use your voice better and protect it.
6.	1. Introduction to the idea of a lesson structure. 2. Discussion of different task types and the nature of each. 3. Brainstorming a list of essential things to consider when planning a lesson.
7.	1. Tasks and activities for introducing a new language. 2. Teacher models some of these first. 3. Learners practise and receive peer feedback.
8.	1. Learners select their theme (in groups of three). 2. Begin to plan a first five-minute teaching slot.
9.	Leaders continue to plan their teaching.
10.	Leaders micro-teach and receive peer feedback.
11.	Leaders extend their planning to a full lesson. Each leader is responsible for 20 minutes' independent delivery BUT the whole hour must cohere, so they must plan together in groups of two or three.
12–14.	Leaders continue to work on their lesson preparation. Leaders teach their first lesson in primary schools and receive feedback from their peers and their teacher.

Week	Activity
Spring term	
1–2.	Leaders reflect on their first lesson and write up their reflections in their log book.
3.	Leaders begin to plan the second lesson (returning to their original notes on tasks, activities, target language lists, etc.
4.	Leaders continue to plan and resource their second lesson.
5.	Leaders continue to work on their lesson preparation.
6–10.	Leaders continue to work on their lesson preparation.
11.	Leaders go into primary schools to teach their second lesson.
12.	Leaders reflect on their second lesson and write up these reflections.
Summer term	
1.	Leaders begin to plan Lesson 3 (returning to their original notes on tasks, etc.).
2–5.	Leaders continue to work on lesson preparation.
6–8.	Leaders continue to work on their lesson preparation and teach their lesson to their peers.
9.	Leaders teach their third lesson in the primary schools.
10.	Leaders reflect on their lesson and what they have learnt during the whole of the Language Leader course and record this in their Log Book.

Frequently asked questions

The details above are merely guidelines for how to implement the award programme in your school. There are many successful variations on the Language Leader Award theme. Teachers need to address the following questions as they prepare the groundwork.

When can we run the sessions?

Sessions can take place in curriculum time, lunch-time or after-school.

Which year group should do the Language Leader Award?

Initially the award programme was aimed at students in Year Ten. However, depending on the demands upon students in Year Ten at your school, you may decide to offer the scheme to Year Nine.

Who should teach the course, and how many groups should there be?

This primarily depends on those who sign up. You may have small numbers in the first instance, which can be taught together. If you have larger numbers, you may find it easier to split into groups according to the separate languages studied by those who have applied. Ultimately it is up to you how to run the course.

Where can the students do their teaching?

Typically students are taken out to local primary schools to deliver the lessons they have planned. This certainly means more work in terms of organising links with the primary schools than it would to teach younger year groups such as Year Seven, but the gains for the Language Leaders and for the primary learners far outweigh the logistical considerations.

When do the students do their teaching?

Students can deliver their lessons in the summer term as they are coming to the end of the programme. However, this can pose some disadvantages in that the leaders have to sustain their interest and momentum over a very long time before ever experiencing the 'teaching' in a real context. It also means they must complete three visits (if you decide to follow the three × 20-minute sessions model) within a short timeframe. It is preferable, therefore, to spread the three teaching sessions over the year, with teaching carried out in January, March and May. This allows student interest and engagement to be maintained.

How do I select the language leaders?

Obviously there is no one answer to this. Much will depend on whether you are doing this award programme as an enrichment activity or as part of the curriculum. However, using an application form which must be endorsed by a signature from a peer and teacher and in which the student must show why they want to be a language leader and what they can offer to the programme, does aid decision-making and encourage commitment.

What other responsibilities or challenges need to be included in the Language Leader programme?

Applying to be a Language Leader involves a commitment to representing languages for the school and taking on an ambassador-type role. Language Leaders can be asked to support the languages department during Open Evenings and Options Evenings as well as any other languages-related events that you might hold. Students tend to respond very well to these opportunities, which add a further dimension to their work as Language Leaders.

Reflections

This project has stood the test of time. Over the past five years ever more students have been attracted to it, so that now approximately one sixth of all Year Nine students in our school complete the award. The challenge involves a winning combination of skill development and different ways of working that appeal to a variety of students. The challenge of planning to teach and then teaching primary (or other) learners generates enthusiasm and creativity and develops confidence and leadership. There is no question that learners come to view their language skills as a tool to use and develop beyond the classroom. Teachers who have already implemented this project have reported it being inspiring for students and teachers alike. We are now seeing Year Nine students completing the language leader award who first encountered it as recipients of the visits when they were in primary school. The impression the Year 9 leaders made on them as younger learners inspires them to take up the challenge when they themselves enter Year Nine.

Rachel Hawkes.

Any language leader would agree that the experience is a fun and exciting way to improve your range of vocabulary, accuracy of pronunciation and leadership skills, as we go into groups of two or three to teach three lessons to primary school students, and I would recommend it to any students that were interested.

Year 9 student, Comberton Village College

The Language Leader Award: Additional DVD materials

1. A sample application form for the Language Leader Award.
2. A sample log book for the Language Leader Award.
3. A list of useful internet sites

Project 4   Reaching out to parents

Project Outline

Requirements: invitations to parents; presentation(s); room large enough to host everyone comfortably; refreshments (if necessary).
Event time: 10–60 minutes (depending on activity/available time).
Languages targeted: any
Impact: medium-high (can be used with small and large groups)

Introduction

Much has been made of the importance of communicating the value of language skills to students at school. These messages are most often delivered by teachers, university staff, undergraduates or business representatives. All endeavour to encourage students to either take up or continue studying a language. However, these efforts can sometimes be negated by parents who believe that languages are not useful or worthwhile and that other subjects are more important. Many parents recall the language lessons they experienced at school and these memories are not always positive! As a result, language learning is sometimes not encouraged or supported. In turn, this can lead to children exhibiting similar negative attitudes. Painting a new picture for parents that languages can be fun, interesting and, above all, valuable and advantageous is key to helping them become advocates for language learning.

Perhaps as a result of their own experiences in the foreign language classroom, or indeed having no experience of language lessons, parents can sometimes feel badly placed to support their child or children in their own language learning. They may not feel confident in offering help with homework or answering questions and consequently may not view the subject positively. Involving parents in their child's language learning can be an effective way to combat issues such as these and can help develop confidence and interest.

Parents arguably have the most direct influence upon what their children study and how they view these subjects. Therefore they can be a useful tool in the promotion and support of foreign-language study. In some instances parents may not know what is useful for a language student, or how best to go about encouraging the more reluctant learner. Providing parents with tips and ideas on how to go about supporting younger linguists goes a long way.

There will always be those who remain unconvinced of the importance of learning a foreign language and this can often present challenges. Some may question why the subject has to be taught at all, or why their son or daughter must participate when they see no real use for it. Certainly, when it comes to choosing options for GCSE and A Level, a case must be made for languages. It can therefore be helpful to consider possible arguments against the study of languages and to come up with some counter-claims to convince even the most ardent of critics.

This section includes ideas on: how to promote languages to parents; how to get parents involved in language learning; how parents can support students studying languages at home; how to tackle those who are unconvinced of the importance of languages.

Promoting languages to parents

Gathering parents together at events such as open days, parents' evenings and options evenings provides good opportunities for promoting languages. Even in a ten- or fifteen-minute slot, a number of benefits that learning languages offers can be presented. Below is a short list of some of the main advantages of learning another language, which can be used as the basis of such a presentation. It can apply to parents of students in all year groups, but may be particularly useful when speaking to parents of students just about to choose their options in Year Nine or Year Eleven.

Advantages of learning another language

1. **Learning another language aids your communication and people skills**

   Learning languages involves perfecting listening and speaking skills (as well as competence in reading and writing). This is vital for interacting not only with classmates and teachers, but with the people from all walks of life whom students will encounter as they progress through school, college, university and the workplace. Being able to communicate with others easily and appropriately is one of the main qualities employers and university admissions tutors look for.

2. **Learning another language helps develop your problem-solving skills**

   The minute a language lesson begins, students are solving problems. They are working out how to process the language they are learning, how to understand and then use it. They must often find answers to problems immediately and think on their feet (for example, when trying to recall vocabulary or figuring out how to say something in the target language). This way of approaching and thinking about problems enables students to develop lateral thinking and creative skills.

3. **Learning another language helps you to get a job/different opportunities**

   Without a doubt learning another language gives students the edge when it comes to vying for jobs in today's competitive market. This does not necessarily mean a student has to be fluent in another language; in fact many employers welcome quite basic language skills, such as being able to greet clients in their native language or conduct short telephone conversations. However, having advanced language skills can of course bring numerous benefits too. Not only are employers often keen to pay more to those who can speak another language, but language skills also enable employees to work and travel abroad.

Advantages of learning another language (continued)

4. Learning another language helps you develop confidence

Students often find that nerves and social inhibitions get in the way of their language learning. It can be daunting to have to speak in front of the class in your own language, never mind in a foreign one! Anxiety over the correct pronunciation, accent or simply looking foolish in front of friends are regularly cited as reasons for not enjoying language lessons. However, persevering in language lessons can help develop students' confidence. The more they are encouraged to speak out in class, to participate in role plays, to prepare for oral examinations, the more assured they will become. Consequently they will be armed with good presentation skills and the ability to speak confidently in front of others – both of which are in demand at university and in the workplace.

5. Learning another language helps you understand other cultures

Learning another language also means learning about other cultures and people. As students go through their lives, they will rarely encounter only people from the same background as themselves. Being able to understand different cultures and traditions will not only be helpful professionally, but also socially. Many students consider travelling or taking a gap year before going to university or starting their career. Being armed with language skills and cultural understanding will enrich those experiences.

If you are talking to parents of students in older year groups, it may be worthwhile including information about how languages can be studied at university or used in various careers. The following points could be added to those already listed above.

Languages at university and work

1. Languages can be combined with almost any subject studied at university

Whilst languages can be studied as a 'pure' degree (for example, a B.A. in French), they can easily be combined with other subjects. Most universities offer courses where part of the time is spent studying a language or languages, with the remainder of the time spent studying courses such as history, politics, media studies, geography, international relations, drama and law to name but a few. Another way of keeping up language study at university is to follow a language module or course alongside your main degree. This enables you to continue with a language you have already studied at school or gives you the opportunity to start a new language from scratch. These courses are often free of charge and available on a 'first come, first served' basis.

Languages at university and work (continued)

2. **Studying languages at university usually involves a period of study or work abroad**

   Depending on the degree course followed, students studying languages usually spend anywhere from a few weeks to a full academic year in a country where the language they are studying is spoken. Students can choose to work or study (or combine the two) providing they meet the requirements set out by their university. This is a fantastic opportunity for students to advance their speaking and listening skills, as well as to immerse themselves in another country's culture. Spending time abroad also encourages them to become more independent and confident.

3. **Languages are useful in a wide range of careers**

   Studying languages doesn't mean you have to choose between becoming a translator, interpreter or teacher. Although many people believe these are the typical career paths followed by linguists, in fact languages can be useful in numerous jobs. Industry sectors in which language graduates have recently taken jobs include: manufacturing; retail; hotels and restaurants; transport, storage and communication; property development; health and social work (HESA, 2011). More specifically, searching employment websites reveals a need for candidates with language skills for the following roles: Human Resources assistant; sales executive; web designer; iPhone application developer; research analyst; sports journalist; medical co-ordinator; marketing manager. This is just a small selection of the many different and exciting positions available for those with languages.

4. **Unemployment rates for languages graduates tend to be low**

   The most recent graduate data show that those leaving university with some form of languages degree tend to experience low rates of unemployment (HESA, 2011). In the year 2009–10 8.6 per cent of languages graduates were unemployed, compared to, for example: 14.7 per cent of computer sciences graduates; 11.8 per cent of those who studied engineering or technology; 11.2 per cent of creative arts and design students; 10.5 per cent of business studies students; 10.3 per cent of those with a physical sciences degree. Only graduates in medicine, veterinary science, law, agriculture and education had lower unemployment rates than those who had studied languages.

5. **Why do employers value those with language skills?**

   A job candidate who has studied languages immediately shows a prospective employer that they possess good communication skills, people skills and problem-solving skills (see the points in the preceding box). Language learners are adaptable, can understand different cultures and are comfortable working in another language. Increasing numbers of companies are realising that conducting business in their clients' and customers' native languages leads to better relations and increased profits. It is widely acknowledged that candidates with language skills have the edge over those who don't.

Other ways of promoting languages to parents could include: language- or country-themed events, such as food tasting or craft activities; presentations by students; language and culture quizzes. Another method is to get them involved in learning a language themselves, either in a parent group or even alongside their child. Ideas on doing this are explored below.

Getting parents involved in language learning

Getting parents involved in language learning can be approached in different ways. Here we will look at two: including parents in their child's language learning and encouraging parents to learn a language themselves.

Including parents in their child's language learning

Whether parents have language skills themselves or whether they have never taken part in a language lesson, involving them in what and how their child is learning can be a valuable way of securing support for foreign languages. At the very least, this will help them to understand what goes on in the languages classroom. In the longer term, establishing strong links between parents and the foreign languages department will prove beneficial, especially when it comes to supporting the subject at various stages such as option choices.

There are many different ways of involving parents. The extent of their involvement depends on individual schools, but even the most basic of programmes can be set up to foster good relations between them and the foreign languages department. Ideas that could be put into practice include the following.

Parent lesson observations. If appropriate, parents can be invited to observe their child's language lesson. This gives them the opportunity to find out what goes on during lessons and provides them with an insight into how to support their child outside the classroom. These could be arranged on a termly basis and, depending on their success, could be developed into a support or mentoring scheme for languages, similar to those often in place for literacy and numeracy.

Languages presentations/presentation lessons. If lesson observations are not feasible (or, indeed, in addition to them) parents can be invited to languages presentation sessions in which students deliver short talks about language learning and/or what they have been doing in class. Such sessions could also include a short demonstration lesson led either by teachers or students. These could be linked with parents' evenings, option evenings and open days.

Using native speaker parents. It is not uncommon for parents to be native speakers of the languages taught in school. If this is the case, it can be very useful to invite these parents into lessons and ask them to speak about some aspect of their language, culture or home country. This can be done on a one-off occasion or introduced as a regular occurrence supporting or supplementing language lessons. Similarly, parents who are native speakers of languages not taught in the school could be asked to run language taster sessions, or even after-school language clubs.

The above are all straightforward ways of getting parents involved in their child's language learning. The prospect of parents descending upon the languages department may sound daunting at first, but, if planned and executed properly, it can be a constructive way of helping to maintain student interest in languages. But there is another way to generate parental support for languages: by encouraging parents to learn a language themselves.

Encouraging parents to learn a language

We have noted that some parents may not feel able to support their child's language learning. This could be a result of previous bad experiences or of not having attended a language class before. Putting parents in the position of students can help to ease some of these sentiments and in turn can help them to encourage their children in their own language study. The simplest way to do this is to invite parents to take part in a language lesson or lessons alongside their child; this could be done in school time or perhaps during a twilight session or after-school club. Below is an example of a lesson well-suited to this type of class. It has been developed by PGCE trainees at the University of Portsmouth and delivered during a parents' session following a Routes into Languages event for student linguists. It is aimed at Year Nine learners of Spanish and their parents.

Lesson: Spanish and Colombian art (based on Fernando Botero)

Duration: 2 × 45 minute sessions with a break in between

Resources needed (for 40 people divided into four groups)

- Flipchart stand with flipchart paper
- Oil pastels (enough for the group)
- Coloured pens or pencils
- A3 plain white paper
- 4 prints of artist's paintings (in this example, pictures by Colombian artist Fernando Botero are used, but others could be substituted)
- 4 envelopes
- 4 sets of 8–10 adjectives (to be placed in the envelopes)
- Sticky putty
- Name labels
- 4 sheets of A4 coloured card
- 5 sheets of A5 white card
- 2 board pens
- A5 quiz sheets on chosen artist (enough for everyone in group)
- Short PowerPoint presentation on chosen artist
- Short PowerPoint presentation showing about 15 different pictures by the chosen artist

Words to be displayed around the room: *grueso/a, oscuro/a, insulto, humor, es, tiene, feo/a, bonito/a, brillante, gordo/a, acción, figura, más, menos, en comparación con*
(NB: these words are relevant to the paintings by Fernando Botero. If you choose another artist, you may need to include different words to describe their work).

Each table should be named: Buenos Aires, Sevilla, Barcelona (add more cities if needed).

Objective: by the end of the lesson you will have created your own piece of art based on the style of Fernando Botero, using Spanish.

Outcome: you will be able to compare and contrast your piece of art with that of Fernando Botero, as well as describe it, in Spanish.

1. **Starter activity (10 minutes)**
   Display Fernando Botero's *Mona Lisa* picture (see the list of useful websites on the accompanying DVD for this project) on the flipchart so that everyone can see it. Using the words displayed in the room, ask each group (or table of students and parents) to write four sentences to describe the painting. Where possible, students and parents should be able to justify their choice of words in Spanish. Give an example to get the activity started.

   After five or six minutes the groups should stop what they are doing and listen to each table read out their four descriptions. Ask each group whether they agree or disagree with each other.

2. **Present the lesson objective and outcome (see above) and hand out quizzes**
   Explain to the group that they will be completing the quizzes whilst listening to the presentation about the artist. Show the PowerPoint presentation and remind everyone to listen carefully for the details which will help them answer the questions.

   Following the presentation allow five minutes for people to swap their quiz sheet with the person sitting next to them. Read out the answers and ask everyone to mark the sheet in front of them and give a mark. Give the quizzes back and compare which answers were right or wrong.

3. **Game**
   Draw a face with teeth on the flipchart paper. Explain that a PowerPoint presentation showing different pictures by the artist will be shown on a loop. Each picture will display for approximately seven seconds and in that time one person at a time must shout out a Spanish adjective to describe it. Remind the group that they can use the adjectives displayed around the room. Players cannot forfeit their turn and if they do not shout out a word in time before the next picture comes up, a tooth from the flipchart picture is 'knocked out'. Start with the person nearest the front and go around the room until everyone has had a turn. Players cannot repeat a word called by the two people before them. The aim is to keep the flipchart face intact with no teeth knocked out. If all the teeth are knocked out, the teacher wins. If the face has at least one tooth still intact by the time everyone has had a turn, the students and parents win.

4. **Break**

5. **Art activity**
   After the break the group is told that each table will be working together as a group for the next activity. Each group is given an envelope containing 8–10

words. These words describe one of the paintings by the chosen artist (each table should have words describing a different picture) and should be used to help the group recreate the corresponding painting. The groups should use the oil pastels and pencils to draw their version of the painting. Allow approximately 20 minutes for this part.

Once all the paintings have been recreated, groups should display their picture for the whole room to see. Then the corresponding paintings are given out so that people can compare their work to that of the original.

The activity ends by giving the students and parents five minutes to think of four brief sentences in Spanish to describe the differences and similarities between their painting and that of the artist. The words displayed in the room can be used for this and groups can also refer to dictionaries. The groups must also try to express an opinion about either their work or that of the artist. Go round each group to hear what they have to say.

END

Helping parents to support language learning at home

Some parents may not want to become involved in their child's language lessons or participate in one of their own. However, they may still wish to find out about ways in which they can support their child's language learning at home. Some parents will feel comfortable doing so and will have explored different ways in which this can be achieved. Other parents may be looking for guidance and will welcome hints and tips. The list below contains a variety of ideas to help with this.

Top tips for parents of language learners

Be positive about other languages and cultures. If you had negative experiences of learning languages, don't let these affect your child.

Support your child in finding out about other languages, countries and cultures. This can be done through simple searches online, visiting the library, watching documentaries on television, visiting other countries where possible.

Try to link your child's language learning to something they are already interested in. For example:

- Play computer games in German;
- Listen to Spanish music;
- Follow a French cooking recipe;
- Look at some Italian fashion magazines.

Dedicate a particular time each week, such as one dinner time, when everyone must speak in the foreign language being studied.

Read books or watch films in a foreign language that your child is already familiar with in English – for example, *Harry Potter* or *Pirates of the Caribbean*.

Label items around the house in the foreign language to aid your child's memory skills and get them used to day-to-day things. You can vary this and increase the difficulty by swapping the labels around and asking your child to match them to the correct item.

If your child has a mobile phone, games console, MP3 player and so on, switch the settings from English to the language they are studying.

Shop for products in other languages. Ask your child to identify the product and use the vocabulary of the language they are studying.

Encourage your child to use the internet (at home, school or in a public library) to practise their vocabulary. Many games can be found online in a variety of languages and these can help with vocabulary and confidence-building. It may also be something you and your child can do together.

Find out whether your child's school runs an exchange or pen-pal scheme with schools in other countries. Pen-pals and e-pals can also be found online.

Keep an eye on the internet/press for details about local events you could take your child to, such as French markets, European days, film festivals and so on. Once there, ask them to spot as many foreign words as they can. If they don't know what a word means, encourage them to look it up when they get home.

Ask your child to teach you what they have been taught in school.

Tackling those who are unconvinced about language learning

Despite the various ways in which parents can be engaged in language learning, be it their child's or their own, some will always remain unconvinced about the point, value or importance of learning another language. In some instances, trying to persuade them that languages are necessary and worthwhile can involve more work than preparing sessions for those who do want to find out more! While it is likely that some parents will never change their opinions and may even pass these on to their children, some may just need to have their doubts assuaged in a comprehensive manner. Here is a list of reasons parents typically give for why their child should not learn a language, along with some counter-arguments that offer a different point of view.

Everyone speaks English! Why bother learning another language?

It may feel as if everyone speaks English, especially when attempts to speak in another language whilst on holiday, for example, is met with a response in English. However, there is plenty that points to the fact that *not* everyone speaks English. Accurate statistics are difficult to come by when it comes to assessing how many people speak which languages, but recent figures suggest that, in terms of the number of speakers per language (the combined number of those who speak it as a native language and those who speak it as a second language), English comes behind Mandarin, Hindi and Spanish (Gordon and Grimes, 2005). Furthermore, it is estimated that 75 per cent of the world's population does not speak English at all. If statistics aren't enough to make this argument convincing, then it is perhaps worth highlighting that those from other countries who do speak English speak it *as well as* their own native tongue (and any other languages they may have learnt). This means that they are already competent in two languages, compared to those English students who are monolingual. In a world where university places, work placements and jobs are fiercely contested, having no other language skills than your mother tongue puts you at a distinct disadvantage.

Well, I don't speak any other languages and I managed to get a job so why does my child have to do a language?

Today's jobs market is very competitive. Employers are increasingly recognising the need for foreign language skills in their workforce. Employers realise that those who have learnt another language have developed a number of other desirable skills, such as problem-solving and good communication. As a result, candidates who have foreign language skills are often chosen above those who do not. Similarly, in some industries employees are paid more because of their aptitude in another language. There are jobs that do not require language skills, but to open up as many opportunities as possible, we would advise that your child continues with their language studies.

My child has already decided that they want to pursue a career where languages are not needed, so why should they carry on with a language?

Your son or daughter may have firm ideas now about the career path they intend to follow after school, college or university, but it is quite possible that their plans and interests may change by the time they enter the world of work. It is also feasible that the career or industry they are interested in may change over the coming years and begin to require employees who are proficient in another language. It cannot hurt to be armed with language skills and then decide not to use them at a later date, but it will be more difficult to pick up a language later in life, if it is needed.

Surely it would be better for students to perfect skills in English rather than another language?

It can be argued that learning another language in fact helps students to use and understand their mother tongue better. This is because students are taught to recognise different parts of the language and how to use them (such as nouns, verbs and adjectives, for example). Furthermore, learning another language helps to develop many different cognitive skills, such as problem-solving and memorisation, all of which can be applied in the student's native language. In addition, the specific focus on reading, writing, listening and speaking when a foreign language is being taught can help students to apply these skills in English.

Reflections

Support for, and promotion of, languages can come from numerous different people or sectors. However, the messages delivered about the importance of languages can be undermined or undervalued if parents – the key people most likely to influence students' choices and attitudes – are forgotten. The ideas and suggestions mentioned in this section have all been trialled and delivered in various ways and with great success. Promoting languages to parents, getting them involved in language learning and answering some of their most difficult languages-related questions can all help to reinforce the idea that language learning is important.

Reaching out to parents: Accompanying DVD materials

1.   List of useful websites

5

Languages, theatre and music

Introduction

This chapter revolves around performance skills and contains four delightful and refreshing projects which can not fail to enthuse your students! *Langauge Live* is presented first, which involves a new 'take' on the familiar story of 'Cinderella'. The project integrates language and drama and brings German to life through the pantomime *Aschenputtel* (Cinderella). It provides creative preparation for AS-level German whilst encouraging others to learn the language at the same time. This is followed by *The Marie Curie Science Project*, which explores the life and times of Marie and Pierre Curie through the medium of French. It offers a carousel of activities for groups of students to enjoy, all based around this theme.

Then comes *Spanglovision* in Spanish combining languages with music in a lively and entertaining way. Presented here as a transition activity with a new Year Seven intake, this project asks students in their year groups to learn and perform a song, one of a number around a central theme in the target language. With excitement building and emotions high, the performance is videoed and then the whole school votes for the winning numbers! In this way, the new intake performs their song in their groups to the whole school via the video recording, helping the whole school community to get to know the new Year Seven students and to cement friendships, as well as exploiting exciting possibilities in the target language.

Finally there is *Die Mauer*, an ambitious project presented here in German and centred around the building and the fall of the Berlin Wall. The resources themselves seek to tap into relevant issues around politics and citizenship, as well as language progression, to provide an interesting and unusual platform for learning. Audio and discussion activities as well as a film form the centre of these imaginative resources which provide an interesting and unusual platform for learning.

Project 1   Language live

Project Outline

Requirements: assembly hall with stage
Event time: one hour performance time
Languages targeted: German (Spanish/French)
Impact: medium (one year group)

Introduction

This lively project, jointly authored by Yvonne Gorrod from Notre Dame High School
and Joc Mack from Framingham Earl School in Norfolk, combines language learning
with theatre studies, bringing German to life through the pantomime Aschenputtel
(Cinderella). This has been found also to motivate those continuing with their German
studies after GCSE, not to mention being great fun for all involved! The performance
of *Aschenputtel* requires the students to do more than learn their lines however. They
write and learn the script, organise costumes and props, sound and lighting; moreover,
all rehearsals take place in the target language. In keeping with tradition, the pantomime,
which has been performed to well over 500 learners of all ages, allows the audience to
interact with the characters on stage.

The writing and performance of a pantomime was originally intended as a bridging
project between GCSE and AS Level, but has since developed into a project for cross-
phase learning. The script presented here encompasses many areas of the Key Stage 4
curriculum (household chores, personal characteristics and descriptions, family
relationships, lost property, to name but a few) and brings that curriculum to life. Students
have a reason to memorise vocabulary in context and all learning styles are addressed in
the rehearsal and production of the pantomime. The familiar story, with its exaggerated
facial expressions and gestures, provides vital clues to the audience, enhancing their
understanding and enjoyment of the language. The whole project won a CILT European
Award for Languages in 2005.

The project presented here is in German, with the script in French and Spanish
included in the accompanying DVD materials. Some tips for implementing drama
techniques in your lessons are presented first. These are followed by the playscript in
German which, in turn, is followed by various language activities designed to familiarise
students with the content of the script as well as encouraging them to focus on linguistic
details. These language activities are extended onto the accompanying DVD as well.

Drama Plus for terrified MFL teachers!

Before you start: get the space ready, preferably with small group of students, before
the activities begin.

Important pointers

- Have with you an attention-seeking device, such as a whistle, soft drum, triangle, singing bowl…,
- or use the "Brown Owl" device: put your hand up and stand still when you want the class to focus on you. This is can have a calming effect, on you as well as the class.
- If in doubt get quieter, not louder.
- Insist on adherence to ground rules right from the first lesson. Be tough on those who shout out and interrupt. Take the whole class outside again if shouting out occurs. It works.

Ideal start, which can become routine

1. Students take a pad and a pen from their bag.
2. They place their bags at the side of room.
3. Students sit in a circle on chairs (which are preferably in place before they arrive).
4. Register the class using a game if possible. Here is an example. Each student has a number or a phrase/movement. Get students to do their own register without you using your voice:

   – *Annie Adams mit blauen Augen*

   – *Brenda Bloggs mit grünen Augen*

   – *Colin Cox mit braunen Augen*

You can use registration to establish something new. Give the first few students their name and a phrase on a slip of paper (for example, eye colour as above) and see if the rest of group can work out the pattern. You can consolidate something already covered, for example:

   – *Annie Adams. Ich spiele gern Tennis.*

   – *Brenda Bloggs. Ich spiele gern Golf.*

More circle activities

The magic box / Die Zauberkiste

The teacher uses a mimed magic wand/*einen Zauberstab* and a spell, for example: *Simsalabimbambasaladusaladim*. The box is transformed into a bath, a guitar, a car, a boat, a cage containing a rabbit, a radio, a TV, a boyfriend and, at KS3 of course, a toilet! The teacher or the students list the words. Use also for a memory game/next week's starter.

Note: the BOX must become something in this game. You can make a new game out of taking something *out of* the box.

Note also: keep an eye on the magic wand. It must never be lost. It can change colour, of course. Ask the holder to describe it.

   – *Der Zauberstab ist jetzt grün mit roten Blumen (darauf).*

All change/Bitte umsteigen

This is a call-and-response game. The teacher stands in a circle of chairs. S/he has no chair in the circle. Demonstrate using bold stance in the middle of a circle as a confident speaker/actor. The voice must carry to all four corners of the room.

Top Tip!

Imagine your voice reaching all four corners, in front and behind.

Use this game to get students used to asking simple questions – confidently and clearly:

> Have you got a sister/a dog/a blue car...
>
> *Hast du eine Schwester/einen Hund/ein blaues Auto...*

or to practise more complex structures:

> Hands up if you have ever been to Italy.
>
> *Melde dich, wenn du je nach Italien gefahren bist*

The person in the middle asks the question or requests a hands-up response. Students respond by sitting still but putting up a hand. The one in the middle claps his/her hands and calls "*Bitte umsteigen*", whereupon all those with a hand up must get to a chair on the opposite side of the circle. The one in the middle also runs to a seat. Someone is left chairless and becomes the new caller.

Circle game without chairs: Copy-cat game/Nachahmungsspiel

The teacher demonstrates until group have grasped dynamics of the game – bold movements, clear and confident speaking.

The teacher takes three steps into the circle:

> My name is Miss Smith and I like [mime tennis].

The teacher returns to his/her place in the circle. On signal, the whole class takes three steps into circle and everybody copies exactly what they have seen and heard – movement, tone, pauses... everything.

Top Tip!

Keep reminding pupils of four corners...*eins, zwei drei, vier Ecken!* so that voice projection is bold and clear.

Extensions:

Memory game. Stand in the middle and look at another player. e.g. *Du bist Fred und du spielst gern Klavier*/plus mime. If correct, take the place of Fred, who goes into middle to speak and mime.

You can really speed this one up, too, on second or third playing.

Teacher in role (TIR) work/Hotseating: Cinderella/Aschenputtel

Tell the class that they have the chance to hotseat a famous person. Generate a few questions to get the ball rolling. The character cannot tell you his/her name. That must be guessed.

The class sit in a semicircle/audience. TIR enters and sits looking lost and forlorn. The questions do come. Click your fingers to come out of role. Delegate the role of facilitator to a pupil if necessary. Others put their hands up to ask a question. The facilitator says "*Fred…du bist dran.*"

Role on the wall/Rolle an der Wand:

Draw around a student standing against the wall to represent the character you are going to work on, be it Aschenputtel or Dr Faustus.

Use different coloured pens to present different aspects of character. For example, a sad face, tatty clothes, dirty shoes …

This is a useful activity at all levels and great for all aspects of character study.

Structured improvisation (in groups of 3 or 4)

Build on TIR work as Aschenputtel.

Scene 1:   Aschenputtel is alone and scrubbing. She talks directly to the audience or responds to the narrator. Questions such as "What is your life like?" or "How do you feel?" should be encouraged.

Scene 2:   Ugly sisters enter. Use modal verbs to boss Aschenputtel around. Set targets: for example, each sister must give three commands.

Action: sisters tell Aschenputtel what to do. She mimes tasks. Useful props may include a dishcloth, an iron, a tea-towel, a broom, a scrubbing brush, a hoover… Take in a washing basket of items of clothing, so that Cinderella can be told "Wash my… socks," etc

Continuation ideas

The teacher writes a letter/invitation to the Ball from *königlichen Palast*/Royal Palace. The ugly sisters read the letter aloud. Each sister wants three new items.

Schwester 1:   *Ich kaufe mir…neue gelbe Schuhe*

Schwester 2:   *Ich kaufe mir neue gelbe Schuhe und einen blauen Rock*

Sisters give Aschenputtel three new commands before they exit.

Wir gehen einkaufen. Du musst hier bleiben. Du musst putzen. Du musst kochen….

Aschenputtel sits alone. Recap Scene 1. At the end of this improvisation ask students to script their version of Cinderella so far.

Hot tips for role play

1. Characters need some background. Here are two examples.
   - **The waiter**, Ludwig Schmidt, 27. He walks with his nose in the air and frequently tosses his hair back **OR** He is a grumpy person with a screwed up face who smokes whenever he can.
   - **The customer**, Frau Weiss, 27. She has thick spectacles and is very shy **OR** She is always texting.

The presentations are more entertaining when pupils can create someone with unique characteristics, for example, a group who sang the restaurant scene in operatic style (Yr 8)

2. Remind students of voice projection skills – four corners/visualise voice reaching its destination. If anyone is changing his/her voice in any way, the target is still clear and bold voice work.

3. Do not let pupils have books in hand. You cannot act and read at the same time. Watching actors reading from a book is deadly. After an initial read-through, use the skim-read technique: look at the line; read it in your head; look up to deliver it. This enables the students to act rather than read the lines. After this run, students should work on five lines and then ten lines at a time.

   > The most productive work can be obtained from structured improvisation.

   > Develop a five-point structure: for example, the neighbours sketch below. Keep the conversation going through five exchanges:

   > Greetings. One neighbour has a card or present for the other one.

   > "Oh, you've got a new dog…"

   > "I like your new…"

   > "I've got a problem with…at the moment."

   > Help, advice and/or goodbyes

4. Get students used to using spontaneous language. For example, set up four customers. TIR as waiter can move from table to table and elicit responses in role. Improvisation gives students confidence. The teacher can repeat and mime to encourage understanding. Do not translate.

5. Warm-up the class before you do rehearsed role play. Students walk around the space saying their lines. They jog. They jump up and down. They do brain gym as they go through lines. You can inject this into the lesson to energise your audience. This can be used as a preparation exercise too. The students choreograph the lines and present to the class. This works because it takes the focus off the words, but you have to deliver the words well to match the big, bold movements.

Deutsch durch Theater: Aschenputtel (ein kurzes Theaterstück)

List of characters	List of props needed
Narrator	costumes for characters
Cinderella	3 magic wands
2 ugly sisters	a golden letter/invitation to the Ball
Step-mother	a washing basket of items of clothing
3 good fairies	a dishcloth, an iron, a tea-towel, a broom
King	a scrubbing brush, a hoover
Queen	a giant pair of pants and an enormous bra
Prince	a packet of confetti
Servant/narrator	L-plates for the third fairy
Dancers/guests at the ball	a football banner and a skateboard
	pair of trainers and a pair of wellington boots
	a yellow and a red football card
	a cushion

Playscript (German version)

Erzähler:
Liebe Kinder – groß und klein
Liebe Lehrer – alt und jung
Liebe Zuschauer
Guten Morgen
Guten Tag
Hallo
Wir präsentieren heute
Ein kurzes Theaterstück
Eine alte Geschichte
Eine traurige Geschichte
Eine romantische Geschichte
Eine berühmte Geschichte
Wir präsentieren heute
Ein kurzes Theaterstück

Alle:	Aschenputtel
Aschenputtel:	Und das bin ich. Ich heiße Aschenputtel. Ich wohne hier in diesem großen Haus mit meiner Stiefmutter und mit meinen Stiefschwestern. Mein Leben ist hart. Ich muss jeden Tag arbeiten. Ich muss den ganzen Tag arbeiten. Ich muss auch am Wochenende arbeiten.
Erzähler:	Sie muss spülen
Gruselina/Tussilein	Du musst spülen
Aschenputtel:	Ich muss spülen
Erzähler:	Sie muss abtrocknen

G &T:	Du musst abtrocknen
Aschenputtel:	Ich muss abtrocknen
Erzähler:	Sie muss fegen
G&T:	Du musst fegen
Aschenputtel:	Ich muss fegen
Erzähler:	Sie muss bügeln
G&T:	Du musst bügeln
Aschenputtel:	Ich muss bügeln
	Und ich muss die Wäsche waschen

(Sie hält einen riesengroßen Schlüpfer und einen riesengroßen BH hoch)

Aschenputtel:	Ich wohne hier in diesem großen Haus mit meiner Stiefmutter und mit den beiden Stiefschwestern. Ich muss so hart arbeiten.Meine Kleider sind alt und zerrissen. Meine Schuhe sind kaputt. Ich fühle mich ganz allein. Ich bin allein und einsam.
Stiefmutter:	Hör auf zu meckern, Aschenputtel. Du gehst mir auf die Nerven. Ich bekomme Kopfschmerzen, wenn ich deine Stimme höre.
	(Es klopft an der Tür)
Gruselina:	Beeil' dich Aschenputtel. Worauf wartest du?
	(Aschenputtel geht zur Tür. Sie kommt mit einem goldenen Brief zurück)
Tussilein:	Sie ist blöd und faul, Mutti. Warum muss sie überhaupt bei uns noch wohnen? Sie geht mir auf die Nerven.
Stiefmutter:	Also, her mit dem Brief, Aschenputtel. Und schnell. Und dann kannst du wieder den Boden fegen. Du bist blöd und du bist faul und du gehst uns auf die Nerven… *(sie liest den Brief)* O, wie schön. Es ist ja wunderbar. So eine Überraschung. Das ist ja super.
Gruselina:	Was ist denn, Mutti? Haben wir im Lotto gewonnen?
Tussilein:	Haben wir ein neues Auto oder eine Reise nach Disneyland gewonnen?
Stiefmutter:	Nein. Wir sind eingeladen. Auf eine Party. O, wie schön. Es ist ja wunderbar. So eine Überraschung. Das ist ja super.
Gruselina:	Eine Party. O wie schön!
Tussilein:	Eine Party. Es ist ja wunderbar.
Aschenputtel:	Eine Party. Aber nicht für mich.
Erzähler:	*(während die Stiefmutter den Brief auch vorliest)*
	Meine Damen und Herren
	Liebe Bürger und Bürgerinnen
	Der König Bäckham und die Königin Posch laden alle auf eine Party ein.
Gruselina:	Ja, ja , ja. Das wissen wir schon. Aber wann? Wann? Wann? Freitag? Montag? Mittwoch? Wann? Wann? Wann?

Erzähler:	**WANN?**

Am Freitag, den zehnten Dezember. Um 20.00h.

Gruselina:	Am Freitag, den zehnten Dezember. Um 20.00h.
Achenputtel:	Eine Party. Im Dezember. Aber nicht für mich.
Gruselina:	Und **wo** denn? **Wo** ist diese Party? In der Disko? Im Park? In der Schule? **Wo** ist diese Party?
Erzähler:	**WO?** Nicht in der Disko. Nicht im Park. Nicht in der Schule, sondern im Poschbäcks Palast. Im königlichen Palast.
Gruselina:	Im Palast. Im königlichen Palast. Mit König Bäckham und Königin Posch.
Erzähler:	Es ist ja eine Geburtstagsfete. Eine Party zum Geburtstag.
Gruselina:	Hat der König Geburtstag?
Erzähler:	Nein
Tussilein:	Hat die Königin Geburtstag?
Erzähler:	Nein?
Gruselina:	Also, **WER** hat Geburtstag?
Erzähler:	Der Kronprinz hat Geburtstag. Der Kronprinz Romeo von Bäckham hat Geburtstag. Und er sucht... **eine Braut.**
Gruselina:	Das bin ich. Ich bin die Schönste im ganzen Land. Ich will Romeo heiraten, Ich bin die Braut. Ich lieeeeeeebe ihn. Ich liebe Romeo.
Tussilein:	Nein. Du bist hässlich. Ich bin schön. Ich bin die Schönste im ganzen Land. Du bist dick und du bist dumm. Ich bin die Braut. Ich lieeeeeeebe ihn. Ich liebe Romeo.
Aschenputtel:	Eine Party. Im Palast. Eine Geburtstagsfete. Und der Kronprinz hat Geburtstag. Ich möchte so gern hin. (*zur Stiefmutter*) Stiefmutter, liebe Stiefmutter? D...d...darf ich auch mitkommen? Auf die Party? Lie...be Stiefmutti...
Stiefmutter:	Was? *Du* willst mitkommen? Bist du verrückt?
Gruselina:	*Du* willst mitkommen? Du blödes, faules Aschenputtel?
Tussilein:	Du bist ja unverschämt. Du wohnst hier bei uns. Du bist blöd und du bist faul. Und jetzt denkst du, du darfst auch mit auf eine Party gehen.
Stiefmutter:	Du kommst nicht mit.
Gruselina::	Du bleibst hier.
Tussilein:	Du bleibst hier, weil du arbeiten musst.
Stiefmutter:	Und jetzt gehen wir einkaufen.
Gruselina:	Neue Kleider für uns... aber nicht für dich.
Tussilein:	Neue Schuhe für uns... aber nicht für dich. (*Die Stiefmutter und die Schwestern verlassen die Bühne*)

| Aschenputtel: | (*Schluchzend*) Eine Party aber nicht für mich. Ich muss hier bleiben – allein und einsam. Ich bin allein auf der Welt. Mein Herz ist schwer. Wer kann mir helfen? |

(*Die guten Feen treten auf*)

Gute Fee 1:	Ich kann dir helfen.
Gute Fee 2:	Ich kann dir auch helfen.
Gute Fee 3:	Und ich kann dir bald helfen.
Die Feen:	Und wir wollen dir helfen.
Aschenputtel:	Aber ..wer seid ihr? Wo kommt ihr her? Was macht ihr hier?
Gute Fee 1:	Ich bin eine gute Fee
Gute Fee 2:	Ich bin auch eine gute Fee
Gute Fee 3:	Und ich bin **bald** eine gute Fee.
Aschenputtel:	Eins, zwei, drei von euch. Hier. In meiner Küche. O wie schön. So eine Überraschung.
Gute Fee 1:	Ich habe meinen Zauberstab dabei.
Gute Fee 2:	Ich habe auch meinen Zauberstab dabei.
Gute Fee 3:	Und ich habe meinen Zauberstab im Bus liegen lassen aber ich habe einen tollen Kuli dabei!
Gute Fee 1:	Und wir wissen, dass du auf die Party gehen willst.
Gute Fee 2:	Ja, die Geburtstagsfete vom Kronprinz Romeo. Er ist sooooooo schön. Ich liiiieeeebe ....Hallo?
Gute Fee 1:	Griselda, hör auf. Romeo ist nicht für dich!
Gute Fee 2:	(*seufzt*) Tja, das weiß ich schon. Er ist trotzdem attraktiv. Nun – was machen wir jetzt? Wir wollen Aschenputtel doch helfen!
Aschenputtel:	Ich möchte so gern auf die Party gehen. Ist das möglich?
Gute Fee 1:	Ja. Aber deine Kleider sind alt und zerrissen.
Gute Fee 2:	Du brauchst neue Kleider. (*die dritte Fee kommt mit einem Ipswich Schal zurück*)
Die Feen:	Nein! Simsalabimbambasaladusaladim (*Aschenputtel zieht den Arbeitskittel aus*)
Aschenputtel:	O wie schön. So eine Überraschung.
Gute Fee 1:	Und dann brauchst du schöne Schuhe. (*die dritte Fee kommt mit einem Gummistiefel zurück*)
Die Feen:	Nein! Simsaladimbambasaladusaladim
Gute Fee 2:	(*Holt Turnschuhe aus der Tasche*) Die besten Turnschuhe auf der Welt. Größe 48!
Aschenputtel:	(*zieht die Turnschuhe an*) O wie schön. So eine Überraschung. Ich jogge gern. Ich jogge jetzt auf die Party.
Gute Fee 1:	Nein. Es ist schon 9 Uhr. Die Party hat um 8 angefangen.
Gute Fee 2:	Kein Problem. Wir helfen dir.
Die Feen:	Simsaladimbambasaladusaladim (*Fee 3 holt ein Skateboard aus der Tasche*)
Die Feen:	Ja! (*sie sehen überrascht aus*)

Aschenputtel:	Ein Skateboard. O wie schön. So eine Überraschung.
Gute Fee 1:	Schnell aufs Skateboard, Aschenputtel.
Gute Fee 2:	Und los auf die Party.
Die Feen:	Kein Problem. Wir helfen dir (*Die Feen ziehen Aschen-puttel auf dem Skateboard los. Sie halten plötzlich an*)
Gute Fee 1:	Du darfst nur bis Mitternacht bleiben.
Gute Fee 2:	Um Mitternacht, um 12 also, musst du weg.
Gute Fee 3:	Oder wenigstens 5 nach.
Feen 1&2:	Nein!
Gute Feen:	Denk daran, Aschenputtel. Mitternacht, Mitternacht, Mitternacht...
Aschenputtel:	Um 12, um Mitternacht muss ich weg. Aber jetzt gibt es eine Party und ich muss hin. Los geht's.

(*Die Feen ziehen Aschenputtel auf dem Skateboard los*)

Szene 2: In dem königlichen Palast. Man hört Fußballmusik.
Der König und die Königin empfangen die Gäste.
Ein Erzähler (als Diener) kündigt die Gäste an.

Diener:	Die Stiefmutter Grossmund und ihre Töchter Gruselina und Tussilein
König:	Guten Abend gnädige Frau. Guten Abend verehrte Gäste.
Königin:	Es gibt Bier, Wein und Orangensaft. Jeeves, her mit den Getränken.
Stiefmutter:	(*nimmt zwei Gläser Wein und trinkt sehr schnell*) Eine Party. O wie schön!
Gruselina:	Wo ist der Prinz? Wo ist mein Romeo?
Tussilein:	Meinst du nicht etwa mein Romeo?

(*Die Schwestern fangen an, sich zu schlagen. Der König zeigt ihnen die gelbe Karte*)

König:	Hören Sie bitte auf. Sie sind doch keine Spice Girls!
Königin:	Aber David. Es macht so viel Spaß. Ich gebe dir einen Klaps... und dir einen Klaps.... und dir einen Klaps... (*sie dreht sich um*) und dir David, auch einen riesengroßen Klaps... Es macht ja so viel Spaß. (*Alle Frauen lachen, schlagen sich und trinken weiter!*)
König:	Aber Liebling, Victoria. Wir haben Gäste. (*Er zeigt ihr die rote Karte*) Du bist schlimmer als Roy Keene und Paulo di Canio!
Königin:	Sei nicht so gemein, David. Du bist mein Schnuckiputz. Her mit dem Wein, Jeeves. (*Zu den Zuschauern*) Wir haben ja einen englischen Butler. Frau Grossmund, Gruselina, Tussilein... noch ein Bier?
Gruselina:	Bitte ein Bit!
Tussilein:	Mir auch.

Alle:	(*Stossen an*) Prost! (*Freeze*)

(*Romeo erscheint. Er sieht traurig aus*)

Romeo:	Ich habe zwar Geburtstag aber ich bin traurig. Ich fühle mich allein und einsam. Ich habe viele Geschenke bekommen - ein neues Auto, ein Rolex und eine elektrische Gitarre. Aber ich bin allein und traurig. Eine Party...Musik...viele Gäste...aber ich fühle mich trotzdem allein und einsam.... (*Freeze*)... (*Aschenputtel erscheint*)
Aschenputtel:	O wie schön. Hier bin ich doch, hier auf der Party. (*Der Diener bringt Wein*) O wie schön.. Der Wein ist gut. Und die Musik! O wie schön.. Ich tanze ja so gern!

(*Alle Frauen und der König tanzen. Romeo tanzt nicht. Gruselina und Tussilein versuchen, ohne Erfolg, den Prinz mit erotischen Bewegungen zu verführen.*

Alle im Freeze, in dem Moment, wo Romeo zum ersten Mal Aschenputtel sieht)

Romeo:	Wer ist sie? Sie ist wohl die schönste Frau auf der Welt. Ihre Augen sind wie die schönsten Sterne am Himmel. Ihre Lippen sind wie die Kirschblute im Frühling. Sie ist die schönste Frau, die ich je gesehen habe. Ich muss mit ihr tanzen. Ich muss mit ihr sprechen. Ich liebe sie. Das weiß ich schon.

(*Romeo nimmt Aschenputtel in die Arme. Sie tanzen zärtlich miteinander. Die Stiefmutter und die Schwestern sehen böse und sauer aus. Die Bäckhams sehen glücklich aus*)

Konig:	O wie schön...Romeo hat endlich eine Freundin gefunden.
Konigin:	O David. Du bist so romantisch. Du bist wohl mein Schnuckiputz. Und Romeo hat eine nette Freundin. Wie schön.
Gruselina:	(*Weint*) Mutti, Mutti. Das ist nicht fair. Ich bin die Schönste. Ich will mit Romeo tanzen...
Tussilein:	(*Weint*) Mutti, Mutti. Das ist nicht fair. Ich bin die Schönste im ganzen Land. Ich will mit Romeo tanzen.
Stiefmutter:	(*Sie tröstet G&T*) Ja, Liebling. Du bist doch schön. Und du, du bist auch schön. Viel schöner als die dumme Kuh da drüben.

(*Man hört die Glocke. Es wird gleich Mitternacht. Romeo will Sektgläser holen*)
(*Die Feen erscheinen*)

Gute Fee 1:	Du darfst nur bis Mitternacht bleiben.
Gute Fee2:	Um Mitternacht musst du weg.
Gute Feen:	Mitternacht Aschenputtel, Mitternacht, Mitternacht...
Aschenputtel:	Es wird gleich Mitternacht und ich muss weg. Ich muss jetzt gehen...weg von der Party, weg von der Musik, weg von meinem Romeo. Romeo, Romeo...

(Romeo kommt mit zwei Sektgläsern zurück)

Romeo:	*(verwirrt)* Wo ist sie? Ist sie weg? Kann das wahr sein? Ich muss sie wiedersehen. Ich muss sie finden. Vater, Mutter – ich muss sie finden.
König:	Wir helfen dir, Romeo. Wir werden sie wohl finden.
Königin:	Wir werden sie suchen und wir werden sie finden.
König:	*(findet einen Turnschuh)* Aha! Ein Turnschuh. Größe 48
Romeo:	*(Streichelt den Turnschuh)* Das ist ihr Turnschuh. Den nehme ich mit. Ich werde sie suchen und ich werde sie finden. Sie ist die schönste Frau in der Welt und sie ist meine Prinzessin.

(Die königliche Familie und der Diener verlassen die Bühne. Die Stiefmutter und die Schwestern weinen sich die Seele aus dem Leib)

Szene 3 In der Küche

Aschenputtel fegt den Boden und singt

Aschenputtel:	Ich wollte tanzen ja und zwar die ganze Nacht. Der Prinz, mein Prinz war schööööööön, Ich wollte tanzen ja und zwar die ganze Nacht. Der Prinz, mein Prinz war schöööööööön

(Die Stiefmutter tritt auf. Sie hat Kopfschmerzen)

Stiefmutter:	Hör auf, so viel Krach zu machen, Aschenputtel. Du gehst mir auf die Nerven.
Aschenputtel:	*(Zu den Zuschauern)* Sie hat Kopfschmerzen. Sie hat zu viel Wein… und Bier… und Whisky getrunken! Sie hat einen Kater!

(Die Schwestern treten auf. Die Beiden haben Kopfschmerzen)

Gruselina:	Mein Kopf tut weh.
Tussilein:	Meine Augen tun weh.
Gruselina:	Ich habe Kopfschmerzen, Mutti. Das tut weh.
Tussilein:	Mutti, Aschenputtel lacht. Hör auf du dumme Kuh. Kaffee brauche ich und zwar sofort.
Stiefmutter:	Hör auf zu grinsen Aschenputtel. Und koche schnell einen Kaffee. Und bringe mir meine Tabletten. Bringe mir zehn Kopfschmerztabletten… und ein Glas Whisky. *(Es klopft an die Tür)*
Stiefmutter:	Also beeil' dich Aschenputtel. Worauf wartest du?

(Die Frauen stöhnen und setzen sich mit Schwierigkeiten hin. Der König, die Königin, der Prinz und ein Diener treten auf. Der Diener hält den Turnschuh auf einem Kopfkissen. Aschenputtel versucht ihr Gesicht zu verstecken.)

Aschenputtel:	(*Zu den Zuschauern*) Der Prinz darf mich nicht sehen. Ich bin nur ein armes Mädchen. Ich bin nicht reich. Ich bin nicht schön.
König:	Guten Morgen gnädige Frau. Guten Morgen Gruselina und Tussilein. Wir haben ein Problem. Könnt ihr uns helfen?
Königin:	Ja, mein Sohn, der nette, junge Kronprinz Romeo hat schon seine Freundin verloren. Wie dumm von ihm!
König:	Victoria, sei nicht so hart. Unser Sohn braucht Hilfe.
Königin:	Er verliert immer seine Sachen! Letzte Woche hat er sein T-Shirt verloren, am Montag hat er sein Pferd verloren und gestern hat er seine Freundin verloren. Unser Sohn braucht doch Hilfe!
Romeo:	Sie ist die schönste Frau auf der Welt. Ihre Augen sind wie die schönsten Sterne am Himmel. Ihre Lippen sind wie die schönsten Kirschblüte im Frühling ...
Königin:	Ja, ja das habe ich schon hundertmal gehört. Jeeves, her mit dem Turnschuh.
Gruselina:	Das ist mein Turnschuh. Ich habe ihn gestern auf der Party verloren.
Tussilein:	Nein, nein. Das war ich. Das ist mein Turnschuh. Ich habe ihn gestern auf der Party verloren.
König:	Langsam, langsam liebe Ladies. Wir haben ein Problem aber wir haben auch eine Lösung.
Stiefmutter:	Gruselina, Tussilein. Zieht euch schnell den Turnschuh an. Eine von meinen Töchtern muss Prinzessin werden.
Gruselina:	(*Versucht den Turnschuh anzuziehen*) Ja ... nein ... ja ... **Ja!** Der Turnschuh passt mir –
Königin:	**Nicht.** Nächste bitte!
Tussilein:	(*Versucht den Turnschuh anzuziehen*) Ja ... nein ... ja ... O ja ... **Ja!** Der Turnschuh passt mir –
Königin:	**auch nicht.**
Romeo:	Es gibt noch ein Mädchen hier. Wo ist sie?
Stiefmutter:	Nein, ich habe nur zwei Töchter.
Romeo:	(*führt Aschenputtel vor*) Bitte, sei nicht schüchtern. Ich helfe dir, den Turnschuh anzuziehen.

(*Der Prinz hilft Aschenputtel zärtlich, den Turnschuh anzuziehen*)

Alle:	**Er passt!**
Romeo:	Versteck' dich nicht. Ach, das bist du. Meine Prinzessin. Meine liebe, liebe Prinzessin.

(*Sie umarmen sich und küssen sich*)

Stiefmutter & Töchter:	**Nein das kann nicht wahr sein. Nein!**
Aschenputtel:	Doch. Ich war gestern auf der Party. Die guten Feen haben mir geholfen.

(Die guten Feen erscheinen)

Gute Fee 1:	Aschenputtel, du hast jetzt deinen Prinz gefunden.
Gute Fee 2:	Und Romeo, du hast deine Prinzessin gefunden.
Gute Fee 3:	Und ich bin jetzt eine richtige, qualifizierte gute Fee!
Beide Feen:	Und wir feiern jetzt eine königliche Hochzeit.

(Sie werfen Konfetti in die Luft)

König:	Aber die Stiefmutter, Gruselina, Tussilein … und Victoria sind öfters schlecht gelaunt und öfters böse und sauer. Könnt ihr mir …. mit euren Zauberstäben helfen?
Gute Fee 1:	Natürlich.
Gute Fee 2:	Und zwar sofort.
Alle:	**SIMSALABIMBAMBASALADUSALADIM**

(Die Frauen sind auf einmal nett und freundlich)

Gruselina:	Ach, Aschenputtel. Mein nettes, liebes Aschenputtel …
Tussilein:	Ach, Aschenputtel. Meine liebe, kleine Schwester …

(Sie umarmen sich und küssen sich)

Gute Fee 1:	Und jetzt ist unsere Arbeit hier wohl fertig.
Gute Fee 2:	Alle sind zufrieden, alle sind glücklich.
Gute Fee 3:	Und wir haben jetzt ein richtiges …
Alle:	**Happy End!**

Language activities: Aschenputtel

Adjective endings

The adjective endings have been removed from the first part of the script. Ask students to complete the two tasks below:

- Highlight all the adjectives from this page of the script, using one colour for those which need endings and another for those which don't. What is the rule?

- Add the correct adjective endings where appropriate.

ASCHENPUTTEL – ein kurz Theaterstück

Erzähler:	Lieb Kinder – groß und klein
	Lieb Lehrer – alt und jung
	Lieb Zuschauer
	Gut Morgen
	Gut Tag
	Hallo
	Wir präsentieren heute
	Ein kurz Theaterstück
	Eine alt Geschichte

> Eine traurig Geschichte
> Eine romantisch Geschichte
> Eine berühmt Geschichte
> Wir präsentieren heute
> Ein kurz Theaterstück

Alle: **Aschenputtel**

Aschenputtel: Und das bin ich. Ich heiße Aschenputtel. Ich wohne hier in diesem groß   Haus mit meiner Stiefmutter und mit meinen Stiefschwestern. Mein Leben ist hart. Ich muss jed   Tag arbeiten. Ich muss den ganz   Tag arbeiten. Ich muss auch am Wochenende arbeiten.

Answers can be obtained by comparing the students' task with the original script presented above. If an adjective precedes a noun it must agree.

Was ist 'pantomime'? (Brief schreiben)

There is no German word for the English word *pantomime,* which refers to the uniquely British form of theatre, popular around Christmas and through to the end of January. *Die Pantomime* in German is the equivalent of the English word *mime,* telling a silent story using exaggerated facial expression, gesture and body language.

British pantomime is never silent! Based on well-known fairy tales, the traditional British pantomime involves singing, dancing and acting. Good battles against evil, as men dress up as women and someone has to play the rear end of a pantomime horse or cow. The Prince or hero is often played by a very attractive actress with long hair and long boots. There is always a pantomime dame – usually a very hairy bloke who dresses in huge padded costumes with gaudy wigs and tacky accessories. The dame is a dreadful flirt and she chats up all the male characters on stage. There are lots of corny jokes as well as soppy romantic lines and songs. The characters interact directly with the audience, asking them to shout out "He's behind you" if they see the baddy, or to join in singing and waving to the musical numbers.

Pantomime stories, like traditional fairy tales, always end happily ever after. The hero gets the girl and the whole of the cast, apart from the baddy and his/her cronies join in the final scene, usually involving a wedding. Everyone is singing, everyone is dancing and everyone is happy.

There are plenty of professional pantomime companies in Britain, but many school and village groups also enjoy putting on a Christmas pantomime. They are popular forms of family entertainment which can be performed by and/or watched by young and old. Professional companies might have huge budgets for ever-changing scenery, costumes and special effects, but a panto in a little village hall, performed by local adults and children, can have a magic all its own.

Our European neighbours often recognise the fairy tales which feature in our pantomimes. They too have versions (often the original ones) of Cinderella, Snow White and The Sleeping Beauty, but no other culture has pantomime as we know it. They are so easy to follow and understand. Why not take your penfriend to see one?

Callum's penfriend Susanne has written him the following letter. She is obviously interested in finding out more about pantomime.

Task

Write back in role as Callum and tell her more about it.

> *Lieber Callum,*
>
> *Vielen Dank für Deinen Brief und die Fotos von Deiner Familie. Ich habe eine Frage. Was ist "Christmas Pantomime"? Pantomime auf Deutsch heißt* mime *auf Englisch. Meine Lehrerin hat uns gesagt, dass* Pantomime *in England sehr lustig ist. Was machen die Schauspieler? Was tragen die Schauspieler? Welche Geschichten spielen die Schauspieler? Hast du eine Pantomime im Theater gesehen?*
>
> *Liebe Grüsse*
> *von Susanne*

Useful vocabulary and phrases

das Theaterstück	play/piece of theatre
mit Musik	with music
das Lustspiel	comedy
lustig	funny
es macht Spass, wenn…	it is fun when…
die Schauspieler singen und tanzen	the actors sing and dance
die Kostüme sind bunt	the costumes are colourful
es gibt eine lustige "Dame"	there is a comic "dame"
sie trägt…	she wears…
sie flirtet mit…	she flirts with…
der Held ist	the hero is…
es gibt immer einen Held	there is always a hero
die Böse	(f) villain/baddy
der Böse	(m) villain/baddy
der Schauspieler	(m) actor
die Schauspielerin	(f) actress
das Märchen	fairy tale
Aschenputtel	Cinderella
Schneewittchen	Snow White
beliebt	popular
Ich habe… im Theater gesehen	I saw… at the theatre
Ich habe die Rolle von… gespielt	I played the role of
es gefällt mir, wenn…	I like it when…
klatschen	to clap
die Zuschauer	audience

Ein Kostüm entwerfen

Draw a costume design for a character from a pantomime. Label the item and colour it. Use the dictionary to help you create a more detailed costume design.

Items	Materials
Button	Silk
Wig	Velvet
Stockings	Wool
Tights	Satin
Shawl	Plastic
Ball gown	Nylon
Boots	Cotton
Slippers	Elastic
Socks	Leather

Accessories are also important of course: handbag, jewellery, crown, sword, bundle on a stick …

Aschenputtel – die Figuren beschreiben

Was für Personen sind sie?

Welche Adjektive passen zu welcher Figur? Ergänzen Sie die Tabelle unten mit den passenden Adjecktiven.

Aschenputtel	Stiefmutter	Stiefschwestern	Prinz	Feen

> *süß   ungeduldig   launisch   gutmütig   böse   hilfsbereit   großzügig   (un)selbstsicher*
> *selbstständig   gemein   intolerant   vertrauenswürdig   nett   freundlich   hart*
> *rücksichtslos   ruhig   aufmerksam   schlau   empfindlich   fleißig   sarkastisch   unhöflich*
> *unverschämt   grausam   romantisch   anpassungsfähig   faul   sauer   schüchtern   reich   sanft   lustig*

Schreiben Sie jetzt eine kurze Beschreibung von einer der Figuren.

Suggested answers (but your students might have other ideas!):

Aschenputtel	Stiefmutter	Stiefschwestern	Prinz	Feen
süß	hart	gemein	reich	großzügig
sanft	böse	faul	gutmütig	selbstsicher
schüchtern	ungeduldig	launisch	freundlich	nett
fleißig	sarkastisch	schlau	empfindlich	hilfsbereit
aufmerksam	intolerant	unhöflich	romantisch	lustig
anpassungsfähig	rücksichtslos	sauer	selbstständig	vertrauens-würdig
ruhig	grausam	unverschämt		

Language Live: Additional DVD materials

1. Photograph of the production
2. Retell the story of Aschenputtel in the present tense
3. Retell the story of Aschenputtel using the imperfect tense
4. Revising modal verbs
5. Describing characters using conjunctions
6. Cinderella playscript in Spanish
7. Cinderella playscript in French
8. Useful websites

Project 2   The Marie Curie Project

théâtre sans
frontières
WORLD THEATRE

Project outline

Requirements: large hall for introductory (and plenary) session(s); science laboratory; classroom for matching exercise; hall or equivalent for drama session; classroom/music room/art room for additional activity if required (ie if there are four rather than three classes participating)
Event time: approximately four hours. Time also needed for preparation beforehand.
Languages targeted: French
Impact: high (100+ pupils)

Introduction

This project was created by Jane Dawson and Mike Butler (School Improvement Advisers, North Tyneside), Karen Jeff (Valley Gardens Middle School, Whitley Bay) and Sarah Kemp of Théâtre Sans Frontières working with students from Valley Gardens Middle School, North Tyneside and Harton Technology College, Jarrow School and St Joseph's RC School, South Tyneside. The original project was conceived and created by Noel Jackson (Head of Education at the Centre for Life, Newcastle upon Tyne), John Cobb, and Sarah Kemp with assistance from: Mark Hanly, Jane Williamson and Simon Henderson (Théâtre Sans Frontières), Margaret Turner and Jacqui Cameron (Hexham Middle School), Hugh Beattie (Corbridge Middle School), Rella LaRoe (Centre for Life) with funding from The Welcome Trust.

The result of this collaborative working was a day in 2008 for pupils to spend at The Centre for Life, exploring the life and works of Marie Curie. The enthusiasm from the pupils and staff involved was such that later the same year, the day was replicated in school as a "Marie Curie Day". This was then repeated the following year. The project presented here contains materials which have been used as part of these days, and is intended to provide teachers with the knowledge and confidence to run a similar day at their school.

The project presented here comprises

1. Five preparatory activities. These are presented first and they set the scene for the themed day which follows.

2. The Marie Curie Day. Three activities are presented which involve up to three classes of students rotating amongst them.

3. The accompanying DVD contains: the audio file for the first preparatory activity; pieces of scientific equipment labelled in French; students' name badges; a photograph of "Marie and Pierre Curie" at work in their laboratory; captions for the six drama scenes in the themed day activity three; a certificate of achievement template for the final plenary; a list of useful internet sites.

This Marie Curie project was "highly commended" in the 2010 European Awards for Languages organised by CILT, the National Centre for Languages, part of CfBT Education Trust (see useful web addresses in the accompanying DVD materials).

Why have a Marie Curie Day?

- It stimulates interest amongst boys and girls, linguists, scientists, artists.
- The cross-curricular approach addresses the requirements at Key Stage 3.
- It gets students thinking.
- It is fun.
- It is something a bit different.

Preparatory activities

The following five preparatory activities are designed to be adaptable and can be delivered over several lessons in advance of the actual themed day. The activities have deliberately been left flexible for you to add your own starters, plenaries and adaptations to meet the needs of your learners, their linguistic abilities, the demands of the curriculum and time scales. The activities presented in this preparatory stage enable key scientific vocabulary to be learnt/practised and for the main facts surrounding the life of Marie Curie to be established.

Learning Objectives for preparatory activities 1, 2 and 3

Aujourd'hui nous allons ...

- *écouter une histoire sur Marie Curie;*
- *apprendre des faits sur Marie Curie;*
- *écrire des mots et des phrases sur Marie Curie.*

Preparatory Activity 1: Une histoire sur Marie Curie

Distribute the sequencing task that follows. Ask the students to listen to the recording twice and, on the second hearing, to sequence the statements in the order in which they are played. Play the audio recording about Marie Curie which is included in the accompanying DVD. Check the students' answers against the transcript of the recording which follows the sequencing task. This will help you to gauge how much pupils have understood and how much they already know. In order to complete the sequencing task below you need to find two images, one of Marie Curie and one of Pierre Curie, her husband (see useful internet sites on the accompanying DVD). Allow students enough time to read the phrases before you play the audio file.

Activité

Organisez les phrases suivantes dans l'ordre correct.

1. *Ils étaient physiciens*
2. *Voici Marie Curie.*
3. *Marie est devenue très célèbre grâce à son travail et...*
4. *Leur travail était dangereux et important.*

5. *Elle était une scientifique importante.*

6. *Ils ont découvert un traitement anticancéreux.*

7. *Irène est devenue scientifique et a continué leur travail.*

8. *Avec sa femme, Pierre a gagné le Prix Nobel.*

9. *Voici son mari, Pierre Curie.*

10. *...elle a visité les Etats Unis.*

11. *Ils ont eu deux filles qui s'appellaient Eve et Irène.*

Answers and transcript

Voici Marie Curie. Elle était une scientifique importante. Voici son mari, Pierre Curie. Ils étaient physiciens. Ils ont découvert un traitement anticancéreux. Leur travail était dangereux et important. Avec sa femme, Pierre a gagné le Prix Nobel. Marie est devenue très célèbre grâce à son travail et...... elle a visité les Etats Unis. Ils ont eu deux filles qui s'appellaient Eve et Irène. Irène est devenue scientifique et a continué leur travail.

Writing up the project (optional)

In class students can start a title page about Marie Curie for their project books. This needs to include images which can be obtained from the internet (see list of useful websites on the accompanying DVD) and text in French.

Preparatory Activity 2: La vie de Marie Curie

You can read this short text about the life of Marie Curie aloud with your students. Or you could devise some simple focus questions to accompany the text. Or you could use the text as a translation exercise, as the English version is provided below. An excerpt from the text would also work well as a dictation exercise.

Maria Sklodowska est née le 7 novembre 1867. Elle habitait à Varsovie en Pologne. En 1891 elle est allée à Paris et s'est inscrite à la Sorbonne, parce que les filles n'avaient pas le droit d'aller à l'Université en Pologne. Elle a rencontré Pierre Curie. Il a travaillé à l'Université Sorbonne à Paris. Ils se sont mariés le 25 juillet 1895 et ils ont eu deux filles, Eve et Irène. Ils ont effectué les recherches sur la Pechblende, un mineral riche en uranium. En 1898 ils ont découvert un élément radioactif: le polonium, nommé en hommage à la Pologne. Puis ils ont découvert le radium. Le radium est dangereux et radioactif. En 1903 avec Henri Becquerel, ils ont reçu le prix Nobel pour leurs recherches sur la radioactivité. Ils sont devenus très célèbres. Ils ont voyagé aux Etats-Unis où ils ont rencontré le Président. En avril 1906 Pierre est accidentellement renversé par une voiture à cheval. Marie est devenue professeur à la Sorbonne en novembre 1906. En 1910 elle a réussi à séparer le radium et a reçu un deuxième prix Nobel in 1911. Elle est la seule femme qui a reçu deux prix Nobel. Pendant la première guerre mondiale 1914–1918 elle a organisé le premier service de radiologie mobile. En mai 1921 Marie et ses deux filles sont allées à New York. Elle est devenue très malade, et le 4 juillet 1934 elle est morte d'une leucémie, probablement à cause de son travail. Maintenant son nom est porté par l'Institut Curie, qui soigne les personnes qui souffrent du cancer. Sa fille, Irène, a continué le travail de ses parents et a gagné le prix Nobel avec son mari.

English translation

> Maria Sklodowska was born on the 7th November 1867. She lived in Warsaw in Poland. In 1891 she went to Paris and enrolled at the Sorbonne because women didn't have the right to go to university in Poland. She met Pierre Curie. He worked at the Sorbonne university in Paris. They were married on the 25th July 1895 and they had two daughters, Eve and Irène. They conducted research into pitchblende, a mineral rich in uranium. In 1898 they discovered a radioactive element: polonium, named in tribute to Poland. Then they discovered radium. Radium is dangerous and radioactive. In 1903 with Henri Becquerel they were awarded the Nobel prize for their research into radioactivity. They became very famous. They travelled to the United States where they met the President. In April 1906 Pierre was accidentally run over by a horse-drawn carriage. Marie became a professor at the Sorbonne in 1906. In 1910 she succeeded in isolating radium and received a second Nobel prize in 1911. She is the only women to have received two Nobel prizes. During the First World War (1914–1918) she organised the first mobile radiology service. In May 1921 Marie and her two daughters went to New York. She became very ill and died on the 4th July of leukaemia, probably caused by her work. Nowadays her name is carried by the organisation Marie Curie Cancer Care, which cares for people who are suffering from cancer. Her daughter, Irène, continued the work of her parents and was awarded the Nobel prize with her husband.

Preparatory Activity 3: Marie Curie

In class students can continue with their write-ups of Marie and Pierre Curie. This should include text in French and images which can be obtained from the internet (see accompanying DVD for a list of useful internet sites). Students now have enough information to write a few sentences in French about Marie Curie using the following headings:

> *date et lieu de naissance/nom de famille/éducation/date de son marriage avec Pierre Curie/ nombre et noms des enfants/la profession de Marie/recherches et découvertes/prix reçus/date du mort de Pierre Curie/contribution à la première guerre mondiale/date de la visite à New York/date du mort de Marie Curie/objectif de l'Institut Curie/travail de sa fille Irène.*

Learning Objectives for preparatory activities 4 and 5

These activities present the scientific language in French which is necessary for the experiment during the actual themed day later.

Aujourd'hui nous allons…

- *apprendre des mots scientifiques en français*
- *reconnaître les mots similaires en français et en anglais*
- *classer les mots*
- *utiliser un dictionnaire*
- *prononcer le son –tion*

Preparatory Activity 4: Marie et Pierre font les sciences

For worksheet *Marie et Pierre font les sciences* students link the scientific words in English on the left to the corresponding word in French on the right (with or without the help of a dictionary) by drawing a line between them. They then highlight the feminine nouns. There are some excellent photographs of pieces of scientific equipment labelled in French in the accompanying DVD materials, which can be used as flashcards to good effect. Students will revisit them in the second activity of the themed day to help them remember these vocabulary items.

Marie et Pierre Curie font les Sciences

boiling point	*la distillation*
Bunsen burner	*un résidu*
crystalisation	*la solution*
distillation	*un filtrat*
evaporation	*l'évaporation*
filtrate	*une éprouvette*
filtration	*un bec Bunsen*
residue	*la filtration*
solution	*la cristallisation*
test tube	*le point d'ébullition*

Answers

nom masculin	*anglais*	*nom féminin*	*anglais*
un résidu	residue	*la distillation*	distillation
un filtrat	filtrate	*la solution*	solution
un bec Bunsen	Bunsen burner	*l'évaporation*	evaporation
le point d'ébullition	boiling point	*une éprouvette*	test tube
		la filtration	filtration
		la cristallisation	crystalisation

Optional extra for the end of the matching exercise activity

Create a mock nineteenth-century science lab, lit by candles with UV light and blackout to simulate radiation – this will be placed at one end of the classroom where the matching exercise is done.

Follow-up task

Work on pronunciation of the sound *-tion* – How many other words can you think of that end in *-tion* in French and English? Students need to recognise that *-tion* words are feminine in French.

Preparatory Activity 5: Organisez les mots

For this second worksheet students classify words into categories. Question words = spot the question marks! Others will be more difficult. The task can be completed with or without the use of dictionaries.

Activité: Est-ce-que les mots scientifiques suivants sont des noms, des verbes, des questions ou des adjectifs? Organisez-les correctement sur la table.

> *Séparer, séparation, filtrer, filtration, concasser, dissoudre, évaporer, évaporation, flotter, flottaison, tamiser, allumer, rocher, cailloux, sable, sel, lunettes, boîte, assiette, composant, combien de…?, il y a…?, chaud, froid, sec, mouillé, rechauffer, qu'est-ce que c'est?, dur, doux, goutte.*

Nom	Verbe	Adjectif	Question

Answers

Nom	Verbe	Adjectif	Question
séparation	séparer	composant	combien de..?
filtration	filtrer	chaud	il y a ...?
évaporation	concasser	froid	qu'est-ce que c'est?
flottaison	dissoudre	sec	
rocher	évaporer	mouillé	
cailloux	flotter	dur	
sable	tamiser	doux	
sel	allumer		
lunettes	rechauffer		
boîte			
assiette			
goutte			

Students will need to use this vocabulary in some way to help embed it. In their project books they could continue the story of Marie and Pierre Curie by writing about scientific experiments. Students will be asked to do this in the second Marie Curie Day activity, so this would be useful practice at this preparatory stage. Examples of exercises are :

Pour (infinitive verb plus noun) *il faut* (infinitive verb plus noun)

For example: *Pour séparer les cailloux et le sable il faut filtrer la solution.*

Students can now write three more sentences using the same pattern and some of the scientific words they have learnt.

An additional exercise is for students to complete sentences such as those below in their project books. The sentences have been taken from the transcript to the second activity for the actual themed day.

Activité

Completez les phrases suivantes avec le mot juste en français.

1. *Il faut* (grind) (the salt).
2. *Puis il faut le faire* (dissolve).

3.   *Maintenant* (the filtration)!

4.   (How many) *millilitres avez-vous?*

5.   *Il me faut* 7 (drops) *dans chaque* (test tube).

Answers

1.   *Il faut concasser le sel.*

2.   *Puis il faut le faire dissoudre.*

3.   *Maintenant la filtration!*

4.   *Combien de millilitres avez-vous?*

5.   *Il me faut 7 gouttes dans chaque éprouvette.*

The Marie Curie Day

Having completed the preparatory activities the themed day itself can take place. The Marie Curie day presented here comprises three activities, preceded by an introduction and ending with an optional plenary/evaluation. Each activity requires approximately 1hr 15 minutes, with the introduction taking about 25 minutes. The plenary depends on the amount of time available. Students first complete the short introductory session and then rotate around the three activities.

The introductory session

One French-speaking 'teacher' needs to animate the initial conversations and, after the addition of a hat, play the role of Marie Curie asleep in her laboratory (the Teacher in Role notes contained in Lesson 6 of *Die Mauer* (Project 4 below) and in *Language Live* (Project 1 above) are useful here). The introductory session takes place in the main hall. Its purpose is to set the scene for the day during which students are working in different subject areas at the same time. The students are now all Polish immigrants, just as Marie Curie was. They should be given a badge/sticker onto which they will write their names. They will be told the purpose and format for the day (three activities around which the three classes rotate), then they will go into role as Polish scientists. You could ask them in French about their journey from Warsaw by train: was it long; how did they travel; how do they feel. Then they could be introduced to Pierre Curie (played by a French-speaking teacher), who will be testing their scientific skills during the experiment to see if they are competent enough to join him working at the Sorbonne. Pierre works very hard, so could be portrayed asleep at a desk. A pupil has to go and wake him up gently in French. A short *"Bonjour, comment vous appelez-vous ? Comment ça va ?"* conversation could then develop, initiated by the teacher.

The children then split up into their three classes and rotate amongst the activities. Photographs of each activity, printed in a sepia style, could be used in follow-up French lessons to recap some of the scientific language used, for example. Students could also incorporate the photographs into their project books (see the 'still images' section in Lesson 6 of *Die Mauer*). The tableaux could also be filmed (see Appendix One for example consent form).

Activity 1 : Paris aux années 1890

This takes place in a normal classroom with blackout possibilities for the drama scene at the end.

Requirements

1. Various images for the six topic areas (see details under each topic heading).
2. Two French-speaking staff members for the short sketch at the end of the activity.

Learning objectives

Aujourdhui nous allons…

■ *étudier Paris dans les années 1890*
■ *travailler en groupe*
■ *lier les textes avec les images*

Présenter en français un thème en groupe

Set the scene

The year is 1898 and the students have just arrived in Paris from Poland. This is a lesson to help them to learn French, as well as to find out more about what there is to see and do in Paris.

Ask questions such as: *tu es de quelle nationalité?*

Students answer questions and give the following information:

je m'appelle…

je suis polonais(e)

j'habite à Paris

Aim

Students should match up sentences with images in order to gain an understanding of what Paris was like in the 1890s, then report back verbally to the rest of the group.

Groups

If they are not already in groups, divide the class into six groups. Give each group an envelope. There are six different envelopes, each containing a different theme, relevant captions and images under the following headings: *le transport; les loisirs; les beaux arts; les sciences et la technologie; le tourisme; le style et la mode.*

Procedure

Explain that students have to match the captions to the pictures. The captions will need to be printed onto card (and laminated for future use perhaps) and the images downloaded from the internet (see the list of useful websites on the accompanying DVD). This activity will introduce students to Paris at the end of the nineteenth century: e.g. to the newly built Eiffel Tower, the Paris Metro, the age of electricity, artists and musicians… the new safe bicycle! Working in groups on different topic areas, the students then make recommendations to their friends in their groups on the most interesting activities they can engage in during their stay in Paris and say what they would like to do. As each group completes the first task, explain that now they have to prepare an oral mini presentation about what there is to do and see in Paris. Only French is to be spoken. Students can read from the cards and add language from memory. They can also mime activities to be guessed by others in the room. Each student must say something in French. Invite groups up one at a time to present.

Differentiation

This task works very well if the groups are mixed ability. Differentiation can then be by teacher support, peer support and outcome. Encourage pupils to look for cognates.

Extension

As well as leading their group and helping the less able, the more able pupils should be able to extend their final presentation to include memorised language such as personal information and opinions.

Plenary

Put on the board a structure to enable the pupils from each group to explain what they would like to do while they are in Paris e.g. *Je vais…*

> …*aller*
>
> …*voir*
>
> …*jouer*
>
> …*faire,* etc.

Ask the question:

> *Qu'est-ce que vous allez faire à Paris?*

Students should think about what they have seen and heard from all six groups and decide what they will do in Paris.

They answer with the structure:

> *Je vais* + infinitive

Add answers from student groups to make full sentences. Students can note these in their project notebooks and add images for homework (see useful internet sites in the accompanying DVD materials).

Here are the six topic areas with captions to be copied onto card. Each topic area also has suggestions for images which can be downloaded to set up the task. Images should be set in the 1890s where possible. A simple Google image search using the key headings provided will provide a range of relevant pictures.

Le transport

> **Suggested images:**
> An old bicycle, Paris metro construction, a sightseeing boat on the Seine, a horse-drawn carriage, an omnibus.

Phrases

Pour se déplacer à Paris vous pouvez prendre l'omnibus.

Ils ont deux étages.

Vous pouvez prendre un deux roues.

Elles ont des pneus pneumatiques.

200 000 ont été vendues.

Ils sont en train de construire le métro.

Les gens ont peur du métro.

Le métro souterrain est dangereux!

Pour voir la rivière et les ponts vous pouvez prendre le bateau mouche.

Faites attention aux chevaux!

Est-ce que vous savez nager?

Les femmes doivent acheter de nouveaux vêtements pour y monter.

Le tourisme

> ### Suggested images:
> A 'pissoir', Place de l'Opéra, construction of the Eiffel Tower.

Phrases

Les premiers pissoirs ont été construits en 1841.

Ils sont seulement pour les hommes!

Maintenant il y en a presque 4 000 à Paris.

Attention, ça pue! Il y a une mauvaise odeur.

L'Opéra a été construit en 1875.

Il y a 2 200 places.

On aime voir Le Mariage de Figaro *ici.*

Ça a été construit par Gustave Eiffel.

C'est le bâtiment le plus haut du monde.

Il y a une belle vue d'en haut.

Elle est d'une hauteur de 300 mètres.

Les rues sont très larges.

Il y a beaucoup d'arbres.

Vous pouvez vous promener ici.

C'est sensationnel!

Les loisirs

> ### Suggested images:
> Poster advert for the Lumière brothers, Renoir's painting *Moulin de la Galette*, poster advert for le Moulin Rouge, photograph of Debussy.

Phrases

Vous pouvez allez voir les premières images qui bougent.

Il n'y a pas de son.

Vous pouvez danser dans les jardins.

Est-ce que vous aimez l'accordéon?

Vous pouvez regarder les femmes qui dansent.

Est-ce que vous aimez le vin?

On va ici le dimanche.

On va ici la nuit.

J'adore le Moulin Rouge!

Vous pouvez écouter de la musique.

On joue du piano.

Debussy est un compositeur célèbre.

Les beaux arts

Suggested images:

A Rodin sculpture (*The Thinker*), a Gauguin painting (*nave nave moe*), photo of the Grand Palais, Statue of Liberty under construction.

Phrases

Qu'est-ce que vous en pensez?

Rodin est un sculpteur très célèbre.

On aime voir des images d'autres pays.

Les femmes de Tahiti sont très belles.

Le peintre a beaucoup voyagé.

Ils sont en train de construire le Grand Palais.

Ça va être un beau musée.

Il va ouvrir en 1900.

Les Français ont envoyé l'original comme cadeau aux Etats Unis.

Gustave Eiffel a aidé à la construction de l'original.

C'est une copie en bronze de l'original.

On va voir des peintures ici.

Les sciences et la technologie

Suggested images:

Photo of John Connon and an early camera, X-ray machine, an early telephone, early print communication, Eiffel Tower illuminated.

Phrases

Vous pouvez aller faire votre photographie.

Vous devez rester immobile pendant 30 secondes.

Vous pouvez regarder les os dans la main.

Est-ce que c'est dangereux?

Vous pouvez parler avec vos amis à distance.

Vous pouvez envoyer un télégramme.

C'est très beau la nuit.

J'adore les lumières.

Ils ont été découverts en 1895 par un Allemand Wilhelm Roentgen.

Vous pouvez l'envoyer à votre famille en Pologne

Attention si vous êtes un criminel!

Le style et la mode

> **Suggested images:**
> Table lamp 'Realdragonfly', Jean Beraud painting of *La modiste sur les Champs Elysées*, photo of Samaritaine department store, man wearing a tie.

Phrases

J'adore faire du shopping ici.

Ici on peut tout acheter.

Les lampes sont très belles.

Elles sont importées des Etats Unis.

J'aime ma nouvelle robe.

On peut acheter les modèles à la mode mais ils sont très chers.

Est-ce que vous aimez mon chapeau?

L'art nouveau est très populaire.

Elles sont faites de métal et de petits morceaux de verre.

Je porte le dernier modèle et je suis très beau.

C'est un très grand magasin.

Est-ce que vous aimez ma nouvelle cravate?

Follow-on

Having completed their presentations, the groups watch a five-minute theatre scene performed by Marie and Pierre Curie (two French-speaking staff members), showing them discovering radioactivity in their 'laboratory'. An image of them at work in their laboratory is included on the accompanying DVD, which also shows suitable clothes that each character could wear.

Playscript: Marie and Pierre discovering radioactivity

Props required: candles, a notebook, a pen, a pestle and mortar, a tin cup, a rose, coloured liquid, a balloon flask, a measuring flask, a test tube, a dropper, a baby (doll!), a UV lamp and bulb.

Marie is in her laboratory. It is lit by candles and very cold. She is writing in her note book.

M: Samedi le 25 novembre 1898 (*coughs and blows on her hands*). Où est le mortier et le pilon? (*She picks up pestle and mortar.*) Voilà, le mortier et le pilon, il faut concasser. (*She grinds crystals and puts them into a pan of water*). Voilà, maintenant il faut le faire dissoudre. (*Coughs.*)

(*Pierre enters with a tin cup and a rose.*)

P: Il fait froid ici. Ça va?

M: Oui, il fait très froid.

P: Tiens, ton café.

M: Merci, c'est bien chaud.

P: Regarde, la dernière rose du jardin.

M: Elle est belle. Merci. (*She carries on with her work*)

P: Ecoute Marie, il est 5h. le train part dans 30 minutes.

M: Le train… 30 minutes… d'accord…

P: Je vais préparer les bagages (*He goes*)

M: Maintenant la filtration… (*she pours liquid through filter into ballon flask*). Maintenant j'ai besoin de 21 millilitres (*she starts pouring liquid into measuring flask, she is still coughing*). 10, 12, 14…

(*P arrives with her coat*)

P: Marie

M: Attends… 16, 18, 19, 20, 21 millilitres. (she writes in note book) 21 par 3, c'est combien?

P: 7. Marie, ton manteau (helps her put on coat)… Dépêche toi. Le train part dans 10 minutes

M: Oui, oui, oui… j'ai presque fini…

P: Je vais chercher le bébé (*exits*)

M: Bon, cherche le bébé. 7 millilitres dans chaque un (*she pours 7 mils into each test tube*). Et, maintenant des gouttes (*She takes dropper*)

P: (*off*) Marie, tu es prête?

M: Attends, j'arrive… (*She uses dropper to add coloured drops to each tube*)

M: 1 goutte ici, 2 gouttes ici…

P: Marie, le train va partir.

M: Attends! Et 3 gouttes ici. Voilà, on laisse ça jusqu'à lundi.

(*Blows out candles and exits. Ultra violet light comes on*)

M: (*off*) Attends Pierre, j'ai oublié mon cahier.

(She returns to lab with baby She sees items irradiated)

M: Viens voir Pierre.

M: Regarde le cahier, le stylo, le mortier

P: et la tasse

M: et la rose, elle est belle.

P: C'est beau…

M: Oui, c'est beau! La radioactivité! C'est beau comme toi!

(She gives him the rose and kisses him.)

M: Allez le train…

(They exit)

Activity 2: Pierre Curie + une expérience scientifique

This activity takes place in the school's science laboratory. The science laboratory requires equipment labelled in French (see the accompanying DVD for the apparatus labels in French) and a lump of rock made up of pebbles, sand, salt and vermiculite made up in advance for each pair (or threesome) of students. The experiment takes the maximum amount of time available.

Resources

1.   Marie Curie rocks.
2.   Two members of staff – one speaks only in French (Pierre Curie), the other speaks in French and English (the science teacher).
3.   Flashcards to help describe the pieces of scientific equipment in French (see accompanying DVD materials)

Marie Curie rock recipe

Sand   Salt   Vermiculite   Pea gravel

(+ a little plaster of Paris, to act as a binding agent, helps)

Method

1.   Mix all ingredients together, with water, until a creamy texture.
2.   Place in mould (ice cube tray).
3.   Allow to dry out thoroughly.

Et voilà – les rochers!

Aim

The students will take part in an experiment to separate lump of rock into its components in line with the methods used by Marie Curie to isolate radium – sifting, filtering, flotation, evaporation. The students have to work out how many components there are and what they are made of. The experiment is conducted with Pierre speaking French and the science teacher English with French where possible.

Learning Objectives

Aujourd'hui nous allons...

■ *découvrir 'combien de composants?'*
■ *faire une expérience de séparation*
■ *expliquer les méthodes en français*

Set the scene

Students are introduced to Pierre Curie who works at the Sorbonne as a teacher and a researcher. He will be testing the students on their separation skills. Students may have already met with the necessary scientific vocabulary in the preparatory French lesson, but they will need reminding of this. They should be able to name equipment in French with the aid of the flashcard labels (see accompanying DVD resources).

Pierre Curie only speaks French. He could be the science teacher or another French speaker. He explains that the students are here to do a separation experiment to see if they are good enough to join him with his research at the Sorbonne.

Show the students the rock and ask:

Il y a combien de composants dans le rocher?

Introduce the scientific equipment in French, using the labels as flashcards. These are all included in the accompanying DVD materials. You may or may not have used them in the preparatory stage (activity 4).

Give safety information in English as well as in French.

Procedure

Distribute the rocks (they should be made in advance of the themed day). Set the equipment out in the centre of the laboratory – students have to decide what to use and when. Students work in groups of two or three to separate the rock. They choose their own apparatus and set it up. They should take note of the apparatus names in French, as they will be required to name them as the teachers go around the class. As each component is separated, the pupils should keep it in a tray for identification. As the pupils separate their rock, ask them:

Qu'est-ce que c'est..?

Que faites-vous?

Some groups may need intervention and guidance. As this is designed as a thinking skills activity, try to avoid giving them the answers!

Differentiation

Lower-ability students have been found to be quite good at the separation techniques, but may need support with speaking about it in French. Use visual resources and flashcards.

Extension

As well as naming the apparatus in French, students should be able to use verbs such as *évaporer* to explain what they are doing. It is challenging to use new language in a new context.

Plenary

Teacher asks: *il y a combien de composants dans le rocher?*

Students should be able to answer this question with *quatre*. If they know the vocabulary they may also be able to name the 4 components: *le sable; le sel; les cailloux; le vermiculite.*

Teacher asks: what did we do?

Give out match-up worksheet. Students have to match the starts of the sentences with the correct ends. In pairs, students draw a line between the start of the sentence and the end. This can be used in a follow-up activity during a French lesson when students can write up the experiment in their project books.

Match the beginnings of the sentences with the correct ends

Concassez le rocher	*pour faire évaporer l'eau et révéler le sel*
Tamisez la poudre	*pour dissoudre les composants solubles et pour déterminer quels composants flottent ou coulent*
Mettez le mélange dans un vase à bec avec de l'eau	*pour séparer le sable de la solution*
Filtrez la solution	*avec un mortier et pilon*
Chauffez le filtrat	*pour séparer les cailloux et le sable*

Combien de composants y a-t-il dans le rocher ?

Answers

Concassez le rocher avec un mortier et pilon.

Tamisez la poudre pour séparer les cailloux et le sable.

Mettez le mélange dans un vase à bec avec de l'eau pour dissoudre les composants solubles et pour déterminer quels composants flottent ou coulent.

Filtrez la solution pour séparer le sable de la solution.

Chauffez le filtrat pour faire évaporer l'eau et révéler le sel.

Combien de composants y a-t-il dans le rocher ? Il y en a quatre.

Activity 3: La vie de Marie Curie drama sketches

This takes place in the hall or another large and empty room. The children work in groups to create a series of tableaux based on captions describing key moments in the life of Marie Curie. This is for a museum exhibition in Paris telling the story of her life. The tableaux are then brought to life by the children using French. These scenes will then be presented to the rest of the group giving the children an overview of Marie Curie's life.

Resources

- six red shawls (to identify Marie Curie in each scene or tableau)
- various props (see suggested list below)
- envelope with phrases
- six title placards

Suggestions for Marie Curie props

School

Girls' pinafores

Boys' caps

Teacher's gown

Slates and chalks

Certificate/medal

Nobel prize ceremony

Jackets and top hats

Nobel prize Certificate

Hat for Marie

Chain for president

Tray and champagne glasses

Flag

First World War

Crutches

Bandages

Nurses' headgear

X ray machine

X ray

Guns

Train journey

Suitcases

Shawls and blankets

Tickets

Guard's hat, jacket, whistle, flag

Letter from Marie's sister Bronya

Pierre's death

Jacket for Pierre

Shawls and caps

Driver's whip

Flower seller's basket and flowers

Pierre's stick or umbrella

USA

Hat, stick and glasses for Marie

Bowler hat and jacket for President

Jackets, flag

Cheque

Reporters' cameras and clipboards

Red cross, aprons and hats

Learning Objectives

Aujourdhui nous allons...
- *étudier la vie de Marie Curie*
- *travailler en groupe*
- *présenter sa vie en tableaux et en scènes*
- *parler en français*

Set the scene

The teacher plays the part of a curator in the Cité des Sciences in Paris (in 2010). They want to commission a scene for their latest Marie Curie exhibition, but only the best will do!

Groups

Make sure you have six groups (mixed ability works well).

Procedure

Introduce the six title placards. Each placard represents an important event in Marie Curie's life. Captions for the drama scenes are provided in French and English in the accompanying DVD materials. In each scene whoever plays Marie wears a red shawl or something similar.

Discuss the drama techniques to be practised this session: *la voix; la composition; le vocabulaire français; le point fixe; le début; la fin.*

Aim

That students understand the six title placards and come up with what makes a good drama scene: opening; strong voices; ending.

Six title placards

- *Tu ne peux pas aller à l'université! (Pologne 1883)*
- *Dans le train pour Paris! (1891)*
- *Marie et Pierre gagnent le Prix Nobel (Suède 1903)*
- *Pierre meurt! (Paris 1906)*
- *La première guerre mondiale (1914–1918)*
- *Aux Etats-Unis (1929)*

Activities

The first activity is for the students to come up with a freeze frame of their scene. Show the example of the *Marie et Pierre découvrent la radioactivité* photograph (see additional materials on the accompanying DVD). It might also be useful to look at the 'still images' section in Lesson 6 of *Die Mauer*. Discuss why it is a good example of a freeze frame. Pupils have five minutes to produce their own freeze frame using the props. A photo of each frame is taken. (These can then be used in a later lesson in the classroom for pupils to create their own dialogues).

The second activity is to act out the scenes. The notes for each scene that follow need to be expanded and rehearsed before being acted out (and filmed). An example of a useful photography/video consent form is included in Appendix One. Students will be marked by the teacher (pretending to work in Paris, who is going to commission the best scene for an exhibition about Marie Curie's life) on the different drama techniques discussed in the starter. Students can use the phrases in the envelopes and/or use their own language to act out the scene in French. Each student must say at least one thing in French (if appropriate).

Here are the notes to the first scene students will find in their envelopes. NB if this scene is used as a demonstration, there are five scenes which follow not six.

1. *Tu ne peux pas aller à l'université! Pologne 1883*

Marie receives a gold medal for being top of her class at school in Poland (aged 15). She is told by her teacher that she can't go to university because in Poland only boys can go at this time.

Tu ne peux pas aller à l'université!	*Félicitations!*
Très bien!	*Je veux aller à l'université.*
Non! Ce n'est pas possible!	*Pourquoi?*
Tu es une fille.	*Ce n'est pas juste!*

Here is the whole scene worked up from the notes above.

Scene 1

Students improvise a classroom with teacher and pupils. Teacher sets some maths problems; children write answers on slates.

Teacher: Ecoutez, 60 plus 45, etc.

Pupils give answers, only Marie gets it right. Teacher calls Marie to front and gives her medal/certificate.

Teacher: Félicitations! Très bien!

Other pupils clap. Teacher tells Marie she can't go to university.

Teacher: Tu ne peux pas aller à l'université!

Marie: Pourquoi?

Boys in class (*laughing*): Tu es une fille.

Marie: Je veux aller à l'université.

Other girls in class: Ce n'est pas juste!

Teacher: Silence !

Marie: Non! Ce n'est pas possible!

Now here are the notes for the remaining five scenes. Students should work on their presentations in their groups before the final performance.

2. *Dans le train pour Paris. 1891*

Marie journeys by train to Paris. Marie reads a letter from her sister Bronya and her husband in Paris. She practises her French with other passengers.

Viens à Paris!	*Paris est superbe.*
Je m'appelle Marie.	*Je suis polonaise.*
Je suis français/française.	*Comment tu t'appelles?*
Où habites-tu?	*J'habite Paris.*
Où vas-tu?	*Je vais à Paris.*
Le train pour Paris! Le train pour Paris!	*Les tickets, s'il vous plaît!*

3. *Marie et Pierre gagnent le Prix Nobel. Suéde 1903*

Pierre and Marie receive the Nobel prize for the discovery of radioactivity from the Swedish president. They are very sick. They drink Champagne with the scientist Becquerel.

Je vous présente le Prix Nobel	*Voilà le Prix Nobel.*
Merci beaucoup.	*Félicitations!*
Du champagne!	*Santé!*
A la science!!	*Formidable!*
Fantastique!	

4. *Pierre meurt. Paris 1906*

Pierre is sick and dizzy. As he crosses the road he is knocked down by a horse and carriage. He dies in Marie's arms.

Au secours!	*Aidez-moi!*	*Un accident*
Qu'est-ce qui se passe?	*A l'hopitâl!*	*Aidez-nous!*
Il est mort.	*Il est stupide.*	*Je t'aime.*
Vite, vite!	*C'est horrible!*	

5. *La Première Guerre Mondiale France. 1914–1918*

Marie is in the trenches with her daughter Irene. They are tending to wounded French soldiers. They x-ray the soldiers' arms.

Aïe, aïe!	*Calme-toi!*	*Ça fait mal!*
J'ai mal à la tête/au bras.	*Mets le bras ici!*	*Voilà!*
Regardez le métal.	*Là et là et là!*	*Il faut une opération.*
J'ai peur.		

6 *Chez le Président. États-Unis 1929*

Marie receives a cheque from the President Hoover of the USA to help her set up a Radium Institute in Warsaw, Poland. She's nearly blind. There are journalists and photographers.

Fromage!	*Voici le chèque!*	*Merci beaucoup!*
Bonne chance!	*Bon voyage!*	*Vive la Pologne!*
A la science!	*Ici, Marie, ici!*	*Regardez la caméra!*
	Au revoir.	

General

Differentiation

Those less able could take a non-speaking part, or a part with little dialogue.

Extension

Those more able can extend themselves with more dialogue and/or use advanced drama techniques.

Plenary

Each group acts out their own scene to the rest of the group. Teacher gives marks /10 for the various drama aspects. Pupils help teacher to evaluate the performances. A winning scene is selected.

At the end of the day, time and space allowing, it is a good idea to get all the pupils together in the hall for a plenary. During this time you can gain valuable feedback about how the day went, which can then inform your planning for the following year. You could also give out evaluation forms for the pupils to complete if appropriate. One idea for the conclusion is to do a prize-giving; awarding certificates for the best scientists, the best dramatists and the best linguists. A certificate template is included in the accompanying DVD materials.

Additional activity suggestions

A fourth activity may be needed if numbers rise for example. This could be an art or music activity, with students exploring the music of Debussy or the paintings of Gaugin or the Impressionists. Alternatively, students could participate in a 'radio show', hosted by an English speaker (the concepts are too difficult for students to debate in French). They listen to arguments put forward by teachers in role as: conservationist, local councillor from Sellafield and nuclear submarine specialist as to the advantages and disadvantages of nuclear power. Students can ask the panel questions and debate the issues, or take on the roles themselves.

Follow-on work

Students complete their project books by writing up in French:

- Details surrounding the lives of Marie and Pierre Curie. This may or may not involve further research.

- The wonders of the 1890s in terms of the six topic headings studied in activity one of the themed day.

- The separation experiment they performed in activity two of the themed day to separate the four elements in the rock. This could involve revision of past tenses.

- The scenes they acted out based on their notes from activity three of the themed day.

Students should use the still photographs taken during the Marie Curie Day to illustrate their work, as well as any other images they may have found useful. Alternatively, they could put the still photos together in a PowerPoint presentation and add speech bubbles and captions to create a photo story.

Another possibility is to re-enact the drama scenes again in different styles: for example, in the style of a musical, an opera, X-factor, melodrama, a clown act, gothic, horror, etc. This is a fun way of revisiting the vocabulary.

A further possibility is for students to make a TV advertisement for the opening of the Marie Curie museum exhibition, showing highlights and giving opening times and prices, etc. This could lead to the creation of a PowerPoint presentation and flyers to advertise the event.

The Marie Curie project: Additional DVD materials

1. A recording of the plenary of Activity 1.
2. Pieces of scientific equipment labelled in French for the plenary of Activity 4 and the themed day Activity 2.
3. A photograph of 'Marie and Pierre Curie' at work in their laboratory.
4. A certificate of achievement template for the final plenary.
5. Useful websites.

Project 3   Spanglovision

routes into
LANGUAGES

Project outline

Requirements: normal language classrooms plus an assembly hall for the final event
Event time: one day for the main event preceded by rehearsal time
Languages targeted: any. The project presented here is in Spanish.
Impact: high. The project presented here was delivered to the whole of Year Seven

Introduction

This project aims to provide the newly-arrived Year Seven students with a focus and
purpose for developing their memory skills in Spanish through the use of a Spanish song
competition. The project combines music with language learning and serves to introduce
them as a year group to the whole school cohort who are involved in the voting process
and selection of the *Spanglovision* winners. As part of *Spanglovision*, each Year Seven group
is given a Spanish song to learn as a group, which is then performed, videoed and shown
to the rest of the school. With the excitement building and emotions high, the whole
school votes for their favourite group, who are presented with the winners' cup! It is a
hugely motivating experience all round that gets the whole of Year Seven (and everyone
else!) singing their hearts out in Spanish just weeks after joining the school.

Rationale for the project

The project combines linguistic learning objectives – the development of pronunciation
and memory skills – with promoting the wider learning attributes of confidence and
performance skills. The development of learners as confident individuals is one of the
key aims of the new secondary curriculum. This project builds on performance skills that
learners often have from their primary education, where they are used to singing and
performing in assemblies and extends them to a foreign language and the bigger
secondary school stage. There is enough overlap of experience here to provide a
reassuring bridge to support transition but, at the same time, to provide a real cognitive
challenge and extension to learning in terms of language development and memory
use. Another aspect of the project that is fully in line with new secondary curriculum
aims is the joining up of experience, so that links between different curriculum subjects
are made and maintained. Here music and languages are successfully combined. In 2009
this project was awarded a prestigious European Award for Languages, which recognises
innovative approaches to language learning and is coordinated in the UK by CILT, the
National Centre for Languages. *Spanglovision* also won the Spanish Embassy Language
Prize, awarded for the best project involving Spanish.

The students

The students involved in this project when it was initiated in 2007 had just arrived in the school from nine feeder primary schools. Most, but not all, had had some experience of Spanish learning during Key Stage Two, but there were inconsistencies in terms of the amount of learning received, the teaching expertise delivering it, and the staging and timing of curriculum provision during Key Stage Two, as well as the usual differences of ability and motivation that a cohort of 260 mixed ability children presents.

When students arrive at the school they often lack explicit knowledge of memory skills and ways of training and working the memory to retain language in the medium to long term. A focus on language-learning skills, in particular on memory, was one of the main foci for this curriculum project. In addition, new Year Seven cohorts frequently need help with transition, to find ways of working together that help them to get to know each other better, to develop a sense of identity in their tutor groups, to learn how to work together as a team and to discover ways to feel connected to the wider school community. *Spanglovision* seemed to enhance this social orientation and provided the second main focus for the project.

We were thus keen for learners to learn:

- how to have fun learning language;
- how to use music and singing as a method of powerfully accelerating memory;
- how to improve their pronunciation and realise the importance of good pronunciation;
- how to improve their levels of concentration and focus in a group;
- how to work together productively as a team;
- how to perform;
- how to use creativity to enhance performance.

Organisation

From the initial idea for a Spanish song competition involving all ten tutor groups in the new Year Seven cohort, the following steps were taken:

1. Ten different Spanish songs were chosen, the lyrics found and printed and the songs downloaded. There was a Disney theme to these songs in 2009 and those used were:

> *Bajo el mar* (Little Mermaid)
> *Busca lo más vital* (The Bare Necessities)
> Formamos un equipo (High School Musical)
> *Lo extraño que soy* (Tarzan)
> *Winnie Pooh* (Winne the Pooh)
> *Hay que llegar* (High School Musical)
> *Hay un amigo* (Toy Story)
> *Nuestra libertad* (High School Musical)
> *Todo el mundo a bailar* (High School Musical 2)
> *Dos mundos* (Tarzan)
> *Hijo de hombre* (Tarzan)

Subsequent years have seen the growth and development of *Abbavision*, featuring Spanish versions of Abba songs.

2. Each tutor group was then assigned a song.

3. The groups' teachers familiarised themselves with the song and the lyrics and planned how to teach and rehearse the songs in lesson time, alongside other language work.

4. Several lessons occurred which included rehearsal and learning time, with the aim of memorising the song ready for performance.

5. On one day during language-lesson time the songs were videoed.

6. The video was edited to produce a video of the best 1 minute of each song.

7. The video was seen by all of year Seven in a Spanish lesson and each student voted for his/her favourite song. In the true tradition of Eurovision, students were not allowed to vote for their own tutor group.

8. Votes were counted and three finalists were to emerge. In the event, four tutor groups were in the final, due to a tie in the number of votes.

9. The video was edited again to produce a shorter video of the 4 finalists.

10. During assemblies all that week, years eleven, ten, nine and eight saw the finalists' video and all students voted – this was highly enjoyable for all students and teachers!

11. In the final assembly of the week, the Year Seven winning tutor group was presented with a cup.

All Year Seven learners were incredibly motivated and engaged in this project. Particular reasons for this were:

- they enjoyed the music and the singing in its own right;
- it was a fun, non-threatening way to develop their form identify and work together;
- they enjoyed the sense of progression and mastery that was achieved through successfully memorising a real Spanish song;
- their confidence and self-esteem was boosted by the knowledge that the older year groups had been impressed with their performances and had been involved in selecting the competition winners.

This organisation of the first two to three weeks of Year Seven teaching time was both different from and the same as that of previous years. It was similar, in that we kept students in mixed-ability tutor groups and sought to revise some basics that they had covered at Key Stage Two. It was different, in that for this series of lessons there was an explicit project focus on developing memory skills and accurate pronunciation and on encouraging students to develop a sense of collegiality, with a group performance being one of the outcomes. In terms of the delivery of this new learning experience, it was the same in that the foreign language class teachers were responsible for the teaching which took place in normal language lesson time. The exception to this was the recording day, when all students used the performance hall to video their songs. Excellent use was made of the digital video to draw the project together and enable the whole school cohort to be involved in the voting process. Although peer assessment was not formally defined, all students in the school had a role in assessing the work of the four final groups, and all students in Year Seven were able to identify strengths in the performances of their peer tutor groups. The sense of 'audience' was a key factor in raising expectations and standards in terms of the learning involved in the song project. The cross-curricular links with music speak for themselves.

Evidence of success

The project generated a huge amount of interest and engagement from students. To enhance the performance they developed their own movement routines and actions to the songs they learned. They worked hard to memorise the language and achieved high levels of accuracy in the pronunciation. They were confident in their performance and the whole experience has been described as key to their successful integration into the school. Since the project, students have continued to participate enthusiastically in language lessons, particularly in learning activities that involve music and song. In terms of confidence and performance skills the gains were very obvious. Learners greatly enjoyed devising gestures and routines to accompany their songs and make the performances memorable. Positive feedback on the project has come from both students and parents as well as from teachers of other curriculum areas within the school.

> Not only was this an imaginative and educationally brilliant way to introduce new learners to the Spanish language, it was also a fantastic way to bring the whole school together.
>
> European Award for Languages judges

Rachel Hawkes at Comberton Village College said:

> *Spanglovision* is at the heart of our European Day of Languages celebrations and reaches every student and every teacher in the school.

Spanglovision: Accompanying DVD materials

1.   List of useful websites

Project 4: Die Mauer

Project outline

Requirements: normal classroom space
Event time: seven 1.5-hour lessons
Languages targeted: German-
Impact: medium (one year group)

Introduction

Die Mauer was developed by: the University of Hull; the Goethe Institut Manchester; Routes into Languages Yorkshire and The Humber; Links into Languages Yorkshire and The Humber. The project itself focuses on the Berlin Wall as a symbol of the ideological differences between communist/socialist East Germany and the capitalist West. Its main aim was to appeal, through inspiring resources, to teachers and students studying A-level German. The materials developed focus on the Berlin Wall (the twentieth anniversary of its fall) and the repercussions of the ideological differences that existed in that period of history. The resources presented here are suitable for use by teachers in secondary schools, sixth-form colleges and other teaching establishments. The resources themselves seek to tap into relevant issues around politics and citizenship, as well as language progression, to provide an interesting and unusual platform for learning. The project involved collaboration with the Drama Department which was the original inspiration for the development of the language and culture resource pack. The approach to the topic is imaginative and fun and uses individual experiences of historical events, whilst the interdisciplinarity of the resource makes it attractive for collaboration across subject areas (for example, drama, history, citizenship).

The original format of the project comprised ten lessons on different topics, including historical events, but also the experiences of the people who lived through this period and who were affected by the Berlin Wall. The extensive materials have been shortened in this book to include seven main lessons with associated teaching/learning materials. The seven lessons can be used independently as well as consecutively/successively.

> There is a huge variety of tasks, encouraging creative use of language and the fact that the experiences of people who lived through this time are explored make the study of history very relevant... An outstanding set of teaching and learning materials.
>
> (*A level teacher, North Yorkshire*)

Lesson 1

Task 1: Das Brandenburger Tor 1988 und heute

Aim: To introduce students to the topic and to see what they already know about the Berlin Wall.

Method: Students compare two photographs

Activity

Show students the first photograph (also contained in colour in the materials for this project on the accompanying DVD). Students respond to questions such as:

- *Was könnt ihr auf dem Bild sehen?*
- *In welcher Stadt befindet sich das Brandenburger Tor?* (the symbol of Berlin)
- *Was seht ihr vor dem Brandenburger Tor?* (the Berlin wall)
- *In welchem Jahr wurde das Foto gemacht?* (before the wall fell in 1988)
- *Wisst ihr, wann die Mauer fiel?* (9 November 1989)
- *Von welcher Seite wurde das Foto aufgenommen?* (from the West)

First clue: *Graffiti* was only possible on the Western side, because only on this side could people get near the wall. On the Eastern side there was the so-called *Todesstreifen* which was heavily guarded. If a citizen tried to escape, soldiers had orders to shoot.

Second clue: You can see the Russian flags on the other side of the wall.

Third clue: You can see the Quadriga on top of the Brandenburger Tor from behind.

Activity

Show students the second photograph below (also contained in colour on the accompanying DVD) and ask them to compare it to the first photograph.

- *Welche Unterschiede könnt ihr erkennen?* (The *Brandenburger Tor* is renovated. The wall has been taken down. People can now walk through the *Brandenburger Tor*. This was impossible during the 28 years that Berlin was divided. You can see the *Quadriga* from the front, which means that the photograph was taken from East Berlin.)
- *Wenn man ganz genau hinsieht, kann man hinter dem Brandenburger Tor ein weiteres Denkmal sehen. Welches ist es?* (The *Siegessäule* in the Tiergarten; 66,89 metres high.)

Task 2: Zeitstrang mit den wichtigsten historischen Daten

Aim: To make students aware of specific important dates and to place those dates into an approximate timeline.

Method: Gapfill (1st activity); multiple choice (2nd activity).

Activity 1

Give students the task below (*Zeitstrang mit den wichtigsten historischen Daten*). They fill in the gaps alongside the dates with what they think happened at the time. Students get no help.

Zeitstrang mit den wichtigsten historischen Daten

What happened on these important dates? Fill in the gaps alongside the dates.

1945	....
1948/1949	....
1953	....
13 August 1961	....
9 November 1989	....

Activity 2: Quiz (Multiple Choice)

Students get some help now from the teacher. Hand out the quiz below and ask students to complete it in small groups/pairs. Check the answers together and ensure the first activity (*Zeitstrang mit den wichtigsten historischen Daten*) is completed accurately.

Quiz: Welche Antwort ist richtig?

1945
- Ende des 2. Weltkrieges: die Alliierten teilen das Land in vier Besatzungszonen und Berlin in vier Sektoren.
- Ende des 2. Weltkrieges: die Sowjetunion besetzt Deutschland und ganz Deutschland wird kommunistisch.
- Ende des 2. Weltkrieges: Deutschland wird neutral.

1948/1949
- Berlin-Blockade: Westberlin ist eine Insel mitten in der sowjetischen Besatzungszone. 11 Monate lang demonstrieren und streiken die Westberliner. Denn sie wollen Teil der DDR sein.
- Berlin-Blockade: die Sowjetunion blockiert alle Straßen nach Westberlin. 11 Monate lang wird Westberlin mit Hilfe von Flugzeugen versorgt. Täglich werden 4500 Tonnen Lebensmittel und andere Produkte nach Westberlin geflogen.
- Berlin-Blockade: Westdeutschland möchte keine Flüchtlinge mehr aus Westberlin aufnehmen. 11 Monate lang darf kein Westberliner nach Westdeutschland einreisen.

1953

- Volksaufstand in Ost-Berlin: Arbeiter streiken im Osten Berlins. Sie fordern bessere Arbeitsbedingungen und freie Wahlen. Am 17. Juni 1953 fahren sowjetische Panzer auf und der Volksaufstand wird blutig niedergeschlagen.

- Präsidentenbesuch: der amerikanische Präsident John F. Kennedy besucht Westberlin und verkündet vor mehr als 400 000 jubelnden Menschen den legendären Satz: "Ich bin ein Berliner."

- Papstbesuch in der DDR: der Papst wird von einer jubelnden Menge empfangen. Vor dem Reichstag versammeln sich über 2 Millionen Menschen.

1961

- 3 Millionen Ostdeutsche sind bereits aus der DDR in die BRD geflüchtet. Am 13. August 1961 ist es der BRD zu viel und sie beschließt, eine Mauer zu bauen.

- Eine Seuche tritt 1961 auf und mehr als 20 000 Berliner sterben. Daraufhin wird die Grenze zwischen Ost- und Westberlin geschlossen und eine Mauer wird gebaut.

- In der Nacht vom 12. auf den 13. August 1961 wird mitten durch Berlin eine Mauer gebaut. Familien werden über Nacht getrennt und dürfen nicht mehr auf die andere Seite. 28 Jahre lang ist die Berliner Mauer Symbol für die Unfreiheit der DDR-Bevölkerung.

1989 (9 November)

- In Leipzig gibt es eine der größten Friedensdemonstrationen in Deutschland. Die Menschen demonstrieren für Redefreiheit, Reisefreiheit und freie Wahlen. Die Demonstration wird von der Polizei blutig niedergeschlagen. 53 Personen sterben.

- David Hasselhoff kommt am 9 November 1989 nach Berlin und singt das Lied "*Looking for freedom*" vor der Berliner Mauer. Die Politiker sind so gerührt, dass sie spontan entscheiden, die Grenze für die Menschen zu öffnen.

- Die friedliche Revolution in der DDR bringt in der Nacht des 9. Novembers die Mauer in Berlin und somit die Grenze zwischen Ost- und Westdeutschland zu Fall.

Answers

1945:	Ende des 2. Weltkrieges: die Alliierten teilen das Land in vier Besatzungszonen und Berlin in vier Sektoren.
1948/1949:	Berlin-Blockade: die Sowjetunion blockiert alle Straßen nach Westberlin. 11 Monate lang wird Westberlin mit Hilfe von Flugzeugen versorgt. Täglich werden 4500 Tonnen Lebensmittel und andere Produkte nach Westberlin geflogen.
1953:	Volksaufstand in Ost-Berlin: Arbeiter streiken im Osten Berlins. Sie fordern bessere Arbeitsbedingungen und freie Wahlen. Am 17. Juni 1953 fahren sowjetische Panzer auf und der Volksaufstand wird blutig niedergeschlagen.
1961:	In der Nacht vom 12. auf den 13. August 1961 wird mitten durch Berlin eine Mauer gebaut. Familien werden über Nacht getrennt und dürfen nicht mehr auf die andere Seite. 28 Jahre lang ist die Berliner Mauer Symbol für die Unfreiheit der DDR-Bevölkerung.

1989 (9. November): Die friedliche Revolution in der DDR bringt in der Nacht des 9. Novembers die Mauer in Berlin und somit die Grenze zwischen Ost- und Westdeutschland zu Fall.

Task 3: 1961 wurde in Berlin eine Mauer gebaut

Aim: To make students aware of how the 'Passiv-Präteritum' is formed and used (revision).

Method: Translation exercise (English to German)

Activity

Students should translate the following sentences into German. They can use the vocabulary list at the end of this lesson.

1. In 1961 a wall was built in Berlin.
   1961 wurde in Berlin eine Mauer gebaut.

2. In 1946 the SED was founded.

   ....

3. Germany was divided into four occupation zones. Berlin was divided into four sectors.

   ....

4. In 1990 Germany was reunited.

   ....

5. In 1953 a demonstration was violently put down in East Berlin.

   ....

6. The border was opened on the 9th November 1989.

   ....

7. German reunification was formally concluded on the 3rd October 1990.

   ....

Answers

1. *1961 wurde in Berlin eine Mauer gebaut.*
2. *1946 wurde die SED gegründet.*
3. *Deutschland wurde in vier Besatzungszonen geteilt. Berlin wurde in vier Sektoren geteilt.*
4. *1990 wurde Deutschland wiedervereinigt.*
5. *1953 wurde eine Demonstration in Ost-Berlin blutig niedergeschlagen.*
6. *Am 9. November 1989 wurde die Grenze geöffnet.*
7. *Die Deutsche Wiedervereinigung wurde am 3. Oktober 1990[1] offiziell vollzogen.*

---

1 *Seither wird jedes Jahr am 3. Oktober der Tag der Deutschen Einheit (Nationalfeiertag) gefeiert.*

Lesson 1: Homework task

Exploring German History (Jigsaw research)

Aim: To motivate students to do their own internet research, to collect data and to present acquired knowledge to the class.

Method: Guided internet research/making a poster and a short presentation.

Task

Give each student one of the boxes (you can print these onto small cards perhaps). Students can work in pairs/small groups if large numbers are present. In the following class (Lesson Two) students should be ready to present their poster (they should try to find pictures on the internet) in about three minutes to explain the key words on the cards and answer the questions.

Karte 1: Ende des 2. Weltkrieges und die Besatzungszonen

Wann und von wem wurde der 2. Weltkrieg beendet?

Welche Besatzungszonen gab es in Deutschland?

Wie wurde Deutschland aufgeteilt?

Karte 2: Arbeiteraufstand 1953

Warum gab es diesen Aufstand?

Wie wurde der Aufstand beendet?

Karte 3: SED und Erich Honecker

Was bedeutet SED?

Wann wurde sie gegründet?

Wer war Erich Honecker?

Wie lange war er im Amt?

Karte 4: John F. Kennedy "Ich bin ein Berliner" und Ronald Reagan "Mr Gorbatschow, tear down this wall"

Wann sagte Kennedy diesen berühmten Satz?

Warum sagte er diesen Satz?

Wann kam Ronald Reagan nach Westberlin und sagte diesen Satz?

Warum sagte er diesen Satz?

Karte 5: Stasi

Was beduetet Stasi?

Wie viele formelle und informelle Mitglieder gab es?

Warum wurden Menschen bespitzelt?

Wie gewann man neue informelle Mitarbeiter?

Was passierte in den Stasi-Gefängnissen, z.B. Berlin Hohenschönhausen?

Karte 6: Der Eiserne Vorhang

Was war mit diesem Begriff gemeint?

Wie verlief "Der Eiserne Vorhang" durch Europa?

Welche zwei Bündnissysteme gab es im Ostern und im Westen?

Was beduetet der Begriff "Der Kalte Krieg"?

Karte 7: Bau der Berliner Mauer

Wann wurde die Mauer gebaut?

Was behauptete Walter Ulbricht nur 2 Wochen davor?

Wie wurde die Mauer im Osten von den Politikern genannt? Warum?

Warum wurde die Mauer tatsächlich gebaut?

Wie viele Menschen flohen bis zum Mauerbau in den Westen?

Karte 8: Luftbrücke und Rosinenbomber

Wann gab es die Luftbrücke zwischen der BRD und Westberlin? Warum?

Warum wurden bestimmte Flugzeuge "Rosinenbomber" genannt?

Karte 9: Gorbatschow: Glasnost und Perestroika

Wer war Gorbatschow? Wann kam er ins Amt?

Warum ist er für Deutschland wichtig?

Was bedeuten die Begriffe "Glasnost" und "Perestroika"?

Warum sagte Gorbatschow angeblich zu Erich Honecker folgenden Satz: "Wer zu spät kommt, den bestraft die Geschichte"?

Was wollte er Honecker damit sagen?

Karte 10: Montagsdemonstrationen in Leipzig

Wer war Pfarrer Führer?

Wann begannen die Montagsdemonstrationen?

Welche Auswirkungen hatten diese Demonstrationen auf den Fall der Berliner Mauer?

Warum war es gefährlich, an diesen Demonstrationen teilzunehmen?

Lesson 2

Task 1: presentations

Aims: for students to present their research and acquired knowledge to the class and to revise the grammar presented in the previous lesson.

Method: presentations.

Activity

Presentations are held in chronological order. Students listen carefully and write down important dates and key words using the timeline below. After the presentations, students should check that they have understood the content correctly. They ask their partner questions such as:

Wann wurde die Mauer gebaut? (Or the teacher could lead by asking these questions.)

Presentations

Task A: Listen carefully to the presentations of your fellow students. Write down the most important dates and keywords on the timeline below.

....

1945   **9. November 1989**

Task B: After the presentations check that you have written down the dates and the facts correctly. Ask your partner some questions such as: *Wann wurde die Mauer gebaut?*

Task 2: Walls – Mauern

Aims: to introduce the concept of "Mauern" in a metaphorical sense (walls in people's minds).

Method: for students to complete and continue a poem.

Task: students fill in the gaps with the words provided on the worksheet. They should write two more paragraphs in the style of the poem as homework.

Student task:

Here is a poem someone has written about walls. Fill in the gaps in the text below using the words in the box.

What can you relate to the term "Mauern"?

Write two more paragraphs in the style of the poem as homework.

einstürzen	Stein	Hoffnung	Zweifel
Angst	Mauern	Liebe	Stolz

MAUERN   …sind aus S___n

sind im Kopf

stehen vielen Jahre

bestehen aus Zw_____

bestehen aus S___z

bestehen aus A_____

Damit es noch H_____ auf L_____

gibt, müssen einige M_____ fallen.

Wie willst du jemals wissen, was sich

hinter der Mauer befindet, wenn du

sie nicht _____ lässt?

Answers

MAUERN   …sind aus **Stein**

sind im Kopf

stehen vielen Jahre

bestehen aus **Zweifel**

bestehen aus **Stolz**

bestehen aus **Angst**

Damit es noch **Hoffnung** auf **Liebe**

gibt, müssen einige **Mauern** fallen.

Wie willst du jemals wissen, was sich

hinter der Mauer befindet, wenn du

sie nicht **einstürzen** lässt?

Task 3: Brieffreundschaften zwischen Ost und West

Aims: Global understanding and focusing on details of listening exercise.

Method: Listening to the *Interview penpals* audio file on the accompanying DVD. A transcription of this interview is also contained on the DVD.

Task: Students should listen to the complete interview first and then answer questions A and B below. They should then listen to the three individual parts of the interview, concentrating on each section and work on the allocated exercises on the worksheet.

Student task

Listen to the complete interview. Answer questions **A** and **B**.

A. *Wie ist die Brieffreundschaft entstanden?*

B. *Was war besonders ungewöhnlich im Osten?*

Listen to part 1 again. Fill in the gaps below and then answer question **C**.

1. *Wir haben in der _____ Klasse – in der Grundschule – Brieffreundschaften mit einer Schule in Stendal angefangen.*

2. *Stendal ist ____ _____ _____ von Ostdeutschland, in der Nähe von Magdeburg.*

3. *Wir hatten jede Menge _____ mit den Informationen über diese Schüler.*

4. *Wir haben uns diejenigen _____, die zu uns am Besten passten.*

5. *Das war _____.*

6. *Wir haben das Ganze dann zum Höhepunkt gebracht mit einer _____.*

7. *Wir haben am _____ teilgenommen und die _____.*

8. *Die Klasse aus Stendal hat den Alltag in _____ kennen gelernt.*

C. *Was ist ein Steckbrief?*

Listen to part 2 again. What is being said? Tick the correct boxes.

☐ *Sport war in der DDR ganz besonders wichtig.*

☐ *In der DDR gab es Ganztagsbetreuung.*

☐ *Im Westen arbeiteten beide Elternteile.*

☐ *Im Westen war schon mittags Schulschluss.*

☐ *In der DDR war alles ungepflegter als im Westen.*

☐ *In der DDR sah alles besser aus als im Westen.*

☐ *Im Westen waren die Mütter zu Hause.*

Listen to part 3 again. Answer questions **D** and **E**.

D. *Ging die Brieffreundschaft auch nach dem Schuljahr noch weiter?*

E. *Warum hörte man irgendwann mit dem Schreiben auf?*

Answers

A. *Kontaktaufnahme mit einer Klasse aus Stendal, Steckbriefe und jeder Schüler suchte sich den Briefpartner aus, der zu ihm passte.*

B. *Sehr viel Sport, Ganztagsbetreuung, alles ein bisschen dreckiger und ungepflegter.*

Part 1

1. *Wir haben in der **vierten** Klasse - in der Grundschule – Brieffreundschaften mit einer Schule in Stendal angefangen.*

2. *Stendal ist **in der Mitte** von Ostdeutschland, in der Nähe von Magdeburg.*

3. *Wir hatten jede Menge **Steckbriefe** mit den Informationen über diese Schüler.*

4. *Wir haben uns diejenigen **ausgesucht**, die zu uns am Besten passten.*

5. *Das war **1991/1992**.*

6. *Wir haben das Ganze dann zum Höhepunkt gebracht mit einer **Klassenfahrt**.*

7. *Wir haben am **Alltag** teilgenommen und die **Familien kennen gelernt**.*

8. *Die Klasse aus Stendal hat den Alltag in **Westdeutschland** kennen gelernt.*

C. *Ein Steckbrief enthält Informationen über eine Person in tabellarischer Form: z.B. Name, Alter, Wohnort, Hobbies, usw.*

Part 2

☑ Sport war in der DDR ganz besonders wichtig.

☑ In der DDR gab es Ganztagsbetreuung.

☐ Im Westen arbeiteten beide Elternteile.

☑ Im Westen war schon mittags Schulschluss.

☑ In der DDR war alles ungepflegter als im Westen.

☐ In der DDR sah alles besser aus als im Westen.

☑ Im Westen waren die Mütter zu Hause.

D. *Ja, für einige noch. So zwei, drei Jahre.*

E. *Weil die Interessen auseinander gingen oder man sich nicht mehr die Mühe machte.*

Lesson 3

Aims: To transfer the "walls" situation to other areas with examples from the play, to create a scene with questions and answers to overcome prejudices, to build confidence in performing to the whole class.

Method: Larger group activity (6–7 students). Groups will work on suitable questions and answers for an interview with either character 1 or 2. The interview will then be presented to the whole class by two members of the group in the personae of an interviewer and either Marta or Livy answering the questions.

Task: First, the teacher should check the homework activity (continuation of the poem "*Mauern*"). Students should next read the profiles below of the two characters they will be working with. They should decide who is going to be the characters and then develop questions as a group to ask that person and find out the details. They should then present their interview to the class. Following this, they should watch the two scenes of the play (DVD: Chapters 7-9 or 23:40-53:00). The play is contained on the accompanying DVD materials. After watching the two scenes, the teacher should initiate a discussion about them.

Note: this lesson is a consolidation unit and no new vocabulary is presented here which students have not already come across before.

Task 1: Theaterstück Not Yet

Read the profiles below. Decide who is going to be the main character and who will be the interviewer. As a group, develop questions to ask your main character (either Marta or Livy) to find out more details. Present your interview to the class.

STECKBRIEF 1

Name: Marta

Wohnort: Burton Road, Immigranten-Wohnheim.

Eltern: Vater arbeitet in der Knoblauchbrotfabrik und nachts als Reinigungskraft, um genügend Geld für die Familie zu verdienen. Mutter gestorben.

Geschwister: Anna älter als Marta, arbeitet auch in der Knoblauchbrotfabrik, muss sich gegen den aufdringlichen Vorarbeiter wehren.

Eigenschaften: Gut in Mathe, intelligent, Probleme mit Englisch.

STECKBRIEF 2

Name: Livy

Wohnort: Wohnung in der Stadt, später Zimmer im Immigranten-Wohnheim, Burton Road.

Eltern: Mutter, keine Arbeit mehr, trinkt, hasst ihre Tochter, findet sie hässlich und nennt sie "Klugscheißer" (*Know-it-all*). Vater abgehauen, kein Kontakt mehr.

Geschwister: Keine.

Großeltern: Eine Großmutter, liegt im Sterben.

Eigenschaften: organisiert die Finanzen der Mutter, spart für Turnschuhe, interessiert sich für die Schule.

Now watch the two scenes of the play *Not Yet* and discuss them with your class and teacher.

Lesson 4

Task 1: Der Lebenslauf eines DDR-Bürgers

Aims: To famiarize students with the life of a GDR citizen until the age of 18.

Method: Asking for missing information (jigsaw reading).

Task: Students work in groups of two. They should exchange information by asking questions and writing the missing information in the first column of the table on the worksheets provided.

Timeline: Lebenslauf eines DDR-Bürgers

Das Leben eines DDR-Bürgers wurde vom Staat geregelt und verlief bei den meisten Menschen bis zum Alter von 18 Jahren mehr oder weniger gleich. Hier ist ein Zeitstrahl, der das Leben eines DDR-Bürgers bis zum 18. Lebensjahr im Überblick zeigt:

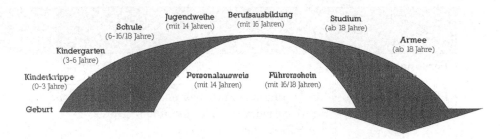

Task 1A

In der Tabelle fehlen einige Informationen. Frage deinen Partner danach und ergänze sie in der ersten Spalte in der Tabelle.

	DDR	England/ Dein Land
Kinderkrippe	In der DDR waren meist beide Elternteile berufstätig. Dadurch war ganztägige Betreuung der Kinder notwendig. Im Alter von 0–3 Jahren besuchten die Kinder die Kinderkrippe.	
Kindergarten		
Einschulung	Mit 6 oder 7 Jahren wurden die Kinder eingeschult. Zum Schulanfang bekam man eine Zuckertüte. Darin waren Süßigkeiten aber auch Schulmaterialien wie Hefte, Bleistifte, Radiergummi usw.	
Schule (POS und EOS)		
Pionier-organisation	Kinder bis 14 Jahre traten in der Regel den Jungpionieren (1.–3. Klasse) und den Thälmannpionieren (4.–7. Klasse) bei.	
FDJ		
Jugendweihe	Mit 14 Jahren wurde man in den Kreis der Erwachsenen aufgenommen. Dazu wurde eine feierliche Zeremonie veranstaltet, zu der die ganze Familie eingeladen war.	

	DDR	England/ Dein Land
Personal-ausweis		
Führerschein	Mit 16 Jahren konnte man den Führerschein für Motorräder machen und mit 18 Jahren den Führerschein für Autos.	
Ausbildung/ Studium		
Armee	Für die Männer bestand eine 18-monatige Wehrpflicht. Sie wurden zwischen dem 18. und dem 26. Lebensjahr in die NVA (Nationale Volksarmee) einberufen. Aber auch Frauen mussten während des Studiums Ausbildungslager für Zivilverteidigung (ZV) besuchen.	

Mögliche Fragen:

In welchem Alter gingen die Kinder in den Kindergarten?

Was heißt POS und EOS?

In welcher Organisation waren die Jugendlichen ab 14 Jahren?

Mit wie veil Jahren bekam man den Personalausweis?

Was konnte man nach der Schule machen?

Task 1B

In der Tabelle fehlen einige Informationen. Frage deinen Partner danach und ergänze sie in der ersten Spalte in der Tabelle.

	DDR	England/ Dein Land
Kinderkrippe		
Kindergarten	Daran schloss sich direkt der Kindergarten an (3–6 Jahre).	
Einschulung		
Schule (POS und EOS)	Von der 1. bis zur 10. Klasse besuchte man die so genannte POS (Polytechnische Oberschule). Danach konnte man bei entsprechenden Voraussetzungen für zwei Jahre die EOS (Erweiterte Oberschule) besuchen, die man mit dem Abitur abschloss.	

	DDR	England/ Dein Land
Pionier-organisation		
FDJ	Die Freie Deutsche Jugend war eine Organisation für die Jugendlichen ab 14 Jahren.	
Jugendweihe		
Personal–ausweis	Mit 14 Jahren bekam man auch den Personalausweis.	
Führerschein		
Ausbildung/ Studium	Nach der Schule konnte man entweder eine Berufsausbildung (mit 16 Jahren) machen oder studieren (mit 18 Jahren).	
Armee		

Mögliche Fragen:

Warum und in welchem Alter werden die Kinder in die Kinderkrippe geschickt?

Wann wurde man eingeschult?

Was war in der Zuckertüte?

In welcher Organisation waren die Kinder bis 14 Jahre?

Wann machte man den Führerschein?

Was ist die Jugendweihe?

War die Armee nur für Männer?

Task 2: Vokabeln

Aims: to review vocabulary introduced in Task 1.

Method: translation of words into English.

Task: students should translate the words into English with the help of the information provided.

Was bedeuten die folgenden Wörter? Übersetze die Wörter ins Englische mit Hilfe der Informationen in der Tabelle.

der Personalausweis =

der Führerschein =

die Wehrpflicht =

die Zivilverteidigung =

die Kinderkrippe =

die Einschulung =

die Zuckertüte =

die Jugendweihe =

Answers

die Kinderkrippe   Institution zur Betreuung von Babys und kleinen Kindern berufstätiger Eltern

die Einschulung   der erste Tag an der Schule nach dem Kindergarten

die Zuckertüte   Pappbehälter mit Bonbons, Schokolade und Schulmaterialien, den Kinder in Deutschland zum Schulanfang bekommen

die Jugendweihe   Zeremonie zur Aufnahme 14-jähriger Jugendlicher in den Kreis der Erwachsenen

der Personalausweis   offizielles Dokument zur Personenidentifizierung mit Foto und Unterschrift des Inhabers

der Führerschein   Erlaubnis zum Auto- oder Motorradfahren nach bestandener Fahrschulprüfung

die Wehrpflicht   Verpflichtung der Männer, für eine bestimmte Zeit nach der Schule zur Armee zu gehen

die Zivilverteidigung   militärisches Ausbildungsprogramm für Mädchen und Frauen

Task 3: Das Leben im ehemaligen Ostdeutschland und in England

Aim: To compare life in the GDR with life in England (up to the age of 18).

Method: Asking for information (see Task 1).

Task: What is life like for a young person in England? How different is it from the life of a person who grew up in the GDR? Students should talk to their partner and write down the information collected in the second column of the table on the worksheets used in Task 1. If the home country of the students is not England, they can talk about that country too.

Wie verläuft das Leben eines Kindes oder Jugendlichen normalerweise in England bzw. Deinem Heimatland? Sprich mit deinem Partner darüber und schreibe die Informationen in die zweite Spalte der Tabelle.

Hausaufgabe: writing a summary

Aim: to summarise the information gathered in class (comparision of life in the GDR to the life in England).

Method: summary-writing (about 150–200 words).

Task: based on the information in the table (Tasks 1 and 3), students should describe the life of someone up to the age of 18, of someone born in

England compared to someone born in the GDR. They should use phrases like *Im Vergleich zu...* (+ Dative) or *anders als in...* (+ Dative).

Beschreibe den Lebenslauf eines Engländers bis zum 18. Lebensjahr im Vergleich zu dem eines DDR-Bürgers (ca. 150–200 Wörter).

Wann werden die Kinder normalerweise eingeschult? Gibt es eine Zuckertüte? In welchem Alter macht man den Führerschein? usw. Verwende dabei Redewendungen wie *Im Vergleich zu...* (+ Dativ) oder *anders als in...* (+ Dativ).

Lesson 5

Task 1: Die Stasi

Aim:	To gain an overview about the institution, methods, people who worked for or were affected by the Stasi.
Method:	Mind map.
Tasks:	Ask students what they know already about the Stasi. They should work in small groups and create a mind map to organise the information. Having compared results, you could tell students about the film *Das Leben der Anderen* and play the trailer (http://www.kino.de/kinofilm/das-leben-der-anderen/trailer/64817.html) in class to prepare them for the subsequent tasks.

Was wisst ihr bereits über die Stasi? Wer oder was war das? Fertigt ein Mindmap an. Ein Film, der dieses Thema behandelt, ist *Das Leben der Anderen*. Darin geht es um einen Stasispitzel, der einen Schriftsteller und dessen Lebensgefährtin, eine Theaterschauspielerin, überwacht und nach anfänglicher Pflichterfüllung Sympathie für seine Opfer empfindet und sie sogar schützt.

Task 2: Die Stasi – Hintergrundinformationen

Aim:	To gain an overview about the institution, methods, people who worked for or were affected by the Stasi.
Method:	Gathering information and reading comprehension.
Task:	All students receive the worksheet below. The other pieces of information (numbered 1–5) should be displayed on separate tables in the classroom. Students go around the tables and gather as much information as possible from each table and write this down on their worksheet. This task could also be done as a group activity, with the students working in five groups and collating one piece of information per group. They then share what they have found out with the rest of the class, so that in the end everyone has the full picture.

Versuche, möglichst viele Informationen über die Staatssicherheit herauszufinden. Mache dir Stichpunkte zu den einzelnen Überschriften.

WORKSHEET

Ministerium für Staatssicherheit
Aufgaben
Mitarbeiter
Methoden und Folgen
BStU

Die Stasi – Hintergrundinformationen 1

Ministerium für Staatssicherheit

Das Ministerium für Staatssicherheit (MfS) wurde am 8.2.1950 gegründet und war Geheimpolizei und Nachrichtendienst der DDR sowie Ermittlungsbehörde für alle strafrechtlichen Untersuchungen, vor allem in politischen Strafsachen.

Obwohl das MfS ein Ministerium war, unterstand es nicht dem Vorsitzenden des Ministerrates, sondern ab 1960 dem Vorsitzenden des Nationalen Verteidigungsrates der DDR, der zugleich Generalsekretär der SED (Sozialistische Einheitspartei Deutschlands) war. Wichtige Angelegenheiten wurden in den 70er Jahren direkt zwischen dem SED-Generalsekretär (Erich Honecker) und dem Minister (Erich Mielke) besprochen.

Das Ministerium für Staatssicherheit war das wichtigste Instrument der SED-Führung, um ihre Diktatur abzusichern. Deshalb wurde es auch "Schild und Schwert der Partei" genannt.

Im Herbst 1989 zunächst wurde das MfS zunächst in "Amt für Nationale Sicherheit" (AfNS) umbenannt, welches jedoch Anfang 1990 im Zuge der politischen Umgestaltung Deutschlands aufgelöst wurde.

Vokabeln

die Geheimpolizei – secret police

der Nachrichtendienst – news service

die Ermittlungsbehörde – investigation agency

die strafrechtliche Untersuchung – criminal investigation

das Schild – shield

das Schwert – sword

die Umgestaltung – reorganisation

Die Stasi – Hintergrundinformationen 2

Aufgaben

In erster Linie sollte das MfS den Sozialismus schützen und die Sicherheit der DDR gewährleisten. Zu diesem Zweck arbeitete die Staatssicherheit eng mit der NVA (Nationalen Volksarmee), den Grenztruppen und der Volkspolizei zusammen. Das MfS war jedoch nicht nur ein militärisches Organ, sondern arbeitete auch als Inlands- und Auslandsnachrichtendienst. Schwerpunkt der DDR-externen Spionage in der Hauptverwaltung Aufklärung (HV A) war die Bespitzelung Westdeutschlands und West-Berlins. Das Hauptaugenmerk lag jedoch auf der politischen Überwachung der eigenen Bevölkerung. Neben Massenorganisationen, Betrieben, anderen Ministerien und den „bewaffneten Organen" (NVA, Grenztruppen und Volkspolizei) wurden auch Einzelpersonen kontrolliert und überwacht. Dies waren hauptsächlich Diplomaten, Journalisten, Künstler sowie Intellektuelle und Oppositionelle, so genannte „Dissidenten", aber auch ganz „normale" DDR-Bürger und ihre Angehörigen im Westen Deutschlands.

Vokabeln

gewährleisten – to ensure/guarantee

der Inlands- und Auslandsnachrichtendienst – national and international news service

der Schwerpunkt/das Hauptaugenmerk – main focus

die Bespitzelung/Überwachung – observation/supervision

der Betrieb – company/factory

bewaffnet - armed

der Dissident – *Andersdenkender, Regimekritiker,* 'someone who thinks outside the box'

die Angehörigen (pl.) – relatives

Die Stasi – Hintergrundinformationen 3

Mitarbeiter

Bei der Stasi gab es offizielle (hauptamtliche) und Inoffizielle Mitarbeiter (IM). Inoffizielle Mitarbeiter, so genannte Spitzel, wurden von hauptamtlichen Mitarbeitern angeleitet und arbeiteten für das MfS, ohne formell dieser Behörde anzugehören. Sie wurden nach sorgfältiger Auswahl angeworben, um aus ihrem beruflichen oder privaten Bereich Informationen zu liefern, die auf offiziellen Wegen nicht beschafft werden konnten.

Die Tätigkeit der inoffiziellen Mitarbeiter konnte so weit gehen, dass sich Kollegen und Nachbarn als "Freunde" ausgaben und sogar Ehen mit den zu überwachenden Personen eingegangen wurden.

Die Mehrzahl der inoffiziellen Mitarbeiter arbeitete freiwillig mit dem MfS zusammen, aber viele wurden auch zur Zusammenarbeit gezwungen und erpresst.

Ab Mitte der 70er Jahre kam im Durchschnitt ein IM auf 100 DDR-Bürger. Heute vermutet man, dass die MfS etwa 90 000 hauptamtliche Mitarbeiter hatte, zu denen noch etwa 175 000 inoffizielle Mitarbeiter kamen.

Vokabeln

hauptamtlich – full-time

sorgfältig – careful

anleiten – to instruct

anwerben – to recruit

beschaffen – to gather

freiwillig - voluntarily

zwingen – to force

erpressen – to blackmail

Die Stasi – Hintergrundinformationen 4

Methoden und Folgen

Das MfS war, obwohl es im Hintergrund arbeitete, den Menschen in der DDR allgegenwärtig. Jede Art von abweichendem Verhalten konnte dazu führen, dass man in die Fänge der Stasi geriet. Daraus resultierte eine permanente Verunsicherung darüber, was man sagen durfte und mit wem man vertraulich sprechen konnte.

Opfer des MfS waren DDR-Flüchtlinge, unbequeme SED-Mitglieder, Mitarbeiter westlicher Parteien auf dem Gebiet der DDR, Journalisten und westliche Agenten. Aber auch ganz normale Bürger wurden von der Stasi überwacht und verfolgt, wenn sie sich systemkritisch äußerten oder etwas taten, das als "staatsfeindlich" eingestuft wurde.

Neben der Überwachung ('Bespitzelung') waren auch Gewaltanwendung, Freiheitsberaubung, Unterdrückung und Einschüchterung gängige Methoden der Staatssicherheit. Bespitzelung hatte für die Opfer meist Behinderung der Karriere, Verlust der Arbeit oder Verhöre und Gefängnisstrafen zur Folge.

Berüchtigt sind die Gefängnisse, in denen politisch Verfolgte verschleppt, vernommen und körperlichen wie seelischen Misshandlungen ausgesetzt wurden. Zu den bekanntesten Haftanstalten zählt das Gefängnis in Berlin-Hohenschönhausen, das heute als Gedenkstätte dient.

Vokabeln

allgegenwärtig – omnipresent

das abweichende Verhalten – deviant behaviour

in die Fänge geraten – fall into someone's clutches

die Verunsicherung – uncertainty

vertraulich – confidential

überwachen – to observe

verfolgen – to persecute

staatsfeindlich – subversive

die Gewaltanwendung – use of force

die Freiheitsberaubung – false imprisonment

die Unterdrückung – oppression

die Einschüchterung – intimidation

die Behinderung – obstruction

der Verlust – loss

das Verhör – interrogation

berüchtigt – notorious

verschleppen – to take someone away

vernehmen – to question so.

die Misshandlung – mistreatment

die Gedenkstätte – memorial site

Die Stasi – Hintergrundinformationen 5

Der Bundesbeauftragte für die Unterlagen des Staatssicherheitsdienstes der ehemaligen Deutschen Demokratischen Republik (BStU)

Die Bundesbehörde der BStU wurde am 3. Oktober 1990 im Zuge des Einigungsvertrags gegründet. Zu deren ersten Leiter wurde 1990 Joachim Gauck gewählt. Von Oktober 2000 bis März 2011 leitete Marianne Birthler die Behörde. Ihr derzeitiger Leiter ist der Journalist Roland Jahn.

Die BStU bewahrt in ihren Archiven die Unterlagen der ehemaligen Geheimpolizei und des Nachrichtendienstes der DDR auf und stellt sie Behörden, Unternehmen, Vereinen und Verbänden, Wissenschaftlern und Journalisten zur Verfügung. Aber auch Einzelpersonen können auf Antrag die Unterlagen zu ihrer Person einsehen.

Das umfangreiche Archiv enthält neben den Akten auch Karteikarten, Filme, Tondokumente und Mikrofiches.

Die BStU hat die Aufgabe, die Tätigkeit des Ministeriums für Staatssicherheit aufzuarbeiten und die Öffentlichkeit über die Struktur, Methoden und Wirkungsweise des MfS zu informieren.

Vokabeln

die Unterlagen (pl.) – documents

die Bundesbehörde – federal agency

die Geheimpolizei – secret police

der Nachrichtendienst – news service

das Unternehmen – company/enterprise

der Verein / Verband – association

zur Verfügung stellen – to make something available

einen Antrag stellen – to lodge an application

umfangreich – comprehensive

die Karteikarte – file card

etwas aufarbeiten – to come to terms with something

Task 3: Substantive und Verben

Aim: to learn about the nominalisation of verbs and verbalisation of nouns with the ending *-ung* and to gain the insight that all nouns with the ending *-ung* are feminine in German

Method: grammar exercise.

Task: students should revisit all texts in the previous task (5 sheets) and write down all the nouns ending in *-ung*. Students should then try to write down the corresponding verb. Equally they should find verbs in the texts and build nouns with the ending *-ung*. Having done that, compare results as a class.

Suche auf den Informationsblättern zur Stasi alle Verben und alle Substantive heraus, die auf *-ung* enden. Schreibe dann das jeweils zugehörige Verb oder Substantiv mit Artikel daneben.

Sustantive auf -ung	dazugehöriges Verb
z.B. die Umgestaltung	*umgestalten*
Verben	**dazugehöriges Substantiv**
z.B. erpressen	*die Erpressung*

Was fällt dir bei den Substantiven auf?

Answers

Nominalisation of verbs and verbalisation of nouns with the ending *-ung*:

Sustantive auf -ung	dazugehöriges Verb
z.B. die Umgestaltung	*umgestalten*
die Ermittlung	ermitteln
die Untersuchung	untersuchen
die Umgestaltung	umgestalten
die Verunsicherung	verunsichern
die Unterdrückung	unterdrücken
die Gewaltanwendung	Gewalt anwenden
die Freiheitsberaubung	jemanden der Freiheit berauben
die Einschüchterung	einschüchtern
die Behinderung	behindern
die Misshandlung	misshandeln
die Verfügung	verfügen über (+Akk)

Verben	dazugehöriges Substantiv
z.B. erpressen	*die Erpressung*
anleiten	die Anleitung
anwerben	die (An)Werbung
beschaffen	die Beschaffung
erpressen	die Erpressung
überwachen	die Überwachung
verfolgen	die Verfolgung
vernehmen	die Vernehmung
aufarbeiten	die Aufarbeitung
verschleppen	die Verschleppung
gewährleisten	die Gewährleistung
bewaffnen	die Bewaffnung

Some of the verbs and nouns in the tables can be found in the vocabulary lists on worksheets 1–5. In the texts themselves are also the following nouns and verbs: *die Aufklärung, die Bespitzelung, die Überwachung, die Bevölkerung, auflösen, gründen, liefern, äußern, aufbewahren*, which can be added to the tables.

All nouns with the ending *-ung* are feminine in German.

Lesson 6: Not Yet

Drama & Citizenship Materials

Exploring the issues

Why should young people in Britain learn about the Berlin wall?

Sarah-Jane Dickenson's play *Not Yet* explores how people put up barriers when they feel vulnerable or threatened.

Here are some Drama exercises you can do with your students to deepen their understanding of the issues surrounding the fall of the Berlin wall and how they might have relevance for young people today. The main material source is *Not Yet* on the accompanying DVD, but some research will have to be done by both teacher and students.

Why use Drama?

Drama is an interactive resource which taps into people's natural learning patterns. Using drama allows students to engage with the topics from a more personal perspective whilst enabling them to put the experience into a wider social or political context. Some of the exercises in the materials allow for the teacher to work as Teacher in Role (TiR).

Teacher in Role (TiR)

After the whole group has watched a scene from the play, the teacher takes the role of a particular character and allows the group to question her (or him) about the character and the situation.

Why use Teacher in Role

Teacher in Role allows the exploration of the motives and implications of a character's behaviour and enables the teacher to engage the students in learning, on a variety of different levels. TiR does not mean that the teacher has to be a good actor. It demands a certain level of improvisation, as there is no fixed script but it is helpful to remember that the role is providing an attitude or a point of view as well as providing information for the students to draw on. It is about reading a situation, drawing on relevant material either from previous experience or research, and presenting the information in such a way that understanding becomes possible. The focus in Teacher in Role is not on acting but to what the role represents. You can step in and out of TiR just by saying something as simple as, "Right, we'll stop the Drama there". At that point, the teacher encourages the students to reflect on what has just occurred and explain their thinking. Then the role can be picked up again quite simply with "OK, we'll start the Drama again now".

In this case the focus is on two scenes in the play:

The scene with Marta, Anna & their father (Chapter 7; 23:40)

The scene with Livy and her mother (Chapter 8; 35:50)

The students will need to watch the *Not Yet* scene on the accompanying DVD.

Pretask

The teacher will have to research or consider the following points.

Economic migrants – To be familiar with the Economic Migrant experience in Britain. For example: what countries in Europe are members of the EU? How does a country's membership affect the employment rights of economic migrants? What are the rights to work of migrants coming from outside the EU?

Young Carers – What is the young carer's experience in Britain, for example, at what age can a young person live on their own? What help is available to young carers from the council or government? How can that help be obtained?

What the teacher wants the students to get out of the scene/s in terms of:

- Personal and social awareness
- Vocabulary and language constructs

Main Task 1: Broader perspectives – Understanding barriers

Aim: To create awareness of how people create and cling to social and personal barriers.

Method: Having watched the scene, students work in groups to ensure a shared understanding of: what is happening; specific vocabulary; the perspectives of individual characters.

Task: Each group has the opportunity to ask the teacher for clarification on factual information and to look up vocabulary. The group will then focus on one of the characters and prepare a number of questions that they would like to ask the character. For example, they could ask about: their fears; their hopes, their attitude to the other person/people in the scene; what they think of their own behaviour in the scene.

Main Task 2

Aim: As Main Task 1 and speaking practice.

Method: The teacher goes into role as one of the characters and allows each group to ask one (or more) question in turn. The teacher answers the question from the perspective of the character based on what is said/implied in the text and mode of enactment, for example, the body language of the character. The teacher talks in the first person and does not explain the character as separate from her/himself. The transition from one question to another can be done in or out of role. For example, out of role: "OK, that's dealt with. Now, next group, what do you want to ask?" Or, in role: "I've answered that one/that's enough on that one/I'm bored with that – what (*pointing*) did you want to ask?"

- The TiR can decide whether they will allow interruptions or supplementary questions depending on the relevance of what is being talked about and whether they want to deepen the discussion at that point.
- The TiR can direct the conversation through her/his responses, leading the conversation in whatever direction they feel is most fruitful.
- The TiR must make it clear when they are *in* role and when they are *out* of role. Time out can be taken to clarify vocabulary and meaning at any point as long as it is indicated. Equally time out of role can be taken to discuss the character in general. The process can be repeated for each character if the teacher thinks that is useful.

Main Task 3

Aim: To deepen theoretical understanding of representation and action.

Method: After a general discussion about the characters in the scene and their situation, the students go back into small groups and create some kind of visual representation of:

- the situation the family are in;

- the way they relate to each other;
- the conflict between them;
- the way society perceives them – and
- the way they perceive society.

This involves the barriers that society puts up to them that are not helpful and the barriers they put up for themselves. They should also consider what help might be available to the family.

Visual Representation

This can take a variety of forms. Groups might work on:

- a spider diagram which represents the family and their situation;
- a table which sets out relationships, feelings and action;
- a comic strip which reflects the situation the family are in.

Or, if they are comfortable with Drama:

- a series of "still images" which illustrate the situation;
- a "sound collage" of the feelings which effect the characters (see Explanation of Drama Terms below).

Homework

Each student will write a letter to one of the characters offering advice on how to handle their situation. The advice should consider the legal and social help that might be available to them.

Explanation of Drama Terms

1.   Still images

A 'still image' is when a group of people create a physical picture which crystallises a situation for those watching. For example, a basic 'still image' representing Livy and her mother might be of one person representing the mother with a drink in her hand looking threateningly at Livy, who has turned away in a position which suggests she is protecting herself.

Another image of the two might represent the mother hugging Livy and Livy looking frightened.

A later image might be of the mother lying drunk in the corner and Livy on the telephone asking for help, or someone helping Livy out of the house.

Words can be added: a phrase from each person in the image, for each image, reflecting their feelings at that point. The images can then be linked by moving from one to another, repeating the phrases for each one.

2.   Sound collage

A 'sound collage' involves each member of the small group thinking of a list of words which describes the feelings of a particular character, preferably an equal number of people for each character. The group then repeats a selection of the words and phrases which represent that person. Each individual repeats their two or three phrases as the others repeat theirs. They can vary pace, volume and levels of intensity. The group perform the sound collage in a line, although they do not have to speak one at a time, and pick up rhythms from each other. This is particularly effective if one member of the group orchestrates by indicating volume, pace and intensity. Please note: This can be noisy, but it is very powerful as a representation of confusion and intensity.

Although the Drama exercises may seem challenging, they are very effective at allowing the students to experience something of the challenging situation, in a safe environment. This deepens reflection.

Not Yet (Ein Theaterstück von Sarah-Jane Dickenson)

Not Yet is a play by the British playwright Sarah-Jane Dickenson and was part of a European-wide drama project commemorating the fall of the Berlin wall in 1989. The piece is about a group of unmotivated pupils who are taught about the fall of the wall by their German assistant teacher, Sigrid Heilmann. But their true learning begins only when they discover the walls that they have built around themselves and others.

In the scene presented here we learn that Sigrid's father, a lawyer, has worked for the Stasi. Sigrid found out about this when she read the Stasi files about her family. The scene gives an insight into the interrogation methods of the Stasi in the former prison Berlin-Hohenschönhausen, but it also gives the opportunity to discuss the process of coming to terms with the past – our own and that of the GDR.

Pretask

Scene from *Not Yet* presented as a reading comprehension (the transcript is contained in the accompanying DVD) to be read for homework. Alternatively, this scene could be watched on the DVD (Chapter 12: 1 hour and 20 minutes) in class and/or be played out by the students in class as a preparation for answering questions 1–6 and discussion about question 7.

Aim: to prepare for the next lesson where the full playscript is introduced and to learn about the methods of the Stasi.

Task

Students should read the scene of the play (the transcript is contained in the accompanying DVD) at home and answer the following questions:

1. Who are the three main characters in this scene?
2. In which situation are they? What are they doing? When and where does the scene take place?
3. What is the defendant accused of? Which 'crime' did he commit?
4. What is the verdict?
5. How did they get to this conclusion?
6. Who is the father of Sigrid? What has he done?
7. Can you understand his arguments? (This question should be discussed in class in groups of three).

Not Yet (Ein Theaterstück von Sarah-Jane Dickenson)

Not Yet ist ein Stück von der britischen Autorin Sarah-Jane Dickenson und Teil eines europaweiten Dramaprojektes, das an den Fall der Berliner Mauer im Jahr 1989 erinnert. Darin geht es um eine Gruppe von unmotivierten Schülern, die von einer deutschen Aushilfslehrerin unterrichtet werden. Auf dem Lehrplan steht der Fall der Berliner Mauer, aber das eigentliche Lernen beginnt erst, als die Schüler die Mauern entdecken, die sie um sich selbst und andere aufgebaut haben.

Lies die Szene aus dem Theaterstück und beantworte folgende Fragen:

1. Wer sind die drei Hauptpersonen in dieser Szene?
2. In welcher Situation befinden sie sich? Was machen sie? Wann und wo spielt die Szene?
3. Was wird dem Angeklagten zur Last gelegt? Welches 'Verbrechen' hat er begangen?
4. Wie lautet das Urteil?
5. Wie kommen sie zu diesem Urteil?
6. Wer ist der Vater von Sigrid? Was hat er gemacht?
7. Kannst du siene Argumentation verstehen?

Lesson 7

Task 1: Fluchtversuche – Facts & Figures

Aim: To familiarise students with historical facts about the Berlin Wall.

Method: Discussing plausible answers with partner.

Task: Teacher hands out worksheet below. On this sheet there are twelve questions, and for each question two possible answers. Go through the list to ensure students have understood the questions. After that, students work in pairs and discuss what could be the correct answer. Finally the teacher goes through the list again to ensure that everyone has answered correctly.

Diskutiere mit deinem Partner, was die richtige Antwort zu den Fragen sein könnte.

Wie viele Menschen sind nach dem 2. Weltkrieg bis zum Bau der Mauer über die Grenze geflohen?	etwa 1,5 Millionen Menschen	etwa 2,6 Millionen Menschen
Wie viele Menschen lebten nach dem 2. Weltkrieg in der sowjetischen Besatzungszone (später DDR)?	knapp 19 Millionen Menschen	knapp 40 Millionen Menschen
Wann wurde die DDR gegründet?	7. Oktober 1949	7. Oktober 1953
Wann genau wurde die Mauer gebaut?	13. August 1961	13. August 1969
Wie lange stand die Mauer?	20 Jahre (von 1969–1989)	28 Jahre (von 1961–1989)

Wie vielen Personen gelang die Flucht über die Berliner Mauer?	über 5 000 Menschen	über 10 000 Menschen
Wie wurden Menschen in der DDR genannt, die in den Westen flohen?	Republik-flüchtlinge (pl.)	Landflüchtlinge (pl.)
Wie viele Menschen starben bei dem Versuch, die Mauer zu überwinden?	zwischen 25 und 106 Personen	zwischen 125 und 206 Personen
Wie viele Hundelaufanlagen gab es entlang der Mauer?	259	476
Wie hoch war die Mauer?	3,60m	2,40m
Wie viel wog ein Mauersegment?	2,6t	1,5t
Wie lang war die Mauer um Westberlin?	155 Kilometer lang	250 Kilometer lang

Answers

Wie viele Menschen sind nach dem 2. Weltkrieg bis zum Bau der Mauer über die Grenze geflohen?	etwa 1,5 Millionen Menschen	**etwa 2,6 Millionen Menschen**
Wie viele Menschen lebten nach dem 2. Weltkrieg in der sowjetischen Besatzungszone (später DDR)?	**knapp 19 Millionen Menschen**	knapp 40 Millionen Menschen
Wann wurde die DDR gegründet?	**7. Oktober 1949**	7. Oktober 1953
Wann genau wurde die Mauer gebaut?	**13. August 1961**	13. August 1969
Wie lange stand die Mauer?	20 Jahre (von 1969–1989)	**28 Jahre (von 1961–1989)**
Wie vielen Personen gelang die Flucht über die Berliner Mauer?	**über 5 000 Menschen**	über 10 000 Menschen
Wie wurden Menschen in der DDR genannt, die in den Westen flohen?	**Republik-flüchtlinge (pl.)**	Landflüchtlinge (pl.)
Wie viele Menschen starben bei dem Versuch, die Mauer zu überwinden?	zwischen 25 und 106 Personen	**zwischen 125 und 206 Personen**
Wie viele Hundelaufanlagen gab es entlang der Mauer?	**259**	476

Wie hoch war die Mauer?	**3,60m**	2,40m
Wie viel wog ein Mauersegment?	**2,6t**	1,5t
Wie lang war die Mauer um Westberlin?	**155 Kilometer lang**	250 Kilometer lang

Task 2: Welche Fluchtarten gab es?

Aim: To learn about how people from the former GDR tried to escape to the West. To build up vocabulary (useful word partnerships). In terms of grammar, to use prepositions, cases and infinitive clauses correctly.

Method: Matching cards and writing short sentences, e.g. *Man versuchte, einen Tunnel zu bauen.*

Task: Students get different coloured cards and in groups of three they have about 5–10 minutes to build as many sentences as possible starting with "Man versuchte, ...zu... ." Students write down their sentences on the worksheet. After that, the groups count their sentences (for each sentence they get a point). Each group reads their sentences aloud while the rest of the students listen and check if the grammar is correct. If a sentence is not 100% correct the group loses 1 point.

Material: Use the words below to create cards (nouns, verbs, prepositions, articles). You need to photocopy the page on differently-coloured paper and cut out the cards for each group.

Reflexiv-pronomen	Prä-positionen	Substantive	Verben
		Tunnel (der)	graben
	über	Mauer (die)	klettern
		Stacheldraht (der)	zerschneiden
	aus	Fenster (das)	springen
		Heissluftballon (der)	bauen
	durch	Fluss (der) (die Spree)	schwimmen
	mit	Pass (der) (gefälscht)	
		Grenze (die)	passieren
		Kleinkind (das)	
	in	Handwagen (der)	verstecken
		Auto (das)	umbauen
		Beifahrersitz (der)	aushöhlen
sich	von	Fenster (das)	abseilen
sich	in	Koffer (der)	verstecken
sich	unter	Motorhaube (die)	verstecken

Welche Möglichkeiten gab es, um heimlich in den Westen zu gelangen? Suche in einer 3er Gruppe möglichst viele Nomen mit dem dazugehörigen Verb und schreibe kurze, sinnvolle Sätze.

ACHTUNG: Manche Verben sind reflexiv und/oder trennbar! Zum Beispiel:

1. Man versuchte, sich im Koffer zu verstecken (reflexives Verb).

2. Man versuchte, ein Auto umzubauen (trennbares Verb).

Task 3: Die Geschichte eines gelungenen Fluchtversuchs

Aim: To give students an example of an authentic escape story which was successful.

Method: Reading activity and putting pieces of a story together in the correct order in groups of three or four.

Task: Students get nine pieces of a story (the sections need to be cut along the lines) of how a woman managed to escape to the West. The order is compared after they have finished the task and the story is read aloud in the classroom.

Aufgabe: Versuche die Teile der Fluchtgeschichte[2] mit deinen KollegInnen in die richtige Reihenfolge zu bringen.

Mit Hilfe eines Seehundes in die Freiheit

Am 19. November 1963 flüchtete Frau Vera Breitwieser aus Pankow, Ost–Berlin, über den S-Bahnhof Friedrichstraße nach West-Berlin. Den Schweizer Pass hatte ihr eine studentische Fluchthelfer-Gruppe der Freien Universität Berlin besorgt.

"Also, erst einmal musste ich meine Personalien lernen. Ich hieß also Sigrid Nüsch, geboren in Basel, wohnhaft in Liestal, in meinem Pass waren auch noch zwei Kinder eingetragen. Da musste ich also die Namen und Geburtsdaten von ihnen lernen. Dann hat der Fluchthelfer meine Tasche gepackt und hat alles rausgeschmissen, was ein bisschen östlich aussah. Er sagte zu mir: 'Sie dürfen kein Stück östliche Qualität an sich haben. Das geht bis zur Unterwäsche, Ihre Schuhe … . Alles muss westlich sein.'"

Während der Flucht trug Frau Breitwieser eine Seehundkappe und einen Seehundkragen, der auf ihrem Mantel war. Diese Sorte von Pelz war in DDR-Geschäften nicht erhältlich.

Bange Minuten hatte sie während der Grenzkontrolle zu überstehen. Hier war es zunächst der Foto-Vergleich, den in dem Pass war das Foto der Schweizerin. Auch hier war die Anweisung des Fluchthelfers "schminken, lächeln, Gesicht verziehen" hilfreich. Das Problem kam danach. Ein Grenzpolizist verschwand mit dem Pass, um ihn auf seine Echtheit zu überprüfen. "Da hatte ich keine Sorge. Der Pass war echt, nur ich war es nicht."

Verunsichert wurde Frau Breitwieser durch eine Grenzpolizistin, die sie die ganze Zeit unentwegt ansah, bis sie feststellte, dass die Aufmerksamkeit nicht ihr, sondern ihrer Kleidung galt. "Plötzlich merkte ich, dass die mich so ansah, als ob sie sagen wollte: 'Du arrogante Schweizer Ziege, du willst wohl was Besseres sein.'"

---

2 The story used for this exercise is a true story, and we would like to thank the "Mauermuseum – Museum Haus am Checkpoint Charlie" in Berlin for letting us use it for educational purposes.

"Ich habe mich also etwas gestrafft, habe versucht, einen etwas arroganten Gesichtsausdruck anzunehmen. Und diese Art, wie sie mich und meine Seehundkappe ansah, das hat mich meines Erachtens gerettet. Vor Fragen .... Die große Gefahr war ja, dass sie mich etwas fragt und ich kein Wort Schweizerisch konnte! Dann war es eine Frage von Sekunden, als der andere Grenzpolizist auf mich zukam, mir den Pass zurückgab und kurz 'Danke' sagte. Ich bekam eine Handbewegung und konnte gehen."

Frau Breitwieser war frei. Am Bahnhof-Zoo angekommen, konnte sie sofort zu ihrem West-Berliner Verlobten fahren.

Umso größer war ihr Schreck, als nur 10 Tage später eine Frau ebenfalls mit Schweizer Pass im Bahnhof Friedrichstraße festgenommen wurde. Die 'Passmethode' der Studenten war schon im November 1961 von einem Spitzel verraten worden. Ein Prozess fand deswegen schon in Ost-Berlin statt. Frau Breitwieser war vermutlich die Letzte, der noch die Flucht mit dem Schweizer Pass gelang. Im Januar 1962 gaben die Studenten diese gerade erst begonnene Methode auf.

Lesson 7: Homework

Students could write a story about a successful or unsuccessful attempt to escape from the GDR to the West (about 300 words). Students can choose the type of text (internal monologue, narrative or newspaper article). The photographs in the picture gallery on the accompanying DVD may also inspire the stories.

Die Mauer: Accompanying DVD materials

1. Two photographs to accompany Lesson 1, task 1
2. *Interview penpals* audio file
3. Transcription of *Interview penpals*
4. Vocabulary Lists: Lessons 1–7
5. Film of *Not Yet*
6. Scene from *Not Yet*
7. Photo gallery of different ways of escaping from East Berlin.
8. List of useful websites

6

Content and Language Integrated Learning (CLIL)

Introduction: What is CLIL?

CLIL is a modern term for an old method which is known by numerous different names, such as immersion (*Språkbad*, Sweden), multilingual education (Latvia) or integrated curriculum (Spain). For Do Coyle, one of the pre-eminent authorities on CLIL in the UK context,

> Content and Language Integrated Learning (CLIL) is a dual-focused, educational approach in which an **additional language** is used for the learning and teaching of both content *and* language. That is, in the teaching and learning process, there is a focus not only on content, and not only on language. Each is interwoven, even if the emphasis is greater on one or the other at a given time.
>
> (Coyle *et al.* 2010: 1)

CLIL is a relatively new method in UK language teaching. A small but dedicated number of secondary schools influenced by the Canadian immersion movement introduced major European languages, such as French, German and Spanish, as the medium of instruction from the 1970s and 1980s onwards. The number of schools, both primary and secondary, offering bilingual instruction in some core subjects, such as History and Geography, increased in the 1990s, and especially since the turn of the millennium (see Coyle *et al.* 2009, Coyle *et al.* 2010 for case studies and information on how to set up CLIL).

CLIL can help stimulate a real interest in language learning because of its focus on using language for a purpose and on authentic, real-life topics. The approach fosters independent learning, develops skills across a range of subjects and enriches the curriculum by focusing on four important dimensions – the four Cs: content, cognition, communication, culture. There are a number of clear benefits of CLIL. It is different from traditional learning; it is time-efficient, because both subject content and language are learned together; it can foster communication and intercultural understanding and development; it refreshes classroom practice and provides teachers with the opportunity to be creative in interpreting the curriculum (see Coyle *et al.*, 2009).

Key characteristics, such as choosing appropriate content and fostering cultural understanding, can support curriculum designers and teachers in developing CLIL in their school contexts (Coyle *et al.*, 2009: 14–15). CLIL can be implemented in various ways, depending on the context of a specific school and the requirements of the curriculum. CLIL can comprise anything from a sequence of two to three lessons to more sustained modules over a term or school year. Finding the balance between content and language, and defining appropriate outcomes for both subject and language development, is a key factor in successful CLIL implementation.

This chapter presents four projects, all of which weave a specific language into a particular educational context. The first two – designed to support teachers wishing to take their first steps with CLIL – mirror each other, with one exploring the continent of Antarctica in French and the second doing the same in Spanish. The focus is on European Geography in the third project, which introduces Austria and Switzerland in German. The final project is also in German, which it combines with domestic science. There are additional materials for this latter project in French on the accompanying DVD.

Project 1   Taking steps towards CLIL (exploring Antarctica in French)

links into
LANGUAGES

Project outline

Requirements: a normal school classroom with PowerPoint facilities.
Event time: approximately 45 minutes – i.e., one lesson.
Languages targeted: French
Impact: medium (30+ pupils)

Introduction

This project in its initial stages sought to introduce a new model of collaboration in CLIL by bringing together:

■ 'novice' teachers who wish to introduce CLIL into their classrooms;
■ 'expert' practitioners of CLIL to act as a model;
■ native speaker teachers of the target language from Aston University to offer support with language and materials. Initially the project was led by staff from Aston University who worked with the novice teachers and native speakers to achieve the following aims.

For learners
The long-term aims were to:

■ make the learning of languages motivating and relevant;
■ give opportunities to use languages in a meaningful way right from the start;

- encourage learners to make connections across subject areas;
- become more independent.

For teachers

Through introducing CLIL into their classrooms teachers can:

- discover innovative and exciting ways of developing pedagogic practice, contributing to their Continuing Professional Development;
- develop teamwork and collaboration across subject areas;
- develop the new curriculum (see the Preface to this book) in line with the needs of their learners.

For schools/colleges

- The introduction of CLIL in schools can:
- provide team-working opportunities for teachers in order to promote CPD;
- develop innovative opportunities for curriculum delivery;
- increase the number of pupils taking languages.

Taking steps towards CLIL was thus designed to meet several needs. It is simple but nevertheless effective and introduces the notion of CLIL in a gentle but motivating way to both teachers and learners. Language learning is embedded in the exploration of the continent Antarctica, and the project presented here in both French (Project One) and Spanish (Project Two) is designed to cover one lesson of 45 minutes. Suggestions for homework possibilities are also included. *Taking steps towards CLIL* was developed under the LINKS into Languages national initiative (see useful websites on the accompanying DVD for further details).

The activities presented are designed to stimulate an interest in the topic of Antarctica as well as present language items. The materials are presented in five main sections: vocabulary; geography; images of Antarctica; landscape and the environment; follow-on. Students can be encouraged to write up a small project on the topic in the target language with appropriate images (these can be found easily on Google images) after the lesson for homework.

Accompanying DVD materials include a list of useful websites which are relevant to the project, whilst excerpts from the film *The March of the Penguins* in the target language support the whole beautifully.

Section 1: Vocabulaire!

Make a glossary to use during the lesson by matching up the words. Copy the English words next to the correct French one. Three are done for you.

antarctique	....	penguins
arctique	....	sun
neige	**snow**	ice
baleine	....	polar

glace	....	mountain
manchots	**penguins**	north
continent	....	fish
polaire	....	antarctic
soleil	....	birds
nuit	....	**snow**
montagne	....	night
nord	....	temperatures
phoque	....	**summer**
sud	....	whale
oiseaux	....	winter
poissons	....	continent
températures	....	seal
hiver	....	arctic
eté	**summer**	south

Answers

antarctique *antarctic*	arctique *arctic*	neige *snow*	glace *ice*
manchots *penguins*	continent *continent*	polaire *polar*	soleil *sun*
nuit *night*	montagne *mountain*	nord *north*	sud *south*
oiseaux *birds*	poissons *fish*	phoque *seal*	températures *temperatures*
hiver *winter*	été *summer*	baleine *whale*	

Section 2: Notre monde

Aim: for students to learn the names of the seven continents in French and to present the seven continents, and in particular the continent of Antarctica, visually.

Ask: *Il y a combien de continents dans le monde? Nommez les 7 continents!*
Voici une carte de notre monde avec les continents.

Conceal the name of one continent and ask students if they can say its name in French.

Ask: *Quel continent manque?* Then do the same with the remaining six continents.

Section 3: Explorez!

Aim: to introduce the continent of Antarctica in a visual way and to revise key vocabulary presented in section 1.

Say: *On va faire un voyage …*

… quel continent est-ce qu'on va visiter? Regardez les images

Section 4: Le paysage Antarctique

Aim: to discover some key facts about Antarctica and its environment.

1. Voici l'Antarctique/Le pôle sud

    Les montagnes sont couvertes de neige et glace.
    Les températures sont toujours négatives.
    La température moyenne est de -57 degrés.

    En été L'Antarctique a 24 heures de soleil.
    En hiver L'Antarctique a 24 heures de nuit.

2. Voici les icebergs

    La glace flotte dans la mer. 90% de la glace du monde est située en Antarctique.
    La majorité d'un iceberg est sous l'eau.

3. Voici des animaux de l'Antarctique

    Des baleines et des phoques habitent en Antarctique.

4. Voici les pingouins (les manchots). Ils habitent aussi en Antarctique.

> *Il n'y a pas des pingouins au pôle nord!*
>
> *Les parents pingouins mangent le poisson*
> *et puis ils le donnent à leurs bébés.*
>
> *Des manchots et des empereurs habitent en Antarctique.*

5. Les gens

> *Roald Amundsen a été le premier homme à arriver au pôle Sud.*
>
> *Il faut porter les vêtements thermiques à cause du froid!*

Section 5: Follow-on

Students may wish to write a short project using the language and information learned in this session. Alternatively they could design a poster in groups (*Un poster de l'Antarctique*), which they illustrate themselves or with downloaded images. The task and the worksheet that follow are designed to help students organise their thoughts in French based on the lesson they have just received, by recapping the language and facts they have learnt.

Activité 1

Les sept continents

Which of the following are continents? Circle the correct ones.			
La France	*L'Asie*	*L'Angleterre*	*L'Europe*
L'Afrique	*Le pôle Nord*	*Le Canada*	*L'Antarctique*
La Chine	*L'Amérique du Sud*	*L'Inde*	*L'Australasie*
L'Amérique du Nord			

Answers

> *L'Asie, L'Europe, L'Afrique, L'Antarctique, L'Amérique du Sud, L'Amérique du Nord et L'Australasie sont des continents. Il y en a sept dans notre monde.*

Activité 2

Which of these is NOT true about *l'Antarctique?*

- *Le pôle Sud est la région la plus froide de notre planète*
- *Des lions habitent en Antarctique*
- *Les températures sont toujours négatives*
- *Les températures sont toujours positives*
- *L'Antarctique est petite comme l'Angleterre*
- *Le continent de L'Antarctique est grand comme l'Amérique du Nord et l'Europe réunis*
- *Des pingouins habitent au pôle Sud*
- *Il y a 24 heures du soleil en été et 24 heures de nuit en hiver*

Answers

These sentences are NOT true:

- *Des lions habitent en Antarctique*
- *Les températures sont toujours positives*
- *L'Antarctique est petite comme l'Angleterre*

Activité 3

Choose five Antarctic facts that you have learnt this lesson and make an illustrated poster together about *l'Antarctique.*

Here are the facts that have been presented during this session.

1. *Les montagnes sont couvertes de neige et de glace.*
2. *Les températures sont toujours négatives.*
3. *La température moyenne est de −57 degrés.*
4. *En été l'Antarctique a 24 heures de soleil.*
5. *En hiver l'Antarctique a 24 heures de nuit.*
6. *Des baleines et des phoques habitent en Antarctique.*
7. *Il n'y a pas des pingouins au pôle Nord!*
8. *Les parents pingouins mangent le poisson et puis ils le donnent à leurs bébés.*
9. *Des manchots et des empereurs habitent en Antarctique.*
10. *Roald Amundsen a été le premier homme à arriver au pôle Sud.*
11. *Il faut porter les vêtements thermiques à cause du froid!*
12. *L'Antarctique est située au pôle Sud.*
13. *La glace flotte dans la mer.*
14. *90% de la glace du monde est située en Antarctique.*
15. *La majorité d'un iceberg est sous l'eau.*

Steps towards CLIL (Exploring Antarctica in French): additional DVD materials

1. Useful websites

Project 2   Taking steps towards CLIL (exploring Antarctica in Spanish)

links into
LANGUAGES

Project outline

Requirements: a normal school classroom with PowerPoint facilities.
Event time: approximately 45 minutes ie one lesson.
Languages targeted: Spanish
Impact: medium (30+ pupils)

Introduction

This project is presented in Spanish and has the same rationale, source and aims as Project One. To avoid repetition, the Spanish exploration of Antarctica starts straight away, but before you use it in class, we recommend that you read the introduction to Project One to 'set the scene' in your mind.

Accompanying DVD materials include a list of useful websites which are relevant to this project, whilst excerpts from the film *The March of the Penguins* in the target language support this project beautifully.

Section 1 vocabulario

Make a glossary to use during the lesson by matching up the words. Copy the English words next to the correct Spanish one. Three are done for you.

Antártida	....	**penguin**
ártico	....	sun
nieve	**snow**	ice
ballena	....	polar
hielo	....	mountain
pingüino	**penguin**	north
continente	....	fish
polar	....	Antarctica
sol	....	birds
noche	....	**snow**
montaña	....	night
norte	....	temperatures
foca	....	**summer**

sur	....	whale
pájaros	....	winter
peces	....	continent
temperaturas	....	seal
invierno	....	arctic
verano	**summer**	south

Answers

La Antártida	Antarctica	*ártico*	arctic	*nieve*	snow
Pingüino	penguins	*continente*	continent	*polar*	polar
Noche	night	*montaña*	mountain	*norte*	north
Pájaros	birds	*peces*	fish	*foca*	seal
Invierno	winter	*hielo*	ice	*sol*	sun
Verano	summer	*ballena*	whale	*sur*	south
temperaturas	temperatures				

Section 2 Nuestro mundo

Aim: for students to learn the names of the seven continents in Spanish and to present the seven continents, and in particular the continent of Antarctica, visually.

Ask: *¿cuántos continentes hay en el mundo?*
Nombra los continentes

Aquí tienes un mapa de nuestro mundo con los continentes
Conceal the name of one continent and ask students if they can say its name in Spanish.

Ask: *¿Qué continente falta?* Then do the same with the remaining six continents.

Section 3 ¡Vamos a explorar!

Aim: to introduce the continent of Antarctica in a visual way and to revise key vocabulary presented in Section 1.

Say: *Vamos de viaje...*
... ¿qué continente vamos a visitar? Mira las imágenes

Section 4 El paisaje antartico

Aim: to discover some key facts about Antarctica and its environment.

1.   Aquí tienes la Antártida/el Polo Sur

Las montañas están cubiertas de nieve y de hielo.

Las temperaturas siempre son negativas.
La temperatura media es de −57 grados.

En verano en la Antártida hay 24 horas de sol.
En invierno en la Antártida hay 24 horas de noche.

2.   Aquí tienes los icebergs

El hielo flota en el mar. Un 90% del hielo del mundo está situado en la Antártida.

La mayoría de un iceberg está debajo del agua.

3.   Aquí tienes los animales de la Antártida

Las ballenas y las focas viven en la Antártida.

4.   Aquí tienes los pingüinos. Ellos también viven en la Antártida

¡En el Polo Norte no hay pingüinos!

Los pingüino padres comen los peces y luego se los dan a sus bebés

Los pingüinos y los emperadores viven en la Antártida

5. La gente

Roald Amundsen fue el primer hombre que llegó al Polo Sur

¡Tuvo que ponerse ropa térmica a causa del frío!

Section 5 Follow-on

Students may wish to write a short and simple project using the language and information learned in this session. Alternatively, they could design a poster in groups (*Un poster de la Antártida*), which they illustrate themselves or with downloaded images. The task and the worksheet that follow are designed to help students organize their thoughts in Spanish, based on the lesson they have just received, by recapping the language and facts they have learnt.

Actividad 1

Los siete continentes

Which of the following are continents? Circle the correct ones.			
Francia	*Asia*	*Inglaterra*	*Europa*
África	*El Polo Norte*	*Canadá*	*Australasia*
La Antártida	*China*	*América del Sur*	*India*
América del Norte			

Answers

Asia, Europa, África, La Antártida, América del Sur, América del Norte y La Australasia son continentes. Hay siete en nuestro mundo.

Actividad 2

Which of these is NOT true about *la Antártida*?

- *El Polo Sur es la región más fría de nuestro planeta*
- *Los leones viven en la Antártida*
- *Las temperaturas siempre son negativas*
- *Las temperaturas siempre son positivas*
- *La Antártida es pequeña como Inglaterra*
- *El continente de La Antártida es grande como América del Norte y Europa juntos*
- *Los pingüinos viven en el Polo Sur*
- *Hay 24 horas de sol en verano y 24 horas de noche en invierno*

Answers

These sentences are NOT true:

- *Los leones viven en la Antártida.*
- *Las temperaturas siempre son positivas.*
- *La Antártida es pequeña como Inglaterra.*

Actividad 3

Choose five Antarctic facts that you have learnt this lesson and make an illustrated poster together about *la Antártida.*

Here are the facts that have been presented during this session.

1. *Las montañas están cubiertas de nieve y de hielo.*
2. *Las temperaturas siempre son negativas.*
3. *La temperatura media es de −57 grados.*
4. *En verano en la Antártida hay 24 horas de sol.*
5. *En invierno en la Antártida hay 24 horas de noche.*
6. *Las ballenas y las focas viven en la Antártida.*
7. *¡En el Polo Norte no hay pingüinos!*
8. *Los pingüino padres comen los peces y luego se los dan a sus bebés.*
9. *Los pingüinos y los emperadores viven en la Antártida.*
10. *Roald Amundsen fue el primer hombre que llegó al Polo Sur*
11. *¡Tuvo que ponerse ropa térmica a causa del frío !*
12. *La Antártida está situada en el Polo Sur.*
13. *El hielo flota en el mar.*
14. *Un 90% del hielo del mundo está situado en la Antártida.*
15. *La mayoría de un iceberg está debajo del agua.*

Steps towards CLIL (exploring Antarctica in Spanish): Additional DVD materials

1. Useful websites

Project 3   European Geography (introducing Austria and Switzerland)

Introduction

This project was designed as a 50–60 minute workshop with beginner-level students in Year Seven or Eight. It was initially designed as part of the Routes into Languages event *Deutsch International!* at Aston University, Birmingham in March 2009 and has been delivered a number of times since in a similar format. The workshop is held entirely in German, which means that the level of language used is fairly simple; it includes vocabulary such as the cardinal points, the names of European countries and Austrian provinces, describing pictures, naming various products.

A suggested session plan for 25 students (in five groups of five) is included here, which is divided into seven different activities with a handout and group work materials. A list of useful internet sites is included on the accompanying DVD. The sequence of tasks can be changed as needed, and any of the activities can be adapted according to the needs of any given group (for example, different pictures in the matching exercises).

Organisation

Forming groups (Gruppeneinteilung)

This introductory activity assumes a group of twenty-five students. Enlarge five of the pictures in this section and place one on each of five tables. Then copy a smaller version of each picture selected for the tables five times and place in a hat or a box. Students pick one small symbol picture at random and sit at the desk that shows a larger version of that symbol.

Instructions: *Sieh dir das Bild an – wer hat es noch? Das ist deine Gruppe! Setz dich mit deiner Gruppe an den Tisch mit deinem Symbol.*

Time frame: no more than 5 minutes

1 *der Bernhardiner*

2 *das Edelweiß*

3 *der Fiaker*

4 *das Wiener Kaffeehaus*

5 *der Christkindlmarkt*

6 *das Riesenrad in Wien*

7 *die Almhütte*

8 *das Matterhorn*

9 *das Rösti*

10 *das Uhrturm in Graz*

11 *der Bodensee*

Österreich/Schweiz Vokabularspiel

Print the pictures and the words separately onto cardboard and cut them out to make memory cards. They can be laminated to make them more durable. Place each complete set in an envelope; each group seated around one table gets one set. Each group should match the word to the correct picture. This vocabulary-matching activity can also be staged at different intervals as a memory game (without the words perhaps).

Instructions: *Nimm die Karten aus dem Umschlag. Jedes Bild zeigt etwas, das typisch für Österreich oder die Schweiz ist. Finde das Wort, das am besten zu jedem Bild paßt. Arbeite mit deinen Freunden in der Gruppe.*

Time frame: 10–12 minutes

Topic 1: German is spoken in which countries? Wo spricht man Deutsch?

Instructions: *Schau die Europakarte gut an. In welchen Ländern sprechen die Menschen Deutsch? Hat deinen Partner/deine Partnerin eine Idee?*

Time frame: approximately 5–7 minutes

Die deutschsprachigen Länder sind:

....

Deutsch spricht man auch in:

....

Answers

Die deutschsprachigen Länder sind:

Deutschland (2), Österreich (9), Schweiz (8), Liechtenstein (1).

Deutsch spricht man auch in:

Luxemburg, Norditalien, Ostbelgien, Ostfrankreich.

Topic 2: Nachbarländer quiz

Students find the names of the countries along the Austrian border by looking at the map of Europe presented previously in Topic 1 above and matching the number to the correct name of the neighbouring country. The task can be made easier by giving the students the names of the countries they are looking for in advance. Here they are:

Liechtenstein, Deutschland, Tschechien, Slowakei, Ungarn, Slowenien, Italien, Schweiz.

Instructions: *Österreich hat 8 Nachbarländer. Sieh dir die Karte nochmals gut an und schreib die Namen der Länder neben die Zahlen.*

Time frame: 8–10 minutes.

Answers

1.	*Liechtenstein*	2.	*Deutschland*	3.	*Tschechien*	4.	*Slowakei*
5.	*Ungarn*	6.	*Slowenien*	7.	*Italien*	8.	*Schweiz*

Topic 3: Puzzle, Part 1 (Puzzle, Teil 1)

Print the map of Austria in this section onto cardboard (you can enlarge it first). Cut it into nine puzzle pieces along provincial borders. Give each group one set of the puzzle pieces in an envelope and ask them to try and put the puzzle together. Go from group to group offering help and advice if needed. When they have finished show them the completed puzzle and go over the terms for the cardinal points. Then complete Part 2 of the puzzle.

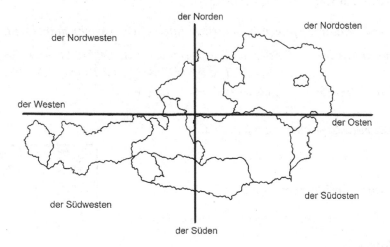

Instructions: *Das Puzzle hat neun Teile. Nimm die Teile aus dem Umschlag und lege sie richtig zusammen!*

Time frame: approximately 10 minutes

Here are the cardinal points in German: *der Norden, der Nordosten, der Osten, der Südosten, der Süden, der Südwesten, der Westen, der Nordwesten.*

Topic 3: Puzzle, Part 2 (Puzzle, Teil 2)

The students see the competed puzzle. They are given strips of paper with the names of the nine provinces, each with its respective direction. Each group is asked to try and name the nine provinces.

Instructions: *Nimm die Streifen mit den Namen der Bundesländer und lege die Namen zu den richtigen Bundesländern!*

Time frame: 10 minutes approximately

Here are the names of the provinces in German:

Niederösterreich, Wien, Burgenland, Steiermark, Kärnten, Tirol, Vorarlberg, Salzburg, Oberösterreich.

3. Niederösterreich
4. Oberösterreich
9. Wien
5. Salzburg
8. Vorarlberg
7. Tirol
2. Kärnten
1. Burgenland
6. Steirmark

Answers

Here is the completed map.

You could ask some focus questions, such as:

Wo liegt Wien? (Wien liegt im Nordosten).

Wo befindet sich Tirol? (Tirol befindet sich im Südwesten)

Niederösterreich liegt im Norden/Nordosten

Oberösterreich ist im Norden/Nordwesten

Salzburg ist im Südwesten

Vorarlberg liegt im Westen

Kärnten ist im Süden

Steirmark liegt im Südosten

Burgenland ist im Osten

Brainstorming: What do you know about Austria and Switzerland?/ *Was weißt du über Österreich und die Schweiz?*

Here are some focus questions which aim to find out how much students already know about these two German-speaking countries and to set the scene for later activities:

Ist Österreich am Meer? (Nein)

Gibt es in der Schweiz viel Schnee im Winter? (Ja)

Was isst man in Österreich? (e.g. Mozartkugel, Marmelade, Schokowaffeln)

Kann man in der Schweiz gute Schokolade kaufen? (Ja)

(Samples of foodstuffs are easily available and can be distributed during this activity to help explain the edible items listed!)

Time frame: depending on group, no more than 5 minutes

Topic 4: Matching I – Who is that? / Wer ist das?

Names can be printed onto card or paper and given to each group. Pictures of the celebrities are also available on the internet to enhance the activity. These can be printed out and distributed at the same time. Students are then asked to match the names of Austrian and Swiss 'celebrities' to the correct description (and picture if included) and then compare their results to those of other groups.

Instructions:	*Du hast vor dir neun berühmten Menschen aus Österreich oder der Schweiz. Du hast auch neun Berufe. Finde den richtigen Namen zu jedem Beruf! Arbeite mit deinen Freunden in der Gruppe.*
Time frame:	5–10 minutes
Names:	Wolfgang Amadeus Mozart, Arnold Schwarzenegger, Roger Federer, Christina Stürmer, Hermann Maier, DJ Bobo, Sepp Blatter, Dietrich Mateschitz, Albert Einstein, Johanna Spyri.
Occupations:	*Schauspieler und Politiker, Autorin, Physiker, Tennisspieler, Popsängerin, Produzent, Komponist, Musiker, Schifahrer, FIFA Präsident.*

Answers

Arnold Schwarzenegger – *Schauspieler und Politiker aus Österreich*

Roger Federer – *Tennisspieler aus der Schweiz*

Christina Stürmer – *Popsängerin aus Österreich*

Hermann Maier – *Schifahrer aus Österreich*

DJ Bobo – *Musiker aus der Schweiz*

Wolfgang Amadeus Mozart – *Komponist aus Österreich*

Dietrich Mateschitz – *Produzent von Red Bull Energygetränk aus Österreich*

Albert Einstein – *Physiker aus der Schweiz*

Johanna Spyri – *Autorin des Kinderbuches* Heidi *aus der Schweiz*

Sepp Blatter – *FIFA Präsident aus der Schweiz.*

Topic 5: Matching 2 – What is that? / Was ist das?

The groups are asked to match products to the country they originate from (Austria, Germany, Switzerland). You could download some pictures of the products to enhance this activity. Before students do the activity, they are given the phrases below to use. Encourage them to give the answers in German!

Instructions:	Acht Produkte sind auf der Liste. Diskutiere mit deinen Freunden in der Gruppe:

- Was für ein Produkt produziert die Firma?
- Aus welchem Land kommt das Produkt? Mach ein X bei dem richtigen Land!

Time frame:	10–12 minutes
Useful phrases:	*Wie heisst die richtige Antwort auf Deutsch?*
	Das ist… Kräuterlimonade.
	Die Firma produziert (Handcreme)

Produkte: *Die Schokolade kommt aus…*

die Schokolade, das Stofftier, das Klappmesser, die Schokowaffeln, die Kräuterlimonade, die Handcreme, das Energy-Getränk, die Uhr.

Firmaname	Produkte	Osterreich	Schweiz	Deutschland
Toblerone®				
Nivea ®				
Swatch ®				
RedBull ®				
Schweizermesser				
Steiff ®				
Männer ®				
Almdudler				

Answers

Firmaname	Produkte	Osterreich	Schweiz	Deutschland
Toblerone®	Schokolade		x	
Nivea®	Handcreme			x
Swatch®	Uhr		x	
RedBull®	Energy-Getränk	x		
Schweizermesser	Klappmesser		x	
Steiff®	Stofftier			x
Männer®	Schokowaffeln		x	
Almdudler	Kräuterlimonade	x		

Shopping list

Students could sample some of the Austrian or Swiss products from the activities, such as Toblerone® chocolates or Männer® wafers. Most of these products are available in British delicatessens or through specialist shops, such as the Austrian cafe-restaurant *Kipferl* in London or online (see list of useful websites on the accompanying DVD). Other products easily available through British supermarkets and which come from Austria or Switzerland are Lindt® chocolates, Pez® sweets and Ricola® sweets.

European Geography: Introducing Austria and Switzerland: Additional DVD materials

1.   Useful internet sites

Project 4   Recipes for MFL success!

Project outline

Requirements: a normal school food technology classroom
Event time: four lessons
Languages targeted: German (and French)
Impact: medium (30+ pupils)

Introduction

This project was developed originally in German by Langley Park School for Girls and was originally offered as a six-week enrichment activity after-school club between 2006 and 2009. Due to its success, it became a fixed part of the curriculum for all Year Sevens from September 2009. Essentially students follow a ten-week Licence to Cook Scheme where they learn practical cookery skills through the medium of German and French. The project *Recipes for MFL success!* received a European Award for languages in 2010 as well as, in the same year, the Mary Glasgow Language Trust Award for the best overall project and the German Embassy Language prize for the best project involving German. The version of the project presented in this chapter is in German, whilst some recipes and additional language activities are included in French on the accompanying DVD.

The main aim of the project is to increase learners' motivation, confidence, pleasure and competence in both language learning and food technology. It also aims to:

- increase cultural knowledge, understanding and cultural communication skills by providing a different perspective on language learning that allows first-hand exposure to target-language culture and access to 'real' language which has a 'real' purpose;
- improve target-language communication skills, in particular oral and listening skills and develop multilingual interests and attitudes;
- allow learners more contact with the target language, without requiring extra teaching hours.

> The course succeeds empahtically in making languages more attractive. Pupils spoke of greater motivation and confidence and were enthusiastic about what they were doing.
>
> Judge's comment, European Award for Languages 2010

Project outline

In the original version of the project, students have two double lessons (two hours and ten minutes) per week for ten weeks. The course is designed to address the standards, skills and knowledge that support food education and enable students to learn to cook and understand the principles of diet and nutrition, health and safety and wise food shopping. Lessons are delivered through the medium of German/French and incorporate the acquisition of many culinary terms, vocabulary, and cultural knowledge. Dishes specific to the target-language country are prepared using authentic recipes, thereby enabling pupils to taste a range of foods from that country, learn to describe them and give opinions on them. Students research aspects of the cuisine belonging to the target language community and present their findings to their class. Students also adapt and design their own recipes. The dishes are designed and prepared, with the language acquired being assessed according to National Curriculum levels for food technology and languages.

A shorter version of the complete twenty-lesson package is presented in German in this section, comprising four lessons selected from the original materials which include recipes for Kaiserschmarr'n, Kartoffelsalat, Apfelstrudel and Kartoffelpuffer. The recipes are followed by some useful expressions in German for describing food as well as some safety tips for the kitchen which can be used in the target language or in English to support the lessons. The four cookery lessons presented here are easily accessible and use clear, concise target language which instils in the students a sense of achievement and independence. They are carefully constructed in order to support and build up reading skills. A selection of recipes in French (making fruity milk shakes, tasting food, vegetable soup, chocolate cookies and making pancakes) is also included in the accompanying DVD materials together with the safety rules and different language activities.

The success of the original project in terms of the students' enthusiasm and motivation in both subject areas (food technology and foreign-language learning) was very plain to see, both in lesson time and in written feedback given by the students. Many students reported that, although they felt apprehensive at first, they very quickly forgot that the lessons were in a foreign language. They almost unanimously expressed the opinion that learning a subject through the medium of a foreign language is beneficial and poses no difficulties to their understanding of the subject. They expressed a real enjoyment in their lessons. All students were successful in achieving Bronze certificates under the Licence to Cook Scheme, with some pupils receiving Silver. Teacher-based assessment within languages has shown a definite increase in the language learners' confidence and a marked improvement in their ability to understand and carry out commands, interpret texts and express opinions. This project demonstrates the real possibilities offered by CLIL teaching, and the methods used could be easily adapted and applied to cross-curricular teaching of other practical subjects, for example Art, ICT and Sport.

Materials for four lessons to support *Recipes for MFL success!* are presented below. Useful expressions for describing food in German follow the four recipes. These in turn are followed by Golden Rules for safety in the kitchen. Selected, related lesson materials in French are included on the accompanying DVD material for this project.

Selected recipes in German: Kaiserschmarr'n, Kartoffelsalat, Apfelstrudel, Kartoffelpuffer

You can easily find images of all the completed dishes on the internet to illustrate the recipes. Other useful websites with German recipes are included in the accompanying DVD material.

Ich koche: Kartoffelpuffer

This is a quick and easy vegetarian dish which is usually served hot with apple sauce (especially at the Christmas markets!). At home the dish can be served with peaches, pears and other fruits, but Kartoffelpuffer often accompany roasts or fish main courses. Kartoffelpuffer are also known as Reibekuchen and Kortoffelpfannkuchen in Germany.

Geräte:

- *Messer*
- *Schüssel*
- *Geschirrtuch*
- *Pfanne*

- *Reibe*
- *Kartoffelschäler*
- *Holzlöffel*

Ich brauche:

- *600g Kartoffeln*
- *20g Mehl*
- *1 Zwiebel*
- *Apfelmus*

- *30g Butter*
- *3 Eier*
- *Prise: Salz, Pfeffer, Muskatnu*
- *1 Esslöffel Zucker*

Ich muss:

1. *Kartoffeln **waschen** und **schälen**.*
2. *Kartoffeln fein **reiben**.*
3. *Saft **herauspressen**.*
4. *Zwiebel **pellen** und fein **reiben**.*
5. *Zwiebel mit Kartoffeln **mischen**.*
6. *Mehl, Eier, Pfeffer und Salz mit den Kartoffeln **verrühren**.*
7. *Butter **schmelzen**.*
8. *Teig in der Pfanne flach **drücken**.*
9. *auf mittelere Hitze fertig **backen**.*
10. *mit Zucker, Muskatnu und Apfelmus **servieren**.*

Notizen

Ich habe..............................gegessen.

(+) *Es war super!*

(−) *Es war nicht so toll!*

Ich koche: Kartoffelsalat

Geräte:

- *Messer*
- *Kartoffelschäler*
- *Sieb*

- *Schüssel*
- *Kochtopf*
- *Schneidebrett*

Ich brauche:

- 500g Kartoffeln
- 1 Apfel
- Für die Soße: 60ml Öl
  30ml Essig

- 1 Zwiebel
- 2 Gurken
- Prise: Salz, Pfeffer, Zucker, Petersilie

Ich muss:

1. Die Kartoffeln **waschen** und **schälen**.
2. In kaltem Wasser 20 Minuten **kochen**.
3. Zwiebel, Apfel und Gurke **fein schneiden**.
4. Öl, Essig, Salz, Pfeffer und Zucker gut **mischen**
5. Kartoffeln mit kaltem Wasser **abgie en**
6. Kartoffeln in Scheiben **schneiden**
7. Alles zusammen **mischen**
8. So e über den Salat **gie en**
9. Mit Petersilie **bestreuen**.

Notizen

Ich habe.............................gegessen.

(+)   Es war super!

(−)   Das war furchtbar!

Ich koche: Kaiserschmarr'n

Geräte:

- Schüssel
- Palettenmesser
- Waage
- Schneebesen

- Holzlöffel
- Sieb
- Pfanne

Ich brauche:

- 120g Mehl
- 3 Eier
- 15–20 Rosinen
- Puderzucker

- 30g Butter
- ¼ liter Milch
- Prise Salz

Ich muss:

1. Milch, Salz und Mehl **rühren**.
2. die Eier **einrühren**.
3. in der Pfanne Butter **schmelzen**.
4. Rosinen dazu **geben**.
5. den Rest in der Pfanne **geben**.

6. *backen lassen*

7. *alles* **wenden**.

8. *schneiden*

9. *Puderzucker* **bestreuen**.

Notizen

Ich habe.............................gegessen.

(+) *Es war super!*

(–) *Es schmeckt nicht gut.*

Ich koche: Apfelstrudel

Apfelstrudel is a traditional Austrian sweet cake from the capital, Vienna (Wien). The German word 'strudel' derives from the Middle High German word for 'whirlpool'.

Geräte:

- *Backblech*
- *Schüssel*
- *Messer*
- *Palettenmesser*

- *Kochtopf*
- *Kartoffelschäler*
- *Kochpinsel*
- *Waage*

Ich brauche:

- *4 × Blätterteig*
- *50g Butter*
- *25g Puderzucker*
- *25g Rosinen*

- *1 Kochapfel*
- *50g Marzipan*
- *25g Pinienüsse*

Ich muss:

1. *Ofen auf 200°* **vorheizen** / *Gas Mark 6.*

2. *Butter* **schmelzen** *– nicht zu heiss!!*

3. *Alles* **abwiegen**.

4. *Äpfel* **pellen** *und fein* **schneiden**.

5. *Äpfel mit ½ Butter und Puderzucker* **mischen**.

6. *Äpfel mit Rosinen, Marzipan und Piniennüsse* **mischen**.

7. *Teig mit Butter* **bestreichen** *× 2.*

8. *Teig mit Puderzucker* **bestreuen**.

9. *Äpfel darauf* **geben**.

10. *Strudel* **bauen**.

11. *Mit Butter und Puderzucker* **bestreuen**.

12. *bei 200°C für 10–15 Minuten* **backen**.

Notizen

Ich habe.............................gegessen.

(+)   *Es war super!*

(−)   *Es ist schlecht.*

Using Expressions to describe food

Which statements are positive and which are negative? Make two lists in the table below:

Es ist wunderbar!	*Es schmeckt nicht gut.*
Das war furchtbar!	*Es schmeckt gut.*
Das war lecker!	*Es ist schlecht.*
Es war super!	*Es war nicht so toll!*
Es ist fettig	*Es ist gesund*
Es ist sauer	*Es ist ungesund*
Es ist bitter	*Es ist langweilig*
Es ist süss	*Es ist salzig*

+	−

What do the sentences above mean in English? Write your translation alongside each expression.

Die goldenen Regeln!

Kochen macht Spaß, aber paß auf heiße Kochtöpfe und Messer auf! Du musst unbedingt einige grundlegende Regeln kennen und beachten. Beachte sie immer, wenn du kochst.

Vorsicht!

1.   *Bevor du anfängst, wasch dir die Hände und zieh eine Schürze an, un dich nicht schmutzig zu machen. Denk auch daran, diene Ärmel hochzukrempeln. Und frag ohne zu zögern um Rat.*

2.   *Lege dir die Zutaten bereit. Wiege die trockenen lebensmittel und miss die Flü igkeiten mit Hilfe eines Messbechers.*

3. *Kontrolliere mit dem Rezept, ob du alle Zutaten hast, ob du alle Küchengeräte zur hand hast und ob du genau wei t, wie du weitervorgehen sollst.*

4. *Vorsicht Messer! Halte sie immer mit der Spitze nach unten und benutze ein Schniedebrett.*

5. *Wenn du den Herd benutzt, stell die Kochtöpfe immer mit dem Griff zur Seite. So vermeidst du, sie umzuwerfen.*

6. *Um deine So en umzurühren, benutze einen Holzlöffel und halte dabei den Kochtopfgriff fest.*

7. *Wenn du das hei e Essen servierst, oder etwas Schwieriges machst, frag einen Erwachsene um Hilfe.*

8. *Zieh einen Kochhandschuh an, bevor du hei e Kochtöpfe hälst oder ein Gericht in den Ofen schiebst.*

9. *Stell die hei en Gerichte nicht direkt auf den Tisch, sondern auf ein Holzbrett oder auf einen Untersetzer.*

10. *Trockne dir gut die Hände ab, bevor du den Mixer oder ein anderes elektrisches Gerät an- oder aussteckst.*

11. *Habe immer einen Schwamm griffbereit. Wenn du etwas verschütterst, mache es direkt sauber.*

12. *Spüle deine Küchengeräte regelmä ig ab. Wenn du fertig bist, räume die Küchengeräte weg und hinterlasse die Küche ordentlich.*

Recipes for MFL success! Additional DVD materials

1. Golden rules in the kitchen in French (*Les règles d'or!*).

2. *Les Fruits*, including identification and matching exercises as well as a word search and a recipe for fruity milk shakes.

3. *Les légumes*, including a translation exercise and a recipe for vegetable soup.

4. Tasting food, including top tips, an interview and descriptive work.

5. Les desserts: *Cookies au chocolat / L'heure des crêpes*

6. Useful websites

7

Languages beyond the classroom

Introduction

This Part takes languages outside the classroom and involves the wider world! The first project presented here is *The Foreign Language Spelling Bee*. It is run on a national basis and played in various rounds, with students learning a set list of words in French, German and Spanish. Whilst the national version is presented here, the whole is easily adaptable to a smaller scale. However it is used, it is bound to be great fun!

The second project is *The Gold Award for Languages*. Students must complete three languages-related challenges to be eligible for the award: work experience; community challenge; personal challenge. The section details the component parts and gives a good overview of what is involved in this exciting language-based challenge.

The mini book-making project, the third one presented here, is inspirational in its simplicity! In essence, it involves students making mini books in a foreign language for other learners. Collectively more than 750 mini books in French, German and Spanish were made in the first instance and displayed in the Central Library in Chelmsford. This total produced has now reached well over 7,500 and the whole project is hugely motivating for students and their teachers alike.

The final project in this chapter is *The Foreign Languages Draw*. Students are encouraged to submit a drawing on any given theme, with prizes being awarded for the most imaginative picture and/or the most correct use of grammar!

Project 1　The Foreign Language Spelling Bee

Project outline

Requirements: invitations to participating classes/schools; classroom for the first class rounds; large hall and three classrooms for the final three rounds.
Event time: ongoing throughout the academic year
Languages targeted: any, but presented here in German, Spanish and French.
Impact: high. The version presented here is a national event.

Introduction

The Routes into Languages *Foreign Language Spelling Bee* was devised by Jane Driver, a language teacher at Comberton Village College in Cambridge. Jane says, "The aim is for students in year 7 to practise and improve their vocabulary, spelling and memory skills in another language to show how much fun it can be." The Spelling Bee was first piloted in the Eastern Region in 2009 and then launched nationally in September 2010 to mark the European Day of Languages, which is celebrated on or around the 26th of September every year to promote life-long language learning and cultural awareness (see also Part III, Project 4). Routes East has been awarded the London 2012 Inspire Mark for all its Language & Sport events, including *The Foreign Language Spelling Bee* project presented here. This project was run in 2010 and 2011 with Year Seven pupils in England learning French, German or Spanish, who were asked to translate words from English into the target language, and then spell them back in that language – the object being to do this for as many words as possible in one minute. Across Wales, a fourth award was developed for pupils learning Welsh. In 2011 The Routes into Languages *Foreign Language Spelling Bee* won a European Language Label Award, and it has now become a national annual event, run by the original team of Jane Driver (now Head of Department of Hinching-brooke School, Huntingdon), Rachel Hawkes (Assistant Principal of Comberton Village College) and Sarah Schechter (Project Manager of Routes into Languages East). There is an excellent dedicated website for the Spelling Bee (www.flspellingbee.co.uk) which was made by a Year 9 pupil at Comberton Village College. Teachers can register on it; pupils can practise; there are videos, photos and much more.

The organization of the *Foreign Language Spelling Bee* is relatively straightforward. There are four main rounds, which take place sequentially. The model presented here is the national version, but the project could easily be adapted to suit a smaller-scale event involving just one or two schools. An overview of the whole project is presented below, followed by further details about each separate stage.

Project overview: Process for the national version

The competition consists of four stages over the three terms:

- Autumn end of term – Individual Class
- Spring half-term – Whole School Competition
- Spring end of term – Regional Competition
- Summer term – National Competition

Students are given 50 words to learn at the first stage of the competition, and a further 50 words are added at each subsequent stage. Vocabulary included is relevant to the curriculum.

The competition is launched at the beginning of the autumn term, and time should be spent in the first few lessons of the year teaching and practising the alphabet in the foreign language, paying particular attention to describing letters with accents.

Unlike a monolingual Spelling Bee, students are given the word in English, which they will first have to translate into the target language and then spell out correctly using the alphabet in the target language.

When participating, students are given one minute to spell correctly as many words as possible.

Students must translate the word with the correct article, but they only need to spell the noun.

Pronunciation must be accurate and spelling clearly enunciated.

If students are spelling a colour that begins with '*de color…*', they need to say that in the translation, but only need spell the actual colour itself.

Students should be allowed to finish a word that they started before the time is up.

Students can pass at any time, but must say 'pass' in the target language.

Words should be allocated in random order.

Accents and other punctuation (note: **not** question marks) must be spelled in the following way:

French	Spanish	German
â ê î ô û – *accent circonflexe* ç – *cédille* é – *accent aigu* è – *accent grave* ë ï ö ü – *tréma* Space – *blanc* Pass – *je passe* Hyphen – *traitd'union* Apostrophe – *l'apostrophe*	á é í ó ú – *acento* ñ – *tilde* Space – *espacio* Pass – *paso*	ä ö ü – *Umlaut* ß – *S-Zett/scharfes S* Space – *Leerzeichen/Abstand* Pass – *ich passe* Hyphen – *Bindestrich*

The names of the winners at each stage of the competition are submitted to the Spelling Bee website (www.flspellingbee.co.uk), so that they can receive acknowledgement for their achievements via a certificate.

1. Class round

Many schools have the *Foreign Language Spelling Bee* integrated into their schemes of work, practising and running the competition in class. Others run it in lunch-break clubs. Some schools combine both. In the eastern region (where the competition has been running for two years already) previous year's competitors, reluctant to relinquish their links with the competition and in their roles as Language Leaders (see also Part IV, Project 3) have run clubs for the Year 7s. Four winners per class receive certificates and go through to the second round. A class organization sheet is included in the DVD materials accompanying this project.

Teachers need to launch the competition to the students at the very beginning of the term and to teach the alphabet in the target language as early as possible in the term, ensuring that students can name letters with accents, etc.

The 50 Stage 1 words need to be allocated to the students, so that they can begin memorising them and practising (the words for the class round are at the end of this project presentation). Students should be tested, and it is suggested that this be done as a starter or a plenary at least once a week, with students testing each other either in pairs or as a whole class. A class competition might be held at the end of the first half-term.

Students should be tested individually and should not use any prompts. They have one minute to correctly spell as many words as possible in the target language. The teacher chooses the words in random order; saying a word in English, whereupon the student first says that word in the target language and then spells it using the target-language alphabet.

Students receive one point per word correctly translated and spelled within the time (if they have begun a word when the timer goes, they should be permitted to finish). In the event of a tie-breaker, a sudden-death round should be played:

Students should take it in turns to correctly spell randomly selected words.

If a student spells a word incorrectly, they are out, and this process continues until both students have been given the same number of words, and there is one winner and a runner-up.

An organization sheet for the class competition is presented below. A similar sheet for the school stage is included on the accompanying DVD.

2. School round

The second round is the school round, with class winners competing against each other. The four school winners in each language get certificates. For schools competing in only one language, all school winners go straight through. For those competing in two or three languages, the school must select four winners to go through (e.g. two French, two German; one Spanish, one German, two French, etc.). An organization sheet for this stage is included in the accompanying DVD materials for this project.

Teachers should allocate the extra 50 words to the stage 1 class winners (the words for this school stage are on the accompanying DVD).

Stage 1: Class Competition (for class use)		
School		
Co-ordinator	**Name**	**Email**
Class Winners		
Class	Forename(s)	Surname
Comments		

Class winners should meet weekly to test each other: this could be done at break or lunchtime. Additionally, the class could test their winners each week as a starter or plenary.

A School Competition should be held at the end of the Spring half-term. The same rules apply as for Stage One, the only difference being that students will be tested on 100 words rather than 50. words.

The names of four winners should be submitted. (Since only four pupils per school qualify for the Regional Final, schools doing more than one language need to tell pupils from the start that only the school winner goes through to the Regional Final, and perhaps the strongest runner-up.)

3. Regional round

Next comes the regional round. Each competitor is given one minute to spell as many words as possible. They will stand at the front of the hall and the words (generated randomly via a PowerPoint programme) will appear on the screen behind them, so that the judges and audience can see. The Spellmaster will read the word in English, and the competitor will first translate it, then spell it (using the formula: say it, spell it). Pupils should be encouraged to speak as loudly and as clearly as possible, although microphones can be used if necessary. After the first rounds, the top four spellers in each language will proceed to the finals. If there are more than four people with the highest scores, a sudden-death round will take place to determine the finalists.

Teachers should allocate the extra 50 words to the Stage 2 school winners (the words for the school, regional and final stages are on the accompanying DVD), and school winners should meet weekly to test each other: this could be done at break or lunchtime. Additionally, the relevant classes could test the winners each week as a starter or plenary.

A Regional Competition is held around March, and each school can send a total of four pupils to compete. The same rules apply as for Stages One and Two, the only difference being that students will be tested on 150 words rather than 50 or 100 words. The Regional Winners are announced on the day, and there is a prize-giving ceremony during which the regional winners receive a certificate. This is included on the accompanying (DVD materials).

Here is a sample schedule for a regional round:

14.00–14.10:	Arrival and registration (teachers to indicate during registration if there are children whose parents did not give photography consent).
14.10–14.15:	Welcome and explanation of the competition.
14.15–14.45:	Room 1: French round one.
14.15–14.45:	Room 2: German round one.
14.15–14.45:	Room 3: Spanish round one.
14.45–15.10:	Break – refreshments available.
15.10–15.40:	Hall: finals in each language (top four from round one).
15.40–16.00:	Prize giving.

4. Final round

The national final is held at the end of the summer term. The same rules apply as for Stages One, Two and Three, the only difference being that students will be tested on 200 words rather than 50, 100 or 150 words.

Thus the top four spellers from the regional rounds are each given one minute to translate and spell as many words as possible (carried out as before, with a Spellmaster and the 'say it, spell it' formula) to determine first, second, third and fourth places. In the case of a draw for any of the places, there will be a sudden death play-off. The first person to spell a word correctly will win, as long as each person has had the same number of words (otherwise the opponent is given a word and, if s/he answers correctly s/he wins, otherwise the sudden-death continues until one of them again makes a mistake).

Teachers should allocate the extra 50 words to the Stage 3 regional winners (the words for this final stage are included on the accompanying DVD). The regional winners should practise weekly, at break or lunchtime with other students. Additionally, the relevant class(es) could test the winner(s) each week as a starter or plenary.

The National Winners will be announced on the day, and there will be a formal prize-giving ceremony during which each finalist receives a shield.

Judges: there is one judge and one verifier per language. These could be university languages lecturers, Student Language Ambassadors or tutors from local schools perhaps. At least one of them must be a native speaker of the language. They confer after each student has had their turn, and their decision is final.

Student Ambassadors: Languages undergraduates and, wherever possible, Language Leaders from participating schools (see Part IV, Project 3) can be on hand to help with the running of the day.

Shopping list

3 stop-watches
Certificates for the finalists in the regional rounds (see accompanying DVD materials)
Shields/trophies for the national finalists
Flowers for the judges

There are a few rules which help with the smooth running of the whole event.

- Contestants face the judges with their back to the screen where the words are displayed. They must speak clearly and loudly. If the judges cannot hear the contestant, the judges will indicate and a re-spell will take place immediately. The judges' decision on whether they heard a letter or spelling is final.
- Contestants cannot alter the order of the letters once they have completed their spelling of the word (unless it is a re-spell), but they can stop in mid-word and start again from the beginning.
- Normally only one re-spell per word will be allowed by the judges. The clock is NOT stopped for these actions.

- No conferring is allowed.
- Contestants must remain quiet when not spelling. Contestants causing disruption will be warned, and if the disruption continues they may be disqualified.
- If a contestant runs out of time before starting to spell the word, no point is awarded.
- If the contestant has begun to spell a word when the time is up they may continue, and, if the spelling is correct, a point is awarded.
- If the contestant is prevented from spelling a word and the time is up (for example, if another contestant is disruptive) the judges may, at their discretion, allow a re-spell.
- The judges' decision is final; their authority is the word list.
- If the judges are satisfied that there has been an incident of cheating, the contestant will be disqualified.
- Mobile phones that remain switched on after a warning is given will result in the contestant being disqualified.
- If guests do not remain quiet during the competition after having been warned, then their contestant may be disqualified.
- If the judges are suspicious that members of the audience are influencing the accuracy of spelling by whatever means, the judges will give a warning. If the activity persists, the judges may disqualify a contestant or contestants.
- Late arrival by contestants and their accompanying teacher or parent may result in disqualification.

Reflections

This has been a particularly fun project to run, and the extent to which the students have engaged with the project in so many different ways is impressive. As one teacher commented:

> I'm really excited by the fact that we will now have thousands of pupils around the country with a strong foundation of basic vocabulary to build on, which they've acquired with such enthusiasm and enjoyment, rather than laboriously and under duress.
>
> Word lists for the class round are presented below in French, German and Spanish. Words for the remaining rounds are contained on the accompanying DVD to this section.

Word List – Stage One Class round, Spanish

	Spanish	English		Spanish	English
1	*hola*	hello	27	*un bolígrafo*	a pen
2	*adiós*	goodbye	28	*un cuaderno*	an exercise book
3	*por favor*	please	29	*un diccionario*	a dictionary
4	*gracias*	thank you	30	*un estuche*	a pencil case
5	*fenomenal*	great	31	*un lápiz*	a pencil
6	*bien*	good/fine	32	*una calculadora*	a calculator
7	*regular*	OK	33	*un libro*	a book
8	*mal*	bad	34	*un sacapuntas*	a pencil sharpener
9	*fatal*	awful			
10	*el cumpleaños*	birthday	35	*azul*	blue
11	*uno*	one	36	*verde*	green
12	*dos*	two	37	*marrón*	brown
13	*tres*	three	38	*gris*	grey
14	*cuatro*	four	39	*negro*	black
15	*cinco*	five	40	*blanco*	white
16	*seis*	six	41	*rojo*	red
17	*siete*	seven	42	*amarillo*	yellow
18	*ocho*	eight	43	*de color rosa*	pink
19	*nueve*	nine	44	*de color naranja*	orange
20	*diez*	ten	45	*de color violeta*	purple
21	*una agenda*	a diary	46	*el español*	Spanish
22	*una carpeta*	a folder	47	*España*	Spain
23	*una goma*	a rubber	48	*¿qué?*[1]	what?
24	*una pluma*	a fountain pen	49	*¿cómo?**	how?
25	*una regla*	a ruler	50	*¿cuánto?**	how much?/many?
26	*una tijera*	a pair of scissors			

Word List – Stage One Class round, German

	German	English		German	English
1	hallo	hello	27	der Taschenrechner	the calculator
2	tschüs	goodbye	28	das Heft	the exercise book
3	bitte	please			
4	danke	thank you	29	das Wörterbuch	the dictionary
5	super	great	30	das Etui	the pencil case
6	gut	good/fine	31	der Bleistift	the pencil
7	ok	OK	32	der Klebstift	the glue
8	schlecht	bad	33	das Buch	the book
9	fürchterlich	awful	34	der Spitzer	the pencil sharpener
10	der Geburtstag	birthday			
11	eins	one	35	blau	blue
12	zwei	two	36	grün	green
13	drei	three	37	braun	brown
14	vier	four	38	grau	grey
15	fünf	five	39	schwarz	black
16	sechs	six	40	weiß	white
17	sieben	seven	41	rot	red
18	acht	eight	42	gelb	yellow
19	neun	nine	43	rosa	pink
20	zehn	ten	44	orange	orange
21	das Tagebuch	the diary	45	lila	purple
22	der Ordner	the folder	46	Deutsch	German
23	der Radiergummi	the rubber	47	Deutschland	Germany
24	der Kuli	the pen	48	was?[2]	what?
25	das Lineal	the ruler	49	wie?*	how?
26	die Schere	the pair of scissors	50	wie viel?*	how much?/ many?

---

* Please note pupils should **not** say the question marks when they spell the words.

Word List – Stage One Class round, French

	French	English		French	English
1	salut	hello	26	dix	ten
2	au revoir	goodbye	27	blanc	white
3	bien	good	28	bleu	blue
4	mal	bad	29	gris	grey
5	bof	so–so	30	jaune	yellow
6	merci	thank you	31	marron	brown
7	s'il vous plaît	please	32	noir	black
8	un cahier	an exercise book	33	orange	orange
9	un crayon	a pencil	34	rose	pink
10	un feutre	a felt-tip	35	rouge	red
11	une gomme	a rubber	36	vert	green
12	un livre	a book	37	janvier	January
13	une règle	a ruler	38	février	February
14	un stylo	a pen	39	mars	March
15	un taille-crayon	a pencil-sharpener	40	avril	April
			41	mai	May
16	une trousse	a pencil-case	42	juin	June
17	un	one	43	juillet	July
18	deux	two	44	août	August
19	trois	three	45	septembre	September
20	quatre	four	46	octobre	October
21	cinq	five	47	novembre	November
22	six	six	48	décembre	December
23	sept	seven	49	l'anniversaire	the birthday
24	huit	eight	50	ça va?[3]	how are you?
25	neuf	nine			

Note: The rules and procedures of theSpelling Bee competition and the list of words are reviewed each year. For definitive details, see the current Teacher's Pack, available on registration at http://www.flspellingbee.co.uk

The Spelling Bee: Accompanying DVD materials

1. An organization sheet for the school stage.
2. Word lists in French, German and Spanish for each round following the class round (i.e., school, regional and national final).
3. Useful internet sites.

---

3 Please note pupils should **not** say the question marks when they spell the words.

Project 2   The Gold Award for Languages

Project Outline

Requirements: copies of the European Languages Portfolio for each student (see below for details); access to languages-related work experience placements.
Event time: this **project** can be organised over as long or as short a period necessary for completing all stages.
Languages targeted: any
Impact: medium-high (can be used with small and large groups)

Introduction

The Gold Award for Languages is a programme comprising three languages-related challenges which students must complete in order to be eligible for the award: work experience, community challenge and personal challenge. It originated in this form as part of the national Routes into Languages initiative (Routes South). It is a very flexible project which can be carried out within various timeframes. It is typically undertaken by students in Year 10 and above, as one of the challenges involves a work-experience placement, but it can be started by students in younger year groups and completed over a number of years. The award not only provides opportunities for students to develop and showcase their language skills but also aims to demonstrate how languages can be applied and valued in a range of different situations. It is a useful platform from which languages can be promoted at school, as it can be linked to a number of other curriculum areas, such as business studies (work experience challenge), citizenship (community challenge), geography (personal challenge), as well as students' own personal develop-ment. It can be completed as part of an enrichment or extra-curricular programme or embedded within the foreign languages curriculum. Once introduced and set up, the programme should require little management time, as students are encouraged to fill in the European Languages Portfolio★⁴ to record their progress and achievements. To attain the award students must present a fully-completed portfolio to their teacher, who then signs it off. Upon successful completion of all stages of the award, students can be

---

4   Before downloading copies of the European Languages Portfolio you may wish to check if your school is registered with the Sports Leader UK Award. This scheme can accommodate *The Gold Award for Languages*. If the school is registered (check with the Physical Education (PE) department), it is possible to extend registration to the Foreign Language Leaders Award (FLLA). A tutor resource pack will be required (approximately £45.00), as will student registrations (approximately £15.00 each). In return students will receive a log book in which they can record their activities. The FLLA will cover the personal challenge and community challenge strands of the Gold Award. You will then need to ensure that students find appropriate languages-related work experience placements. Details of these can be recorded in the log book.

presented with *The Gold Award for Languages* certificate, which should be signed by the head teacher as well as the head of the languages department.

This section outlines the three different stages of the Gold Award for Languages. It contains explanations of the challenges along with some examples of what students can do to fulfil the challenge requirements and reflections. The accompanying DVD also includes a short presentation to introduce the award to students, a list of frequently asked questions for employers; a 'letter of understanding' for employers providing work experience placements and the Gold Award for Languages certificate.

Introducing the Gold Award for Languages to students

It may be useful to introduce the Gold Award to students by way of a short presentation. This can be a brief outline of the project, along with some statements about the value and importance of language skills. This can help to reinforce similar messages you may already have been promoting during language lessons and may encourage the more reluctant learner to think about signing up for the award. A sample PowerPoint presentation can be found in the accompanying DVD materials for this project.

The award challenges

As mentioned above, the Gold Award is split into three separate challenges, and students must complete all three and collect evidence of this to be eligible for the award. Challenges can be completed in any order.

The work experience challenge

The work experience challenge aims to emphasize the importance of language skills in the workplace and the many different ways in which they can be used. It can be completed when students would typically undertake their period of work experience or can be done independently (for example if your school does not offer work experience, or if students begin the Gold Award in lower year groups).

Finding work experience placements

Ideas for work experience that immediately spring to mind include placements in translation or interpreting companies, teaching, tourism offices or attractions, call centres and so on. However, it is always worthwhile considering less obvious industries, as this helps to reinforce the notion that languages can be applied in a wide variety of jobs and careers. Examples of these could include law, video games and software development, finance, market research, science, engineering, web design and many more. A useful way of generating ideas is to ask your students to carry out a simple job search via online recruitment agencies (see the example in the list of useful websites for this project on the accompanying DVD). Once a range of possibilities has been identified, businesses can be approached according to the work experience regulations in place at your school. To assist you in securing placements, you may wish to provide prospective companies with the following information.

What is work experience?

- It is an opportunity for a student to spend an agreed period of time in the workplace, usually two weeks.
- The placement is unpaid, and the student carries out set tasks according to the Job Description agreed with the employer.

Since September 2004 there has been a statutory requirement that all young people should experience some work-related learning within the curriculum at Key Stage 4 (age 15–16 years).

Work-related learning is defined as: planned activity that uses the context of work to develop knowledge, skills and understanding useful in work, including learning through the experience of work; learning about the experience of work and working practices; learning the skills for work.

Therefore the statutory requirement is for schools to make provision for all students at KS4 to:

- Learn through work, by providing opportunities for students to learn from direct experiences of work (for example, through work experience or part-time jobs, enterprise activities in schools and learning through vocational contexts in subjects).
- Learn about work, by providing opportunities for students to develop knowledge and understanding of work and enterprise (for example through vocational courses and careers education).
- Learn for work by developing skills for enterprise and employability (for example, through problem-solving activities, work simulations, and mock interviews).

All young people need work-related learning as an essential part of full preparation for adult life in which they will contribute to the country's economic well-being. Making it statutory ensures clarity, coherence and quality of provision.

What is the Gold Award for Languages?

The award is based around the existing two-week work experience that school students undertake but within a language learning framework. They complete three challenges: work experience; community challenge; personal challenge. Students undertaking these activities will be awarded the Gold Award for Languages by Routes into Languages South (see www.routesintolanguages.ac.uk/south).

We are looking for employers to support the work experience strand of the Gold Award for Languages

What are the benefits for your business?

- Interviewing and supervising students on placement provide excellent opportunities for staff development in the company.
- The profile of the company is raised amongst students, parents and teachers.

- Support for the local community is demonstrated, providing good public relations.
- Students bring their own skills, enthusiasm and a fresh perspective with them to the work placement. This can be surprisingly valuable for many companies.
- Young people can be assessed by the company for part-time or full-time work.
- Feedback can be given by employers to education, so that young people are better prepared for the job market.
- Students are offered an insight into the company, which may encourage them or their friends to think of it when looking at future employment.

If you and your business can identify with one or more of the following statements, please get in touch with:

....

☐ I am an employer who values languages in the workplace;
☐ I am an employer who has staff who routinely use languages, other than English, in the workplace or as part of their international activities for our business;
☐ I am an employer who has branches within the UK or overseas where staff use their language skills;
☐ I am an employer who would like to work through our Corporate Social Responsibility Programme (or equivalent) to offer local students opportunities to understand the value of languages;
☐ I am an employer who can provide language-related work placements for one or more students for one or two weeks each year.

A list of further frequently asked questions and their answers can be found in the additional materials for this project on the accompanying DVD.

Employers may wish to interview prospective work experience students or arrange a pre-placement meeting. This is useful for both parties in terms of getting to know each other, finding out what to do on the first day and advising of any medical conditions or disabilities. Following their placements, students may be asked by employers for feedback about their experience. This could be in the form of a short questionnaire or brief interview before they leave. Students should also be encouraged to write a letter of thanks following their placement. Copies of any feedback forms as well as the letter of thanks can be included as evidence in the ELP.

If your school does not offer work experience, or you cannot secure appropriate placements...

If work experience is not offered at your school, or you and your students have difficulty in securing languages-related work placements, there are alternative ways of completing this strand of the award. Providing there is a demonstrable link to the workplace, students may design, implement and evaluate a short project or series of activities that simulate a work experience placement. A good example of this is outlined in the following case study of students at Invicta Grammar School for Girls in Kent.

Case study: Japanese Project

As it is increasingly difficult to gain work experience related to the use of foreign languages, we had to think of an alternative for the work-related module for the Gold Award. We are fortunate enough to have a very good relationship with a school in Tokyo, Japan, and they send students to us every year to learn more about English culture and language. We therefore decided to take advantage of this to build in the work experience element for those unable to find placements involving languages.

The first thing we did was to invite someone in to provide basic Japanese lessons. The English students were taught how to greet Japanese visitors, introduce themselves and talk about their families. They also learnt about cultural differences and, most importantly, how to prepare and eat Japanese food!

Invicta students then researched what would be of most interest to our Japanese visitors and organised the 10-day programme accordingly. They decided upon a programme in which language and cultural experience were of equal importance. Daytrips both within and outside Kent were planned, with relevant information provided, so the foreign students could get the best out of their visit. Questionnaires, maps, explanations of useful historical knowledge, and so on, were included.

When our guests arrived, the English students delivered a welcoming speech in Japanese and explained the 10-day programme they had organised themselves – from Easter egg hunts to day trips, lesson content to London shows.

The Invicta students delivered the lessons and organised all resources themselves. One of the highlights was a fashion show they asked the Japanese to put on after teaching them the relevant vocabulary. The Kanto students strutted their stuff down a catwalk to modern music and detailed explanations of the items given to them to wear. Another memorable event was when they were taught the plot and music to the musical *Wicked* before going to see it. The harmonised singing was so emotive it actually brought tears to the eyes of those listening.

The Japanese fully benefited from the programme offered, and Invicta students built such good relationships with their guests that some have since been to Japan to visit their newly made friends on their home territory.

This element of the Gold Award has proved the most rewarding and is the part our new students are looking forward to most. This year they are planning an itinerary for some visitors from Finland and have already come up with some new and innovative ideas. I can't wait to see the finalised programme!

The community challenge

The community challenge strand of the award offers students the chance to engage in promoting language learning to different groups within the community. There is scope here for many different ideas, and students should be encouraged to think creatively. In the first instance it is useful to identify the various community groups which could benefit from the challenge, such as: primary school pupils; students in lower secondary year groups; parents and guardians; senior groups. This section provides some ideas for this part of the award which can either be replicated or used as food for further thought.

Teaching a foreign language to a community group

Students may wish to teach the language(s) they are learning to members of different community groups, such as those listed above. This would involve identifying the group then promoting, planning and delivering the lessons. Such a challenge could be completed in pairs or small teams. Students should be encouraged to prepare a short scheme of work, lesson plans and materials. They could focus on any aspect of the language they wished, such as one or two related topics, basic grammar or languages and culture. Copies of any materials prepared and used should be kept and added to the European Languages Portfolio as evidence. Students should also allocate time for personal reflection on the challenge, as this often helps them to consolidate their own language learning.

Hosting languages and cultural events

The planning, delivering and assessing of languages and cultural events provides students with numerous opportunities to put their creative thinking to good use. They may want to choose one specific country and organise a short series of events to showcase its language and different cultural aspects: for example, events focussing on traditions, food, dress, history, and so on. Alternatively, students may wish to focus on a particular cultural aspect that links a number of different countries, and prepare events in relation to that. Again, all steps taken to put on such events or activities should be recorded in the European Languages Portfolio.

The personal challenge

The personal challenge element of the award inspires students to think about how they might challenge themselves in a languages-related environment. There is a broad scope here for many different types of challenge, as, obviously, what may prove challenging to one student may not apply to others. Whilst some ideas are provided below, students should be encouraged to think of a challenge of their own if possible. They should record their progress and steps taken to successfully complete their challenge in their European Languages Portfolio.

Personal challenge ideas

It may help students to develop their personal challenge ideas by thinking of areas of language learning they might wish to improve. For example, less confident students could challenge themselves to speak up in the target language (TL) in class for five or even ten consecutive lessons. Along similar lines, perhaps a group of students who are not comfortable speaking in the TL could set up a lunchtime or after-school conversation club.

Those who are confident in their use of the TL or who have been identified as Gifted and Talented students could think about really extending and deepening their language skills by learning a new language. This could be done independently, but if there is a group of students in the same position, why not encourage them to set up a small class of their own?

Some students may be fortunate enough to be able to travel abroad, either with the school or with their friends or families. Even a short trip to another country can provide ample opportunities for personal challenges. Students could set themselves a target of interacting in the TL with native speakers on a certain number of occasions (perhaps even recording their experiences). They could use their time in the foreign country to carry out a short project on a topic of their choice, perhaps related to tourist attractions in the area they are visiting, specialities the region is known for or famous people from the area.

In short, the list of ideas for personal challenges is endless. It is up to the student to choose something that will genuinely provide a challenge for them, so that they have something to work towards and something that will help them develop and perfect their understanding of another language and its culture.

Reflections

Although this is a larger-scale project than something that can be completed in a day, it does serve to offer students a wide variety of languages-related challenges. These challenges can help them to see language skills as a tool to use and develop beyond the classroom. Teachers who have already implemented this project have reported it as being inspiring for students and teachers alike. Students have risen to the challenges, and the fact that the majority of the award revolves around their own individual input helps them to remain engaged and focused. Teachers have appreciated the scheme's (from their point of view) "light-touch" aspect, and in some instances it has been so successful it has been embedded into the languages curriculum.

The Gold Award: Additional DVD materials

1. A short presentation to introduce the award to students
2. A list of frequently asked questions for employers
3. A 'letter of understanding' for employers providing work experience placements
4. The Gold Award for Languages certificate
5. Useful websites

Project 3   The mini-book-making project

Introduction

The Mini-Book-Making Project was instigated in 2008 by nine schools in Essex to increase student motivation with regard to reading and writing skills. The nine schools are part of the former Quartier Rouge network set up by the Local Education Authority and led by Jane Breen, Advanced Skills Teacher and Director of Language College Outreach at King Edward VI Grammar School, Chelmsford. Other schools in the network were: Chelmer Valley High School, Moulsham High School and St Peter's College, all in Chelmsford; Bentfield Primary School, Stansted; Helena Romanes School, Dunmow; Mountfitchet Mathematics and Computing College, Stanstead Mountfitchet; The Plume School, Maldon; and Saffron Walden County High School. The network has now evolved and the schools listed above are part of an Essex-wide network working in conjunction with Cambridge University, *Languages First in Essex*).

The project is not only delightfully simple in concept, but also hugely motivating for both students and their teachers alike. In essence, it involves students making mini-books in a foreign language for other learners. Collectively more than 750 mini-books in French, German and Spanish were made in the first instance (see picture gallery on the accompanying DVD) and these were displayed in the Central Library in Chelmsford. In 2009 the mini-book-making project won a European Award for Languages organized by CILT, part of CfBT Education Trust (see useful web addresses in the accompanying DVD materials). It has since reached out across the world with more than 7,500 books being made to celebrate European Day of Languages on 26th Sept 2009 (see also Part III, Project 4). In the first instance the mini-books were shared physically, with students going to the library, and then the books were exchanged between schools. Then 2011 saw the development of a related cross-subject, cross-school project called *Talking Texts*. The language part of this project will be to film students reading both their own books and books other students have made. The films can then be shared across schools.

The mini-book-making project aims to motivate students to read more, to celebrate world languages and language learning and to enable students to share their written work beyond the classroom and with the wider community. In addition to meeting these objectives, the project is important because it:

- encourages students to read *spontaneously* to and with each other;
- encourages students to start *voluntarily* learning a new language!
- underpins and promotes all three strands of Community Cohesion: teaching and learning; equity and excellence; engagement and ethos;

- gives students the unique opportunity to interact with and learn from each other's work;
- provides an inclusive learning opportunity for all students, where success is not determined by academic ability.

Shopping list

To make the mini-books you need:
- 1 sheet of paper
- Coloured pens
- Imagination!

Organisation

One one-hour lesson is needed to get the class to fold the paper and make the books (see accompanying DVD for the short film on folding paper correctly). This stage needs to be taken slowly, making sure everyone has completed each step before going onto the next. You can do this in the target language successfully if the process is demonstrated clearly. Students then need to *plan* the content in rough (otherwise they start without thinking through and make mistakes with content) and finally they can begin their books. I would tell students to bring in pens, colouring pencils, etc. At least one homework is needed to finish the books. In the following lesson, students bring in their books, read to each other and share their work. Give students a feedback speaking frame so they can evaluate in the target language.

The books can be on any theme from basic numbers to the geography of France, a history of the German boy band Tokio Hotel or a day in the life of an alien. It is best if students choose a topic related to the unit they are currently learning, or have covered previously and try to present the language as imaginatively as possible. The target audience for the book is younger readers. Some students like to create lift-the-flap books. Students plan the text of their book in rough and then create the books in lesson time and share with their class and other students in the school. The project works best when as many students as possible take part and when they do the work together in class. The sharing of ideas inspires creativity, and the exchange of books generates an enthusiasm for reading rarely seen in foreign language classes. The project works best as a spontaneous activity and is excellent for the end of term or end of year. There is also no need for teachers to mark or correct books. The planning stage in class gives teachers the opportunity to intervene when necessary, and, if there are mistakes in the books, then spotting these and/or questioning accuracy provokes good meta-linguistic conversations and dialogue. Some schools introduced the mini-books as a revision tool at the end of a unit of work. Students were so insistent that mini-books were an excellent way to

> When students are involved in making the mini-books they are enthusiastic and determined to do the best that they can to show their language skills off to the full, being conscious that these books are to be displayed and read by others. Students really enjoyed making the mini-books and the quality of the books produced was outstanding and amazing to see. Students put a lot of effort into their mini-books to ensure not only the quality of the language but also to make them visually attractive to readers. A real success story in terms of increasing student motivation and developing their reading and writing skills.
>
> The Plume School

revise and reflect on a unit of work that mini-books have been incorporated into schemes of work.

Reflections: what did I learn as a teacher?

1.   That students' choice of the "best" books and my choice were sometimes very different. Whereas I tended to favour longer, more complex text, students often seemed to prefer books that were immediately accessible.

2.   I had assumed, incorrectly, that for books to be of benefit they had to contain a good amount of text and neat pictures – this wasn't borne out in student feedback.

3.   In my drive for ever more challenging literacy activities, I had overlooked students' need for simple vocabulary-learning tasks.

4.   The books provide an excellent introduction to language learning.

5.   Students really benefit from materials created by learners in the wider community – perhaps there should be more of this across all subjects.

6.   We were able to share the books between schools. In one lesson I placed a pile of books in the middle of each table and told students to read, evaluate and put a post-it note with feedback on each book they read. What struck me immediately was how the boys paired up and started to read aloud to each other spontaneously, sharing and enjoying the books. They were engaging in a deeper, personal interaction than that normally facilitated through reading activities – a relationship reminiscent of the parent–child relationship that builds up when reading aloud to children. The boys were also very keen to read books in new languages and learn vocabulary.

> The students really enjoyed making the mini-books, and the quality of the books produced was outstanding and amazing to see. Students put a lot of effort into their mini-books to ensure not only the quality of the language but also to make them visually attractive to readers. A real success story in terms of increasing student motivation with regard to the development of their reading and writing skills.
>
> The Plume School

> The mini-book-making project is great, as students can not only work on looking back on their notes but, once completed, they can read each other's work, and then I display the work in our school library.
>
> Chelmer Valley High School

Our groups really enjoyed making these. Pupils were given a choice as to what they wrote them about, with topics including 'Ma famille', 'Le sport', 'Les Animaux'. Pupils drafted text in their exercise books before copying this into their booklets and adding decoration for homework. The language used was creative and varied. They really took pride in them, and, for once, every single person in my group handed their homework in on time! Other teachers reported similar successes, and we'll definitely look at building this kind of task into our Schemes of Work.

Saffron Walden County High School

The mini book-making project: Additional materials

1. Picture gallery
2. Folding paper correctly (short film)
3. Useful websites

Project 4   The Foreign Languages Draw

Project Outline

Requirements: a long wall in a central venue: e.g. a school foyer, an assembly hall
Event time: one day for the main event
Languages targeted: any
Impact: high (this project can be delivered on school to regional levels, and potentially at national level too)

Introduction

The Foreign Languages Draw was inspired by the National Drawing Campaign in 2011 (see list of useful websites on the accompanying DVD). It was first delivered by Routes South on a small scale at a German Christmas event in 2011 and then again on a larger scale in 2012 to celebrate the London Olympic and Paralympic Games. This project was awarded a Springboard Grant from the University of Brighton in 2012, which enabled a formal final awards ceremony to be held for the winners of the categories from schools across West and East Sussex. However, the event can be organized on a simpler scale, involving just one class or year group in your school.

The basic shape of The Foreign Languages Draw is very simple and, as long as there is a suitable, central venue available, relatively easy to organize. The main aims of this project are:

■   to enable students to celebrate a topic-related theme in a foreign language;
■   to learn new vocabulary items and related genders (where relevant);
■   to have fun whilst using the target language and being creative.

Essentially, students are asked to draw a picture (or pictures) around a theme. The subject of the picture should be a noun or even a simple sentence and the heading for each picture should be presented in the foreign language, with the appropriate gender where relevant. Any foreign language can be chosen. The two model invitations provided in this project are, firstly, in German to celebrate Christmas at a German-style Christmas event, with Christmas vocabulary and, secondly, in any language to celebrate the 2012 London Olympic and Paralympic Games, with vocabulary based around the theme of sport. The additional DVD materials for this project include a picture gallery of some of the artwork presented at the German Christmas event in December 2011, which was held at The University of Brighton for a group of visiting Year Nine students. The invitations serve as a good example of what can be done on a larger scale to stimulate and sustain an interest in foreign languages, although, as previously mentioned, the project can also be delivered on a much smaller scale.

Organisation

In order to organise the Foreign Languages Draw, the organiser needs to

1. **Choose a meaningful theme.** This could relate to a particular celebration – e.g. the *Day of the Dead* (see also Part III, Project 2) – or a special event that is taking place, for example, the 2012 Olympic and Paralympic Games in London.

2. **Identify a suitable location.** This could be for example a local church hall, a school assembly hall, a town hall, a library, a long corridor in your school or your local college/university, the walls of your school canteen, etc.

3. **Identify a day** when students can come to the central venue, bringing with them their decorated picture(s) on a piece of A4 paper. Enough time needs to be left for teachers to disseminate the information and for students to complete the artwork.

4. **Identify your judges.** The artwork judge could be a local figure, or else someone who is simply interested in drawing as a hobby. The language judge should ideally be a native speaker of the language(s) involved. This person could however be a *Language Leader* (see Part IV, Project 3) or a different language teacher perhaps. It is not advisable for the regular class/school language teacher to act in the role of judge – a more neutral outsider is probably best.

5. **Identify participants.** Invite as many students to take part as appropriate. Your *Foreign Languages Draw* can be organised as a whole-class event or across several classes. It could be an inter-school competition or organised across a region. Potentially the regional finals could feed into a national final with the winning pictures being used for further publicity;

6. **Set up the task and prepare the invitations.** Here is a sample one used to help celebrate the German Christmas market (see Part III, project 1) which was held at the University of Brighton in December 2011. A second model invitation follows, which advertises a larger-scale *Foreign Languages Draw* and was used to invite students to a central venue at the University of Brighton to celebrate the diversity of languages united by the theme of sporting activities involved in the London 2012 Olympics. This Sussex *Foreign Languages Draw* was held in April 2012 and also provided a good opportunity for Language Leaders to contribute to the occasion (see Part IV, Project 3).

Example One: Celebrating Christmas at a German-style Christmas market with Christmas vocabulary.

The Foreign Language Christmas Draw

Looking for an exciting way to celebrate Christmas? Wondering how to combine German with another subject? Then look no further!

As part of our German Christmas celebrations, we are holding a *Foreign Language Christmas Draw,* which will be held at (venue) on (date) from (time). All your students have to do to enter is to complete the word *Weihnachts-* with a suitable noun (and its gender) which they should illustrate and decorate!

Prize

There will be three prizes awarded at (the event venue). One prize will be for the best artwork, one prize will be for the most effort made, and one prize will be for the most imaginative noun with the correct gender. Prizes will be awarded by (the foreign languages team). (Name of artwork judge) will judge the artwork, and (name of linguist to judge the foreign language) will award the language prize.

Rules

1. Pictures should be drawn on A4 paper (one per word). The correct gender of the noun should also be included as part of the heading.
2. Pictures can be sent in advance or brought along on the evening to be displayed on our wall frieze. Individuals may enter as many items as they wish.
3. Pictures must be the artist's own, original handwork (i.e. computer graphics are not acceptable).
4. Only one artist should draw and decorate each picture. The name and age of the artist should be clearly indicated on the **front** of each picture.
5. Pictures should be either sent in advance to (name) or brought in to the German Christmas event on (date) at (venue).
6. Prizes will be awarded at the end of the celebrations on (date) in three categories: best drawing; most imaginative noun with the correct gender; most effort made. The judges' decisions in all cases are final.

Here are three examples of the types of picture your students could produce and decorate.

das Weihnachtsaquarium   der Weihnachtspinguin   die Weihnachtskarte

Don't forget we are looking for the most creative drawing and the best artwork!

Example Two: celebrating the 2012 London Olympics with vocabulary based around the theme of sport. The rules are the same as for The Christmas Draw above.

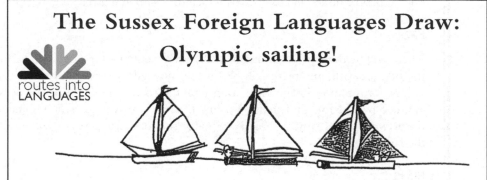

The Sussex Foreign Languages Draw: Olympic sailing!

© Emma Ball

At the 2012 London Olympic and Paralympic Games we shall be host to athletes and spectators from more than 220 countries across the globe. Help us to celebrate this richness of languages and cultures by entering The Big Sussex Draw. All you have to do is to choose a sport, draw a picture of it, decorate your picture, label it in any language other than English (including the correct gender where appropriate). One entry per student is allowed, and the picture must be your own original handwork (not computer drawn/coloured).

Prizes will be awarded in two age categories: 15 and uinder; 16+. In each category there will be one prize for the best artwork and one prize for the most imaginative (and correct!) use of language. Local artist (name) will judge the artwork, whilst (name) will be the language judge. Their decision in each category is final.

All entries must be received by (date and time). Please send your entries to (contact name). One entry per student will be accepted which must be drawn on one sheet of A4 paper. Please put your name, the language you have chosen and your age on the front of your drawing. Winners will be notified by (date) and invited to a final presentation at (venue). Good luck!

Shopping list

- Sheets of display paper onto which the submitted pictures are pinned
- Some means of sticking up the pictures: e.g. glue, pins, staple gun or sticky tack, etc.
- Prizes for the various categories
- Tokens of appreciation for the judge(s)
- Card if formal invitations are to be posted

Reflections

The Foreign Languages Draw which was as part of the German Christmas event held at the University of Brighton on Thursday December 8th 2011 was a great success, with some lovely artwork on display (see picture gallery on the accompanying DVD). Prizes were awarded in two age groups (15 and under; 16+) and in two categories: best drawing; most imaginative noun with the correct gender. Next time the draw takes place there will be three categories in the two age groups: the additional one being for most effort made, as some of the pictures demonstrated a lot of effective and creative work, even though they did not fall into the two original categories.

It was a good idea to invite a local artist from outside the university to join in the evening and judge the artwork. Her presence avoided any conflict of interest, as she was a stranger to the schools and staff present. Students need to write their details clearly on the *front* of the pictures (not the back) to assist the prize-giving.

The Foreign Languages Draw: Additional DVD materials

1. Picture gallery of the artwork displayed on December 8th 2011
2. List of useful websites

8

Continuing Professional Development

Introduction: What is CPD

Successful CPD inspires and helps us to be even better teachers. It shares best practice, gives us practical and immediately applicable ideas for our classrooms and reinvigorates our energy, confidence and desire to improve the language-learning opportunities we provide for our students. This Part considers the role of Continuing Professional Development (CPD) in the language teacher's professional practice and explores a variety of different opportunities open to you. Its format is thus slightly different to the others, as it considers key questions to be asked regarding the role of CPD and helps you to set up your own training opportunities. This chapter is all about how you can get involved in providing both small and large-scale CPD opportunities for yourself and your colleagues and is based on real experiences at Hove Park School and Language College in Brighton. It outlines how you can step outside the normal 'cascade' opportunities in Foreign Languages departments to run your own workshops and your own conference. A range of support materials are included on the accompanying DVD to support your Continuing Professional Development: a sample planning sheet for setting up your CPD; a sample running order of an appropriate workshop, sample evaluation forms and a picture gallery of the actual *Airport* event delivered to students.

Why get involved in delivering CPD?

There are many reasons and you only need one. For example, if you have attended an inspiring workshop, presentation or conference, then you have had a great first-hand experience. You will want or need to pass on what you learned to your colleagues, but second-hand is sometimes second best. Departmental meetings usually allow and encourage colleagues to 'cascade' their findings, but are necessarily limited by time constraints and busy agendas. Writing a report or emailing colleagues your notes and the original workshop presentation or materials is helpful but lacks the immediacy and impact of the first-hand experience that you had. Colleagues reading your email at the end of a day in the classroom will have other issues on their minds and may or may not be receptive, so what was great CPD for one person may be lost on others. Impact becomes minimal. Why not provide them with a similar first-hand experience instead?

If you were inspired yourself then you are probably the best person to set up the CPD, because you know exactly what was provided for you, how it worked and what could be improved or adapted to suit your audience. Alternatively, you may be in a situation where good CPD is lacking but you recognise the need to update, develop and motivate yourself and colleagues. Taking the initiative yourself means that not only will the CPD take place, but you can customise it to fit the requirements of your audience. The Training and Development Agency for Schools (2011a) has recommended that CPD is only effective where it is directly relevant, practical and applicable to each participant. CPD should thus be enjoyable and inspirational too. Why not help to make this happen?

Getting started

First sit down and list the key questions. This will help you think through the process of setting up the CPD and provide a simple structure to help you consult with, for example, your Head of Department, Director of CPD, Headteacher or other line manager. It is much easier to explain and enlist the support of others if you have already done some clear thinking early on. When you talk to others, sound confident but open to suggestion – they may have some great ideas to add to yours.

Key questions to address
- What is the aim of this CPD?
- Who is it for?
- When will it happen?
- Where?
- How will it be structured?
- Who will lead the CPD?
- How much will it cost?
- How will I know if the CPD is successful?
- What is the likely impact?
- How will I measure the impact?
- Who do I need to tell?
- Who can help me?

Focus on each question and make notes about details as they occur to you.

Aims of Continuing Professional Development

The main aims of all CPD in schools is to improve and enrich the experience and learning of the students and build the confidence and competence of staff. Good CPD supports and encourages the sharing of best practice within your institution. It raises expectations, broadens horizons, encourages experimentation and a climate of openness and mutual support. It helps the institution move forward on its agreed priorities for development and action. Helping to set up and deliver CPD shows your willingness and ability to support wider school effectiveness, a crucial aspect of current professional Core and Post-threshold standards, along with communicating and working with others, personal professional development, team working and collaboration (Training and Development Agency for Schools, 2011b).

Who is the audience?

If your department is small, think about opening up this training to others who could share it with you. Consider other colleagues and departments both within and outside your institution, including partner schools and feeder primary schools. For example, CPD about a specific language can be offered to other Languages departments in local or regional schools. CPD about strategies for learning can be shared with other departments within your institution, as well as with other schools and institutions, such as your local Initial Teacher Training providers. Shared CPD offers opportunities for colleagues to broaden supportive networks and brings fresh perspectives and differing experiences into the mix.

Ask your institution for a list of all staff, their roles and contact details, so that you can consider whom best to invite. The staff in the main office will usually have a list, as will the school's CPD Co-ordinator and the person responsible for teaching and learning. Talk to colleagues and your CPD Co-ordinator about who could also benefit from the proposed CPD, including teacher trainees, teaching assistants, foreign language assistants and support staff.

Look up the names of other schools on your Local Authority's website. Ring up schools and ask for the names and roles of each member of the Languages Department and their contact details. Then make a point of inviting people by name. Experience has shown that a personal invitation is more likely to elicit a response than a blanket invitation to a whole department or anonymous colleague, Co-ordinator or Head of Department. If you begin by writing or emailing, it is worth making follow-up calls to elicit positive responses from your invitees. You will need names to compile a register for attendees to sign at the CPD itself.

Send some detail about the training and presenter to potential attendees. Include simple bullet points about the training and its intended impact, a short biography about the speaker and a note about the handout or materials for attendees to take away at the end. The more informed people are, the more likely it is that appropriate colleagues will apply or turn up for your event.

When will this CPD happen?

Start looking as early as possible to identify the best opportunity for your CPD and talk to the right people about slotting in your proposals. School and institution timetables are usually scheduled many months in advance and include some inflexible dates, such as examinations and In-Service Training (INSET) days, which are reported to parents and the local authority. Sometimes local schools will link up for joint liaison INSET days specifically to allow schools to share CPD. The most convenient CPD times are those already on the calendar, but you will need to check that your Head of Department or school CPD Co-ordinator has space to include your proposals. If possible, avoid dates close to Parents' evenings, school shows and other directed late events such as Open Evenings.

Where?

If the CPD is about classroom practice, then one of the best venues to use is a classroom itself. It instantly places attendees in role as learners, just like their own students. A classroom helps teachers consider the students' perspective during the training. Most teachers love to see other classrooms, as it is often a great way to pick up new ideas, just by seeing the layout and displays in the room. A familiar venue over which you have control will be easier for you to set up for the training, so your own classroom in your school or institution can work well. However, it is worth considering other spaces in your school building, or outside school (such as your local sixth-form college or university), if they offer a better, smarter or more convenient place for the training.

Can I afford this venue?

Your local authority is likely to have a smart and convenient teachers' development or training centre with a variety of room sizes to hire. Benefits include trained administration staff and technicians to support you, easy parking, a range of equipment for presentations, smart furniture, good toilet facilities and, usually, a great choice of food and beverages. The downside is that most authorities have to charge for use of rooms, use of equipment and separately for catering, so you may need a starting budget of about £100 to be able to make a booking. Visit the website of your local teacher development centre and you will usually find useful and clear information posted about room and equipment hire and catering. Call them to talk through your needs.

Is the venue appropriate?

Remember that first impressions count. If you are using a school room, let the cleaners know what is happening and give them time to prepare the room. Tidy away anything that looks messy. Check chairs and tables for graffiti and chewing gum (!) and arrange to swap some furniture with another colleague if necessary. Move desks and chairs around to create the seating arrangement you need for the training. A carousel arrangement of group tables and chairs is usually the most inviting and relaxing for attendees. Remember to put everything back in its place at the end of the session.

Is it easily accessible from the entrance?

If not, you may need to post up some temporary signs to guide people to the room. Inform your Reception staff about what is happening in advance, so they can help attendees find their way to you.

Is there easy access to parking, toilets and refreshments?

Making people feel comfortable and welcome is essential in helping to create a positive atmosphere for training, particularly if it is a twilight session at the end of a teaching day. Check that there are enough parking spaces for visitors and enlist the support of your site manager or caretaker if extra space needs to be found. Check also that there are male and female toilets nearby. Put up temporary signs to help attendees find them. Check your supplies of loo paper, or ask your site manager/cleaner to do this for you.

Always provide refreshments, or access to them. Most attendees welcome a choice of hot or cold drinks and a nibble. Ask your Headteacher's Personal Assistant or Reception staff and you will probably find that you can borrow the hot-water urns and equipment used for Governors' and Parent/Teacher Association meetings. Check supplies of cups and teaspoons. Purchase throwaway cups if needed. Provide milk, sugar, tea, coffee and biscuits – chocolate biscuits are always popular! Provide water, including a jug or glass of water for your attendees and speakers. Put a decent bin or waste-paper basket in a handy place for all to use.

Does the technical equipment work?

Double-check before and on the day that all necessary technical equipment is working. Tell your technicians about the event and ask for their support. If you are using a visiting speaker, then ask well in advance about their technical requirements. Ask presenters to email or send you their presentation ahead of time, so that technicians can check that audio or video clips, internet links, etc., all work at your venue.

Are there Health and Safety requirements to meet?

Do you know the fire drill? If not, find out and make a quick announcement at the beginning of the training – just in case! Ensure that you have a register which lists names, institutions and contact details. Ask every attendee to sign as they enter the training venue. You will need to grab this list and take it with you in the event of an emergency.

How will the event be structured?

Training is about showing people how to do things, rather than telling them what to do. Aim to make your training interactive. Enable attendees to participate in practical activities, in the same way as you hope students will do as a result of the training. The Airport Workshop which is presented below is a good example of this, as teachers take on the exact roles of the students during the CPD event. Always give some time for feedback or questions to facilitate a dialogue about the training. Some of the best ideas and examples of good practice are often those shared from the floor by attending colleagues. Sample evaluation forms are included on the accompanying DVD for this project.

Decide on the style of your event: will it be a workshop, carousel of workshops, table-top discussions, conference or other? If you are delivering your own workshop, then consider your total training time. Break it down into chunks of time, so that you vary the pace and activities within the session. A sample running order of an appropriate workshop is also included on the accompanying DVD. Be on hand to meet and greet attendees, as they arrive, with a warm smile and directions to the refreshments and toilet facilities. Thank them for attending at the end.

Who will lead the CPD?

Will it be you, a colleague or an extenal speaker? If you are by yourself, then consider asking a colleague to co-present. Not only will you already be cascading your knowledge by allowing your colleague a more in-depth insight into what you already know, but you will find it much easier to share the work in planning and setting up the training. Co-presenters can help each other stay relaxed and confident, keep to timings, and offer to help out with technical equipment. Plan together and ensure you each have a copy of all paperwork.

If funding is possible, ask the original presenter of the training – the person who inspired you – to deliver the training. Expect to pay them for travel costs and a presentation fee – although this may be negotiable, so it is always worth asking. Check their requirements for equipment and resources in advance. Ask them to send you some bullet points about the workshop and a short biography, so that you can send this out to potential attendees. If they provide a handout you will need time to print and photocopy this on behalf of the speaker.

At the end of the event, remember to thank all presenters. Often presenters appreciate an email which thanks them and refers to the positive impact of their training session – one to keep for their own Curriculum Vitae or CPD purposes.

How much will it cost and who is paying?

Starting costs may be no more than a packet of biscuits and a litre of milk, but you will need to list everything that might require money and work out costs for each item. A sample planning sheet for setting up your CPD is included on the DVD accompanying this project. Co-presenting training with a partner school or institution means you can share the costs. Consider consulting with national language organisations to see if they can support the training at your school, or advise on funding streams to follow.

How will I know if the CPD is successful?

Always include time for attendees to complete an evaluation or feedback form at the end of the training (see samples on DVD). Collate the results and prepare a summary of these for yourself and your CPD Director or other interested line manager. You need to know how the training was received, what suggestions attendees might have for improvements, or what further training they would like to receive in the future.

How will I measure the impact of the CPD event?

Ensure that your evaluation form allows attendees to write a short note about how they intend using this training in their own classrooms. You can follow this up with an email some time later to ask if they have trialled the ideas and have any further feedback or samples to share with you.

Within your own institution, you can bid for follow-up time during departmental or liaison meetings, collate or scan samples of relevant work for a portfolio of best practice, carry out classroom climate or monitoring visits to view practice, or even just talk to others. Continue the dialogue in a variety of positive, encouraging ways. One way of measuring success is to see that the good practice you tried to pass on is subsequently embedded into schemes of work and becomes a norm for all colleagues.

Whom do I need to tell?

Every institution contains a large number of people who either need to know, or consider that they should be told. List all the people who are essential for the success of your training. These could include your site manager, cleaner, computer technicians, office staff, CPD Co-ordinator and/or colleagues who also use the space where you are holding your event. Ask your Multi-media Manager or another helpful colleague to take photographs of the event to post on your school or institution website, or in a newsletter. Think about whether your event is newsworthy, particularly if it involves colleagues from local schools and call your local newspaper to see if they are interested in reporting the event. Developing a high profile in this way makes future funding applications more likely to be successful.

Who can help me?

List anybody who can help you with any aspect of this training (for example, administrative or teaching support assistants, teaching colleagues, student helpers, CPD Co-ordinator, line manager, Headteacher, Local Authority Advisers, as well as local, regional or national organisations) and find the right moment to ask them for support – a Tuesday morning may be more successful than a Friday afternoon! If you are looking for inspiration for training ideas then start by attending some training yourself. Look for a conference or workshop, or post a message on a language forum for advice. Some suggestions for these professional associations are included on the accompanying DVD. **Be inspired yourself, then inspire others!**

Sample airport workshop

This workshop has been tried and tested at numerous CPD events and has proved to be great fun as well as an effective activity once cascaded back in school.

How to set up the Airport Workshop

The Airport Workshop is based on a whole-school thematic event and is designed to equip attendees with the knowledge and personal experience to replicate this model in their own schools. It therefore includes a role-play situation and the venue layout echoes the layout used originally for pupils. This links to *Fly the world from your own school Airport!* in the Primary companion to this book (*Living Languages: An integrated approach to teaching foreign languages in primary schools*) where the student version of the project is presented.

Presenters	Two – Presenter A and Presenter B
Venue	Large classroom or conference room
Essential equipment	Projector, screen, speakers, laptop, microphone & tannoy system
Room layout	Arrange tables and chairs as a departure lounge, check-in and aeroplane aisles. The arrangement of chairs must be in front of the screen so you will need to arrange the other furniture accordingly. It is important that attendees experience a 'journey' around the airport before being seated on the aeroplane.

Resources	<ul><li>Powerpoint presentation – includes audio track of aeroplane take off, departure information and weather chart</li><li>Laminated signs (in target language) and Blu-tack</li><li>CD of background music</li><li>Passport cards, tickets, departure sheets</li><li>Foreign newspapers and magazines</li><li>Samples of pupils' work (in target language)</li><li>Security tape</li><li>Number cards</li><li>Pens</li><li>Sticky tape & scissors</li><li>Inflight shopping magazines and First Class menus (made in target language by pupils)</li><li>Laptop/keyboard & telephone</li><li>Stamp</li><li>Realia from airports – luggage labels, security posters, leaflets</li><li>Bunting</li><li>Silver foil</li><li>Doormat</li><li>Chime bars & stick</li><li>Cable-tester (or something which emits a buzzing sound to order)</li><li>Fluorescent safety jacket</li><li>Uniform</li><li>Two trays of sweets</li><li>Workshop handout (on CDs)</li></ul>

Running order for one hour Airport Workshop

Timing in minutes	Activity
10	Roleplay entry to airport and journey through Departure Lounge, Check-in and Security (use target language & English)
5	Roleplay security announcements (in target language) & take-off.
3	Introductions to Partner A & B and workshop aims
10	Partner A begins presentation, Partner B moves on PPT slides to co-ordinate pictures with talk.
5	Pause PPT. Partner A shows samples of pupil work, attendees look at pupil newspapers, inflight shopping brochures and menus.
5	Continue PPT & presentation.
5	Pause PPT for Refreshment break (offer in target language)
5	Continue to end of PPT
5	Partner B questions Partner A about impact of this model on pupils and school community.
5	Questions and evaluations
2	End of workshop. Attendees depart airplane. Hand out CDs & thank attendees for flying with us today.

Room layout

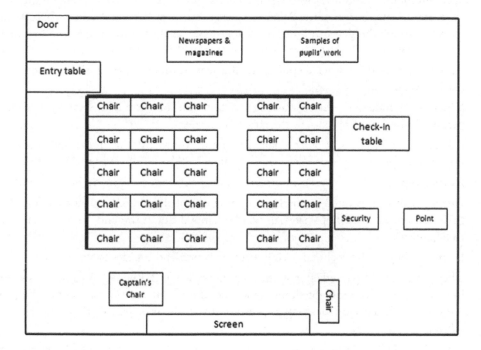

Workshop Description

Set up the venue so that seats for attendees are lined up in front of the screen like seating on an aeroplane, with a narrow aisle down the middle. Cordon off the 'aeroplane' by tying security tape around the seating so that attendees can enter by only one route.

Hang bunting around the room to create an international atmosphere.

Place one table by the entrance to the room. Lay out passport cards, tickets and departure sheets for attendees to pick up as they enter. Provide pens for them to write with.

Play CD of background music to help create atmosphere.

Partner B meets and greets attendees as though at an airport, gives them passport, ticket and departure sheet and asks them to fill in some details on the passport and departure sheet. A PowerPoint of alternating slides of departure information and weather from around the world plays during this role-play, so that attendees can see the information they need for completing their departure sheets.

Attendees move into the Departure Lounge (hang up signs in target language to help indicate different areas). Lay out selection of foreign newspapers and magazines, plus pupil work in the target language, for attendees to peruse while they wait.

Meanwhile, Partner A calls out security announcements in the target language on the tannoy system, with tannoy tuned so it echoes slightly.

When all attendees are in the Departure Lounge, Partner A announces that Check-in is open. Partner B moves to the Check-in desk and role-plays checking passports, taking tickets and issuing boarding cards to each 'passenger' in the target language.

Partner A role-plays a Security Officer. Two chairs are set up to create a narrow walkway between them. Drape silver foil over the chairs and place a doormat between the chairs to create the impression of the Security Gates at airports. Partner A asks each 'passenger' to step through the gates and uses the Cable-tester as though testing for hidden metals on each passenger. Press the buzzer on occasion as though finding something wrong.

Passengers take their seats according to the seat number on their ticket. Each seat is marked with a number card.

When all attendees are seated, Passenger A & B role-play the final security announcements and indicate fire exits, in the target language.

Partner A takes the Captain's chair. Partner B turns off the lights and works the PowerPoint presentation to show take-off slides with accompanying sound effects.

Partner B pauses the PowerPoint presentation to announce the in-flight entertainment.

Partner A & B introduce themselves and the aim of the workshop. Partner A explains that a CD of all workshop materials will be handed out at the end, so there is no need to take notes.

Partner A begins the main talk while Partner B works the slides to coincide.

The PowerPoint is paused after about 10 minutes while Partner A asks attendees to look in more detail at the inflight shopping leaflets and menus on the backs of chairs (stuck there with Blu-tack or sticky tape) prepared by students as part of their experience at school.

The talk and PowerPoint continue until it is paused again to offer in-flight refreshments – two trays of sweets are taken down the aisles of the plane by Partner A and B.

The talk and PowerPoint continue and finish.

Partner B asks Partner A to explain the impact of this Airport experience on pupils' learning and community cohesion.

Questions are invited to Partner A while Partner B hands out evaluations.

Workshop ends. Attendees are thanked for 'flying with us today' and invited to 'disembark' by the front aeroplane entrance. Partners A & B hand out CDs of all workshop materials as attendees leave.

Continuing Professional Development: Accompanying DVD materials

1. A sample planning document for a CPD opportunity
2. A sample running order of an appropriate workshop
3. Draft languages conference programme
4. Sample evaluation forms
5. List of professional organizations
6. A picture gallery of the actual *Airport* event delivered to students

Routes into Languages

Parental Consent Form for Use of Images of Children and young people

I/we,.. the parent(s)/guardian(s) of:

(child's full name)...

(child's full name)...

(child's full name)...

hereby give 'Routes into Languages' permission to use any still and/or moving images such as video footage, photographs and/or frames and/or audio footage depicting my/our children named above, for any of the following uses: advertisements; marketing; leaflets; website; any other use such as training, educational or publicity purposes.

The above consents will apply throughout England and be for an indefinite period.

Signed .... Date ....

Signed .... Date ....

Address...

....

.... Postcode ....

This information will be used for Routes Into Languages purposes only. Your details will not be released to third parties, or used for any purpose not related to Routes activities. Data held by Routes into Languages is subject to the provisions of the Data Protection Act 1998.

Routes into Languages is an £8 million group of projects funded by the Higher Education Funding Council for England and the Department for Children, Schools and Families and aims to increase the take up of languages at GCSE and beyond.

For further information on the Routes into Languages project visit www.routesintolanguages.ac.uk

References

Coyle, D. (2007a): "Content and Language Integrated Learning: Towards a connected research agenda for CLIL pedagogies". In *International Journal of Bilingual Education and Bilingualism*, 10:5, 543–562.

Coyle, D. (2007b): "20 United Kingdom, England". In Maljers, A., Marsh, D. and Wolff, D. (eds): *Windows on CLIL. Content and Language Integrated Learning in the European spotlight.* The Hague: European Platform for Dutch Education, and Graz: European Centre for Modern Languages (http://archive.ecml.at/mtp2/CLILmatrix/DOCS/Windows/ Windows%20on%20CLIL%20England.pdf).

Coyle, D., Holmes, B. and King, L. (2009): *Towards an integrated curriculum: CLIL National statement and guidelines.* London: Languages Company. (http://www.languagescompany. com/images/stories/docs/news/clil_national_statement_and_guidelines.pdf).

Coyle, D, Hood, P. and Marsh, D. (2010): *CLIL – Content and Language Integrated Learning.* Cambridge: Cambridge University Press.

Crystal, D. (2003): *The Cambridge Encyclopedia of the English language*, 2nd ed. Cambridge: Cambridge University Press.

Dalton-Puffer, C. (2007): *Discourse in Content and Language Integrated Learning (CLIL) classrooms.* Amsterdam/Philadelphia: John Benjamins Publications.

Dearing, R., and King, L. (2007): *Languages Review.* London: Department for Education and Skills.

Felder, R., and Henriques, E. (1995): Learning and teaching styles in foreign and second language education, *Foreign Language Annals*, 28:1, 21–31.

Gordon, R.G., and Grimes B.F. (2005): *Ethnologue: Languages of the world*, 15th ed. Dallas: SIL International.

Graham, S. (2004): Giving up on modern foreign languages? Students' perceptions of learning French, *The Modern Language Journal*, 88:2, 171–191.

HESA (2011): http://www.hesa.ac.uk/index.php?option=com_content&task=view&id=1899 &Itemid=239 Table 4B. Accessed December 2011.

Johnson, K. (2008): *An introduction to foreign language learning and teaching*, 2nd ed. Harlow: Pearson Longman.

Jones, T., and Ereira, A. (2005): *Terry Jones' medieval lives*. London: BBC Books.

McCall, I. (2011): Score in French: Motivating boys with football at Key Stage 3. *Language Learning Journal*, 39:1, 5–18.

Marsh, David, and Wolff, D. (eds) (2007): *Diverse contexts – converging goals. CLIL in Europe*. Frankfurt am Main/Vienna: Peter Lang.

Rowling, J.K. (1998): *Harry Potter und der Stein der Weisen*. Hamburg: Carlsen Verlag.

Training and Development Agency for Schools (TDA) (2011a): www.tda.gov.uk under *Career prospects and development*. Accessed November 2011.

—— (2011b): See *Professional standards for teachers* (*C6, C10, C40-41, P9-10*) at www.tda.gov.uk. Accessed November 2011.

Watts, C. (2004): Some reasons for the decline in numbers of MFL students at degree level, *The Language Learning Journal*, 29:1, 59–67

Index